Praise for *A Year in the*

"*A Year in the Enchanted Garden* is the bo bookstores! This guide is filled with all the things that makes a Witch's heart happy: gardening, nature, plants, magick and ritual! With a monthly focus, this book draws you in as a reader and gets you excited about the months ahead. It's so inspirational, I started immediately making lists for my upcoming garden and Wheel of the Year celebrations. It's a book I know I will refer to again and again." **—Lisa Wagoner, author of *Positive Pagan***

"A beautiful, poetic, and inspiring guide for those seeking to experience the magickal wonder of nature through gardening. Divided by months, each section contains practical rituals, spells, crafts, and recipes to help readers awaken a magickal connection with the land to empower their own personal practice. This beautiful book should be included in every Green Witch's collection." **—Laurel Woodward, author of *Backyard Garden Witchery***

"Master Gardener and seasoned Witch, Monica Crosson, shares an incredible wealth of plant-based knowledge in this delightful book—magickal gardening ideas, foraging tips, and witchy recipes, crafts, rituals, and spells. She expertly teaches you how to work with the rhythms of nature and encourages you to forge a personal path." **—Susan Ilka Tuttle, author of *Green Witch Magick***

"An inspiring guide to embracing nature's rhythms and tapping into your unique magick. Filled with spells, crafts, recipes, and rituals that align with the Wheel of the Year, this book encourages hands-on connection and intuitive practice. Whether you're a beginner or an experienced practitioner, Crosson's wisdom empowers you to find your own path in the garden of magick." **—Ambrosia Hawthorn, author of *The Spell Book for New Witches* and *The Contemporary Witch***

A Year *in the* Enchanted Garden

About the Author

Monica Crosson has been a practicing Witch and educator for over thirty years and is a member of Evergreen Coven. Monica is the author of *The Magickal Family, Wild Magical Soul,* and *Summer Sage* and is a regular contributor to Llewellyn's almanacs and datebooks as well as magazines such as *Enchanted Living* and *Witchology*. Monica lives in the woods near Concrete, Washington.

To Write to the Author

If you wish to contact the author or would like more information about this book, please write to the author in care of Llewellyn Worldwide Ltd. and we will forward your request. Both the author and the publisher appreciate hearing from you and learning of your enjoyment of this book and how it has helped you. Llewellyn Worldwide Ltd. cannot guarantee that every letter written to the author can be answered, but all will be forwarded. Please write to:

Monica Crosson
℅ Llewellyn Worldwide
2143 Wooddale Drive
Woodbury, MN 55125-2989

Please enclose a self-addressed stamped envelope for reply, or $1.00 to cover costs. If outside the U.S.A., enclose an international postal reply coupon.

Many of Llewellyn's authors have websites with additional information and resources. For more information, please visit our website at http://www.llewellyn.com.

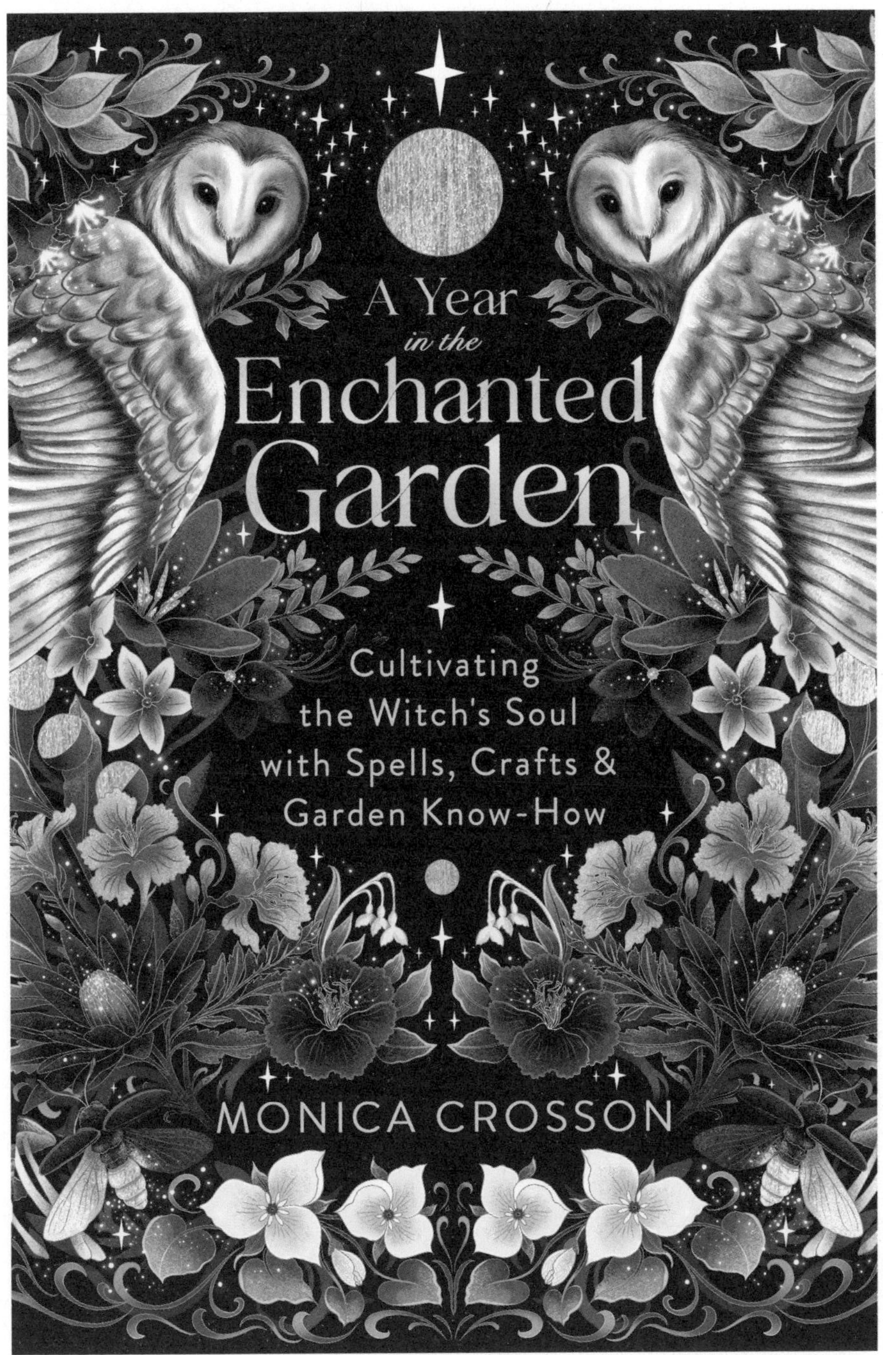

Llewellyn Publications
Woodbury, Minnesota

FIRST EDITION
First Printing, 2024

Book design by Christine Ha
Cover art by Pixie Cold
Cover design by Shira Atakpu
Interior illustrations by the Llewellyn Art Department

Library of Congress Cataloging-in-Publication Data (Pending)
ISBN: 978-0-7387-7367-4

Llewellyn Publications
A Division of Llewellyn Worldwide Ltd.
2143 Wooddale Drive
Woodbury, MN 55125-2989
www.llewellyn.com

Printed in the United States of America

Also by Monica Crosson

The Magickal Family: Pagan Living in Harmony with Nature

Summer Sage

Wild Magical Soul: Untame Your Spirit & Connect to Nature's Wisdom

Disclaimer

This book is not intended to provide medical advice or to take the place of medical advice and treatment from your personal physician. Readers are advised to consult their doctors or other qualified healthcare professionals regarding the treatment of their medical problems before beginning any herbal regimen. Neither the publisher nor the author takes any responsibility for any possible consequences from any treatment, action, or application of medicine, supplement, herb, or preparation to any person reading or following the information in this book. Consult your veterinarian before giving your pet any herbal remedy or diffusing essential oils.

Contents

Introduction
An Enchanted Garden of My Own

A long, long, time ago, when blackberries tasted the sweetest and my feet never felt the inside of a shoe, I would walk approximately two miles down an old back road that led through second-growth forest until it opened to a long-abandoned homestead. At one time, the little farm had belonged to my great-grandparents, who grew raspberries and sold them at local markets. Much to the chagrin of my mother and her siblings, my grandparents sold the ten-acre plot along with the adjoining woodland acreage for just around $2,000 in the 1960s when they hit hard times. The new owners, who were from out of state, quickly tore down the small, dilapidated house my grandmother was raised in and built a small cabin in the forest. They rarely visited more than once every couple of years, which left me free to roam the property where the ghosts of my ancestors resided.

In this forgotten garden, the raspberries were long gone, the field left with only traces of their existence—bent cedar posts that marked old rows and wire that lay tangled in grass and blackberry canes. Where the house once stood, daylilies, daisies, and sweet william could be seen struggling to reach above the tall field grass. But the foxglove thrived near the forest's edge and California poppy had spread unabashedly from its restraints. The honeysuckle that once covered the front porch made a new home twisted around the trunk and branches of a vine maple tree, and the witch hazel, which I imagined my great-grandmother using as part of her herbal medicine chest, still thrived and welcomed the spring with bright yellow blossoms.

Lying in the grass, I would watch as butterflies darted and cottonwood fluff floated, like faery clouds, above me. Sometimes, I would bring a book or a journal to draw in, or I would stick my feet in the small stream that trickled near the edge of the forest. Here I gathered material for my first spells (though, at the time, I didn't have a name for my magickal play). I brought home herbs to make into teas or balms. I talked to the spirits of my great-grandparents and sang songs to the spirits of nature. As a child, I felt as if it were my very own magickal garden—a place to play, dream, create, and commune with nature.

I consider it my first magickal garden, and I haven't stopped creating magick in the dirt since. In fact, I've been a Master Gardener for over thirty years and have used my knowledge to help create community and school gardens throughout the county, to teach container gardening for the Department of Social and Health Services to relieve food insecurity, and to help develop the children's gardening curriculum for our local university extension office.

Defining a Witch's Garden

Close your eyes, if you will, and try to visualize the perfect magickal garden space. What did you see? A formal garden with perfectly trimmed topiaries and rosebushes that encircle your ritual space? How about an old-fashioned vegetable garden with a pumpkin patch and a scarecrow? Maybe you visualize yourself sipping herbal brews in an English cottage garden or studying spellwork in a tropical garden where the scent of jasmine bewitches you. Others may visualize an amazing herb garden just steps from their kitchen—or a gothic Witch's garden tangled with mystery and secret knowledge.

What about desert-inspired gardens, where the element of fire sets our hearts ablaze, or a shady woodland setting, where faery energy can be felt just under the fern fronds and moss makes a cool carpet for our dancing feet? There is also something enchanting about a snow-covered landscape that sparkles under moonlight—reminding us to take the time to tend the garden that is our inner self. Gardens are as varied as the Witches who tend them, be they amazing arrays of potted plantings on a balcony or fields of wildflowers. The most important aspect of your magickal garden is that it feeds your soul.

How to Use This Book

This book was written to inspire you as you journey along your chosen path. I wish to encourage you to get your hands dirty and learn to work with the rhythms of nature in your own specific region, to get to know the spirits of your land and tap into energy that is unique to your own magick. I will take you with me, month by month, and give you a glimpse into my own personal magickal journey, teaching you the very basics of working with the land through gardening and foraging. And along the way, I will introduce you to some powerful archetypes and herbal allies. This book is also filled with spells, crafts, recipes, and rituals to enhance the celebration of the ever-turning Wheel of the Year.

At the end of every section, you will find gardening to-do lists for varying gardening zones and a list of magickal correspondence for the given month. Remember, magickal correspondences are not always the same for every practitioner—mine are a starting point. Let your intuition be your guide, because there is no wrong way to practice magick. As we walk together through the seasons of the enchanted garden, you will also discover the following:

The Importance of Connection with Our Ancestors

I have written a lot about seed saving and plant sharing because I feel it is an important way not only to produce food that is better adapted to your region but also to connect us with our ancestors. Be it a cutting from my grandmother's prized rose or seeds that have been passed down for generations, for me, part of the magick of my own garden is that it's a place where I can feel my ancestors near me.

Another way to connect may be more historical in nature. Take a look at an old grimoire, receipt book, or an herbal almanac. Are you drawn to these plants because of their medicinal, historical, or magickal values?

Growing your own magickal plants is a great hands-on way of learning more about the craft and connecting with long-gone hedgewitches and cunning folk who walked between the worlds in days gone by.

The Importance of Our Connection with Nature

Being a part of life's process helps us understand that our connectivity with nature is truly a symbiotic one. We lovingly tend to the earth to grow our own food, which in turn helps sustain us. Flowers, shrubs, trees, and water features that we add to our landscapes not only are beautiful but also provide food, water, and shelter for other creatures; attract pollinators; and provide oxygen. As magickal practitioners, you may notice more faery activity. The blessing of nature spirits is abundant when we are in sync with our natural surroundings.

The Importance of Earthing (Grounding)

Being in contact with the earth has calming effects that may lower stress and help improve sleep.[1] Magickally, it helps balance and equalize the flow of energy and avoid the negative side effects unbalanced energy can have on your spellwork. Plunging your witchy hands into the soil is a great earthing technique—in fact, recent studies show that there is a soil microbe called *Mycobacterium vaccae* that has the same mood-enhancing effect as antidepressants.[2] Barefooting is another way to make that contact with earth's balancing energy. Wiggling your toes in fresh upturned soil or walking on fresh spring grass are great ways to ground and create a sense of ease. How about tilting your face to the breeze? Let the element of air blow away negativity and stimulate your creativity. Balance your energy by dipping your feet in a stream,

1. Kirsten Weir, "Nurtured by Nature," American Psychological Association, April 1, 2020, https://www.apa.org/monitor/2020/04/nurtured-nature.
2. Catharine Paddock, "Soil Bacteria Work in Similar Way to Antidepressants," Medical News Today, April 2, 2007, https://www.medicalnewstoday.com/articles/66840#1; Christine L. Foxx et al., "Effects of Immunization with the Soil-Derived Bacterium *Mycobacterium vaccae* on Stress Coping Behaviors and Cognitive Performance in a 'Two Hit' Stressor Model," *Frontiers in Physiology* 11 (January 2021): 524833, doi:10.3389/fphys.2020.524833.

lake, or other body of water. Dance in the rain or simply sit by a garden water feature and let the trickling sound of water cleanse and equalize your spirit.

A Sense of Accomplishment

As I look at the jars of dried flowers and herbs that line my witchy pantry, I can take pride in the knowledge that I cultivated my magickal ingredients myself. I like knowing what went into the cultivation of my garden: everything from the compost that the seeds are propagated in to the astrological timing of when they were sowed to the moon phase of when the plants were harvested is all under my control and contributes not only to the success of my plants but also to the success of my spell crafting.

How to Customize Your Magickal Herbal Needs

What are your magickal needs? Would you like to make your own smoke-cleansing bundles? Adding sage to your garden sounds good. Maybe you want to work with lunar energy—how about growing lemon balm, gardenia, or willow? No problem. Growing your own means you can customize your garden to fit your needs.

How to Create a Place for Meditation and Ritual

This is your sanctuary. You will learn to take advantage of focal points, such as a favorite tree, vine, water feature, or view that soothes you, and how to create a sense of safety and enclosure to make your ritual space comfortable and maybe give it just a hint of mystery.

So come with me as we stroll through the garden gate and down a stony path to sit beneath the willow who whispers her eloquent tales of a Witch (like you, like me) who weaves their magick with a green-tipped wand and dirt stains under their fingernails and finds solace in the company of growing things.

JANUARY

I walk as if in a dream, drawn to the souls of old trees who whisper of spring's return.

JANUARY CORRESPONDENCES

Nature Spirits: Gnomes, brownies

Colors: White, blue-violet, black

Herbs and Flowers: Snowdrop, crocus

Scents: Musk, mimosa

Stones: Garnet, onyx, jet, chrysoprase

Tree: Birch

Animals: Fox, wolf

Birds: Owl, blue jay

Deities: Freyja, Cailleach, Holle

Zodiac: Capricorn, Aquarius

Work spells for letting go of the past, planning projects, self-love, protection, release, new cycles, and inner truth.

Chapter 1
Dreams to Grow By

For me, there is a longing that happens during the cold, dreary days of January in the Pacific Northwest, an itch to plunge my hands once again into the dark, loamy soil—to take in the scent of bee balm and to pluck fresh strawberries off the vine. At night, though the wind howls and the rain beats out a wild rhythm on my rooftop, I dream of the Green Man as he walks with me along the garden path and, with the voice of a songbird, sings to me songs of fertility and life. Second by second, day by day, inch by inch, I make note of the light's progress as the sun rises and falls.

"Did you see that, Steve?" I ask my husband. "The sun is above the willow now. He wasn't last week."

"Yes," Steve says, not bothering to look up from his magazine. "The light is coming back, and you'll be out there once again."

It's my mother who reminds me to be patient. "Enjoy January," she says. "It's not going away, so just sit back and take in its stillness."

And she's right. In January the Crone rules over my magickal garden. It is her dark mantle that cloaks the frozen landscape and draws us (and the garden) ever inward to gather energy so we can bloom once again.

January is a time to dream. As Witches who tend magickal gardens, we may spend the long, cold nights thumbing through seed catalogs or drawing up new garden designs. How about a faery garden for that shady corner near the fence line or a rowan tree for that bare spot in the backyard?

I love nothing more during January, when the nights are at their longest, than to curl up with a few gardening magazines and a seed catalog or two and find new plants that might enchant my garden with their lovely presence.

If you're an established gardener, you may have seeds that you saved over the growing season. This is a great time go through your seed stores to reminisce, plan, and check their viability. If you're new to magickal gardening, this is the time to study up.

Basic Garden Needs

In my first book, *The Magickal Family: Pagan Living in Harmony with Nature*, I wrote in depth on how to begin a new gardening endeavor. Here I will touch on some of the things to consider when dreaming up your first garden (or adding to an established one).

First, evaluate the sun exposure on your property. Spend a few days observing shade patterns from outbuildings and tall trees and record how many hours of sun per day your planned planting areas receive. Different plants have different light needs:

Direct Sun: Many fruiting plants require six hours of direct sunlight. These include tomatoes, squash, cucumbers, sunflowers, yarrow, and daisies.

Partial Sun: Some plants and root crops can get away with a little less light and only require four to six hours per day. These include carrots, beets, foxglove, bee balm, and hydrangea.

Partial Shade: Plants that require only three to four of light per day include your greens (lettuce, spinach, arugula, and chard), hosta, fern, and astilbe.

Consider the wind patterns in your area as well. Too much wind will determine the type of plants and landscaping elements, such as fencing or taller trees, that can act as a wind break for your garden.

Start out small. If you are new to gardening, start out small and grow as you succeed. A few containers or a small raised bed is all you need to begin. Huge plots can be overwhelming, especially for new gardeners.

January, named for the two-faced Roman god Janus, is a time for both putting aside the past and looking ahead to the future. What does the future of your magickal garden look like? This would be a good time to start your own magickal garden Book of Shadows. List the herb, plant, and tree allies you would like to share your magickal space with. What kind of energy do they emanate? Write down magickal correspondences and draw up garden designs that resonate with your witchy style. Throughout the year, use your garden Book of Shadows to take notes—what spells worked best for you and which herbs did you use? Your garden BOS is also a great place keep track of favorite soap, balm, tincture, anointing oil, and tea recipes.

One thing I like to do that adds a bit of charm to my BOS is glue pressed leaves and flowers next to their correspondences. If using a larger leaf, I first paint a coat of sealer on it, let it dry completely, glue it to the page of my BOS, and then write the spell directly on the leaf. It not only looks beautiful but makes a great botanical reference.

Manifesting Your Dreams

With the cold and darkness of winter comes a cleansing and purification—a clean slate, if you will, that allows us to dream anew. January can be very dark and dreary where I live, so I can typically be found with a hot mug of tea, stacks of gardening books, and a journal, dreaming up new ideas for my garden. Garden dreams can be easily manifested—but like with any form of manifestation, keep your intention, or goal, in mind and then take action toward that goal.

You want a pond in your backyard? Or how about a series of raised beds? Don't talk yourself out of it with excuses like "I'm not a landscaper" or "I could never build anything like that."

I remember, years ago, chatting with a friend of mine over coffee. She had just constructed an arbor on her own, and I told her I could never build an arbor because I wasn't good at carpentry. She blinked and said, "Then I guess you never will."

I was completely gobsmacked; she was right. I went home and immediately started putting together a notebook filled with simple arbor ideas. I instructed my husband (who is a carpenter) not to help me, and over the course of several months, I watched YouTube videos and practiced simple carpentry techniques. I built my own arbor, then designed and created my own life-size gothic garden statuary to sit under it.

One thing that helped me was a vision board—a visual representation that included pictures, quotes, words of power, sigils, and symbols that represented my intention. In my case it was a collage with pictures of arbors, strong women who worked in construction, and powerful affirmations that reminded me that I was capable of the task at hand. I hung it in my bedroom, so it was the first thing I saw when I rose in the morning and the last thing I saw as I tucked myself in every night. Whether your goal is magickal or mundane, vision boards are a great tool for keeping yourself focused on your goal.

Vision Boards

Our words, thoughts, and intentions have power. If we tell ourselves something isn't possible, it isn't. And the opposite holds true if we believe in ourselves and are willing to take action to make a goal attainable. Creating a vision board keeps us focused on our goal and reminds us that anything is possible.

Before making your vision board, make sure you have a clear objective in mind. Once you've established a goal, make sure it is achievable. Wanting a sunny perennial bed in a heavily treed area of your backyard? Probably not going to happen without taking out some trees. You say you like your trees? Okay, let's tweak the garden idea and create a beautiful shade garden that adds a touch of mystery to a darkened area. Now that you have a concrete idea, follow up with a realistic timeline and set goals accordingly.

Once you have a clear and attainable goal in mind, research ideas, layouts, plants, and other supplies. Print images from Pinterest and other sites that offer lovely pictures, words, quotes, and phrases that represent your goal, and cut them out in an artistic way. With everything all cut out, it's time to put together your vision board.

A vision board may feel like a fun craft, but if used correctly, it is a form of magick. Before getting to work, make sure you are centered and ready to set your intention—light a few candles, play soothing music, and make yourself a cup of tea to set the mood.

Using poster board, tagboard, canvas board, or something comparable, glue or tape your images into a collage that feels inspiring to you. Take your time and focus on your goal as you do this. Embellish your vision board with powerful words, symbols, or sigils using markers, pens, or paint. You may even want to glue on charms, coins, or other textural pieces to complete your "vision." You may choose to frame it or hang it up as is. Just make sure it is situated where you will see it every day.

As you hang it, state your vision. Say something simple like,

This is my garden. As I will, so it will be.

Every time you see the board, restate your vision, and remember to also take active steps toward realizing the goal. That means to continue to do research, learn a new skillset, and set aside money if needed. This technique can be applied to your magickal intentions as well—it makes a great complement to spells for abundance, strength, or wisdom, and is proof that if we can visualize it, we can make it happen.

Visions in the Dark

I think January is when my intuition is at its most powerful. Maybe it's because the world around me is at its most quiet, allowing me to perceive in a way I am unable to when I am filled with the raucous energy that sets in with the arrival of spring. With the onset of winter, I am more attuned with the energies around me, which is both a blessing and a curse. I have been known to wake suddenly in the middle of the night, my chest pounding with anxiety—an indication that something is terribly wrong with a loved one, and I am always right.

On the plus side, I have an intimate understanding of the natural world that surrounds me and am able to gain wisdom from the Otherworld through meditative practices. During the long, dark evenings of January, I set aside time for divinatory practices as well. I hone my skills with the pendulum and tarot, but my most effective tool is the black scrying mirror. Visions appear easily in my mind's eye as I gaze by candlelight into darkened glass. It's no surprise, as I have always been a visual person. No matter your divinatory tool of choice, enhance the experience by making sure that you are relaxed and that the area you will be working in is cleansed and charged. I also like to have a cup of "visions tea." It helps with relaxation and aids in opening the third eye and tapping into the intuitive self.

Visions Tea

There are many herbs that can be gathered during the bright summer months (which will be discussed in later chapters), dried, and stored to provide you with material to enhance your magickal practice throughout the winter. I have included some of my personal favorite herbs:

Ginkgo: Mental clarity, accessing ancient wisdom

Lavender: Aligning your third eye, quieting your mind

Mugwort: Astral projection, inner journeys, psychic awareness

Peppermint: Unblocking your third eye, peacefulness, prophetic dreams

Sage: Accessing ancient wisdom, balance

Yarrow: Communication, psychic ability, vivid dreams

I find that tea combined with my own grounding techniques is the key for me to align with my intuitive self and ready myself for divinatory practices such as tarot or scrying. You can experiment with your own tea combinations using the herbs listed above or use my own favorite recipe, which follows. I include lemon verbena for its brightness and spirit-cleansing abilities. This tea can help open the third eye and is a great complement to meditation, yoga, or other centering practices that are an important factor in preparing for divinatory practices.

You will need:

- 4 parts lavender (aligning your third eye)
- 2 parts lemon verbena (purifying body/mind/soul)
- 1 part sage (accessing ancient wisdom)
- 1 part mugwort (psychic awareness)

Fill a tea ball and place it in a cup. Pour hot water over it and cover, allowing it to steep for 5 to 8 minutes.

Black Scrying Mirror

Magic mirror in my hand, who's the fairest in the land? Since the dawn of modern humanity, mirrors and reflective surfaces have been infused deeply into our myths and spiritual belief systems. Our fascination with mirrors came not only because of a mirror's practical use but also because of the deeply ingrained belief that a mirror's reflection can reveal to us what is in our soul.

In Egyptian mythology, the goddess Hathor fashioned the first magic mirror from her shield that was thought to show everything in its true light. Nostradamus is believed to have employed a small bowl of water as a scrying tool into which he gazed and received images of future events. In older versions of *Beauty and the Beast*, Beauty uses a mirror to watch over her family, and Lewis Carroll used a mirror as a magickal portal in his novel *Through the Looking-Glass.*

Scrying is a form of divination using transparent or light-catching surfaces and has been practiced since ancient times to penetrate the veil between worlds, talk to the dead, reveal the future, and unveil the truth—but black mirror scrying (typically polished obsidian) is by far the most used historically. Today, it is still used by many modern seers and magickal practitioners. You can easily find an obsidian mirror online or in many metaphysical shops, but making your own black mirror is inexpensive and imbues your divinatory tool with your own personal power.

On those deliciously decadent nights of winter, blanketed with a dark velvety sky spattered with stars, light a few candles and turn out the lights, for this is the perfect time to look deep within your soul by use of a scrying mirror. What does the mirror have to say to you?

You will need:

- An inexpensive picture frame (Round is nice, but pick one that calls to you.)
- 1 to 2 cans black matte spray paint (depending on your frame size)
- Water steeped with mugwort

Remove the glass from the frame and clean both sides of the glass thoroughly. When dry, spray the paint on one side only of your glass carefully, holding the can approximately 12 inches from the glass and moving side to side. Do this in thin layers, allowing each layer to dry before starting the next, until you can no longer see light through the glass. If you want to paint the frame, do this while waiting for the glass to dry.

Put the glass back into the frame. Make sure that the unpainted side of the glass is facing outward. Before use, cleanse the glass with a little of the mugwort-steeped water.

Chapter 2
Here We Go A-Wassailing

In northwestern Washington, winters can be particularly dreary. We have known people who have moved to our beautiful valley during the summer and by September declared, "The rain isn't as bad as I thought it would be." We chuckle at their naivety and say, "Just wait until November." Where I am in eastern Skagit County, the mountains that surround us trap the clouds, so we can sometimes go months without a break in the weather. By the time spring arrives, we open our doors bleary eyed and suspicious of the big, bright round thing that dominates an unfamiliar blue sky.

One particularly cold, soggy January afternoon, after weeks of continual drizzle, my five-year-old daughter said to me, "Mama, can't we just shoo it away, so the sun will come back?"

I smiled, then said, "I wish I had a spell to make it disappear."

She went back to playing with her dolls and had soon forgotten all about the gray dampness that kept her indoors, but it got me thinking about rituals meant to scare away the winter and encourage the arrival of spring. I knew all about Carnival celebrations that would be happening in February, whose pre-Christian roots began with festivals to usher in the spring, but the ritual I was most interested in was the mid-January ceremony known as wassail.

Long, long, ago, British people set out in small groups, sometimes led by a wassail king and queen, into the bitter cold of a January evening. As they walked, they banged drums and rang bells down winding paths that led to their orchards to frighten away winter spirits. Along with them was brought a special brew of cider or beer that had been prepared with herbs, sugar, spices, eggs, and cream. This would typically take place on the eve of

Twelfth Night on January 5 or on January 17, depending on which calendar was used.

Typically, they surrounded the oldest fruit-bearing tree, chanted rhymes, and sang songs to "wake up" the spirit of the tree. In some traditions, the trunk of the tree was beaten with a stick to get the sap moving. As an offering, pieces of dried bread would be dunked into the wassail bowl, and the elected queen placed them in the hollow or supporting branches of the tree. Some of the wassail brew would then be poured about the roots or upon the tree's trunk and the rest shared among the revelers.

It was that very evening that my daughter, Chloe, who was rightly elected queen, and my sons, Joshua, aged twelve, and Elijah, aged nine, followed me down a winding path, equipped with apple cider and some bells, to our small orchard. As we walked, we shook our bells and cried out, "Go away winter! Ye have been banished!"

The kids ran circles around a gnarly old apple tree who produced the smallest and knobbiest apples you can imagine. "Wake up, wake up!" they screeched and jingled their bells. Chloe, taking her role of elected queen very seriously, ceremoniously dunked toasted bread into our wassail bowl and tucked it into the crook of one of the lower branches. "Here you go, nature spirits," she said. "I hope this helps you wake up and make all this rain go away."

We sang what verses we could remember from that old carol "Here We Come A-Wassailing," then spilled a little of the wassail onto the roots of the old tree before sharing the rest among ourselves. "Here's to a good try, old friend," I said, and raised the bowl. Of course, after taking a big swig from our wassail bowl, Joshua had to spray the contents from his mouth all over the tree's trunk.

"Joshie!" Chloe screamed and started hitting him with her bells.

"I was just blessing the tree," he said, blocking her blows with a now sloshing bowl of apple cider. This statement threw my nine-year-old into a fit of laughter, to which Chloe responded with a set of bells between his eyes.

"It's time to go in," I said as calmly as I could. I watched as my three little Witchlings ran screaming and laughing back to the house, then I turned toward the tree. "I know you get it," I said and patted the twisted trunk. "Blessed be, dear spirit."

Planting Your Bare-Root Tree

Bare-root trees and shrubs are typically available to buy at your local nursery between January and March. What's great about buying bare-root plants is that it is an easy and affordable way to add fruit-bearing or flowering trees and shrubs to a new garden. Also, most bare-root trees sold are typically a dwarf or semi-dwarf variety, so spacing isn't as big of an issue as if you were to purchase a standard-size tree.

When to plant your bare-root tree will vary from region to region, but ideally you want to plant trees when they are still dormant. In warmer regions, that means late fall to early winter. In colder regions, plant just after the ground has thawed.

When you are ready to plant your bare-root tree or shrub …

- Take off the protective packaging and gently untangle the root system.
- Soak it in water for approximately 3 to 6 hours before planting.
- Dig a hole that is at least double the size of the root spread. Break up the sides of the hole to accommodate growth.
- Mix equal parts garden soil and good compost and partially fill in the hole.
- Place the tree in the hole and fill soil in around the roots. Make sure the root collar (where the roots meet the base of the tree) is level with the ground. Pack the soil in well.
- Build up the soil a little around the tree to form a water basin and give your tree a good watering.
- Cover a 3-foot-wide and 2-inch-deep area around the base of your tree with mulch to hold in moisture.
- Water every 7 to 10 days until well established.

Fruit Outside the Door

Fresh fruit can be an expensive treat for a family on a budget. Growing fruit in your backyard garden can supply you and your family with bushels of homegrown goodness that you know is completely organic and can be picked at its peak for optimum flavor.

There are many varieties of fruit trees (including dwarf) that can grow in just about every region, from cold-hardy fruits like apple and cherry trees to heat-loving citrus fruits. The key to a successful planting is doing the proper research for varietals that tolerate your hardiness zone and microclimate. To find out which varieties are best for your garden, contact your local extension office and talk with a Master Gardner.

Because it is important to provide both the leaves and fruit of your orchard tree access to light and fresh air, be prepared to learn proper pruning skills. Once again, this can be done through a class offered by your local extension office, or online. Try these common orchard favorites:

Apple (*Malus* spp.)

This member of the rose family, a tree of Venus and the element of water, can be used in spells for love, health, immortality, or garden magick. This favorite tree of Witches (I know it is one of mine!) is popular for making wands. Also known as the food of the dead, apples are typically seen on altars at Samhain. For disease resistance, consider the varieties dwarf 'Enterprise' and dwarf 'GoldRush'. Zones 4 to 8.

Cherry (*Prunus* spp.)

A popular Venus tree associated with water, cherry can be used to make wands for divination. Use it in magick for unification, love, and intuitive insight. If you're using an older spell that requires blood, cherry juice works well as an alternative. For sweet cherries, consider 'Rainier' or semi-dwarf 'Stella'. For the tarter pie cherry varieties, consider 'Montmorency' or dwarf 'North Star'. Zones 4 to 8.

Peach (*Prunus* spp.)

Peach is another tree in the rose family that is associated with Venus and the element of water. Use peaches for love magick. Make a peach pie for your loved one at Lughnasadh. It is also used for wisdom and fertility. The wood of the peach tree can be used for exorcism or in spells for longevity. Use branches for divination. If you live in a northern region, consider dwarf 'Frost Proof Peach', or try dwarf 'Starking Delicious' for peaches perfect for canning and freezing. Zones 5 to 9.

Pear (*Pyrus* spp.)

This is a watery tree connected to Venus. It is said that dancing with your consort beneath a pear tree will help stir up passion. Use it in spells for love and lust. If you're new to growing pears, try the beginner-friendly 'Baldwin', a cold-hardy variety that bears fruit in two years. Zones 4 to 8.

Plum (*Prunus* spp.)

This Venus tree connected to water can be used in magick for protection and for love. The branches of the plum tree were once hung above the entrance of the home to guard against intruders.

Japanese plums produce firm-skinned, firm-fleshed, heart-shaped fruit that is great for eating fresh or for canning and freezing. For a heavy-producing Japanese plum tree, consider growing 'Methley'. European plums boast soft-skinned, soft-fleshed oval fruit that is great for cooking, canning, or drying to make prunes. Consider the dwarf European plum 'Stanley' for abundant crops. Zones 4 to 9.

Fig (*Ficus* spp.)

Associated with Jupiter and the element of fire, figs are used for fertility magick. Some folkways include carrying a piece of fig wood with carved phallic symbols if you wish to conceive and eating fresh figs to overcome infertility. Plant a tree in your yard for protection, and use fig for divination and in love magick.

Consider dwarf varieties 'Black Jack' and 'Violette de Bordeaux'. Zones 7 to 10.

Orange (*Citrus* spp.)

Orange is a fiery fruit connected with the sun. Use orange peel in prosperity spells. Flowers, seeds, and peel can be used in spells for love or added to charm bags. Orange can be used in spells for divination, friendship, and luck. Folklore dictates that an infusion of orange peel will guard against drunkenness.

If you want to try a hardy orange tree that grows fast, consider 'Valencia'. Zones 9 to 11.

Lemon (*Citrus* spp.)

Lemon is associated with the moon and the element of water. Use lemon water to wash negative vibrations from secondhand magickal tools, amulets, and jewelry. Use the dried peels and flowers in love magick and charm bags and in spells for fidelity, longevity, luck, and home blessings. Use lemon in lunar magick. If you want an easy-to-maintain dwarf variety that can be grown in a container, try 'Eureka'. Zones 9 to 11.

A New Twist on an Old Ritual

Now that you have your new tree or shrub firmly planted in your garden, why not bless it with a new twist on an old-fashioned wassail ritual? This ritual is a great way to bless your new addition to your garden, and it also blesses the birds who call your garden home.

This tree blessing can be done in your established garden, backyard, or orchard during the dormant period, or anytime after you have planted a new tree or shrub.

Try your hand at making my dairy-free and egg-free version of old-fashioned wassail (see page 24). Or how about picking up some locally brewed hard cider or beer?

You will need:

- Evergreens (real or artificial)
- Floral wire
- Wassail, beer, or hard cider (pretty wassail bowl is optional)

- Bells, pans, whistles, etc. for making noise
- Small bird feeder filled with seed

Elect someone from your group to lead the procession. (Though this ritual is more fun worked as a group, it can also be performed solitarily.) Twist the greens with floral wire to form a crown. This will be worn by the elected leader who represents a Green Man or Green Woman character.

Your leader will carry the wassail bowl (or container holding cider or beer bottles). All others will carry the noisemakers, which may include bells, whistle, pots and pans, and so on. Don't forget to have someone carry the filled bird feeder. As you make your way to the tree, bang those pots and shake those bells—be as noisy as you please! Yell out for winter spirits to flee. Remember to make it fun—dance about and make merry!

Your elected king or queen will then lift the wassail bowl or open container and spill just a bit over the roots of your tree. As this is done, all say something like this:

Health to thee, my (fill in type of tree) tree
Steadfast upon the ground
Be it weather good or foul
May every sprig flourish well
Upon your leafy crown

Then have your elected leader take the bird feeder and hang it from a branch. As this is done, all say something like this:

Hail thee birds who grace this tree
Your presence brings us cheer
We hope this offering of seed and mirth
Eases your stay here

Now everyone can cheer and share in the libation.

Wassail

- 4 small apples
- ¼ cup brown sugar
- 1 quart apple cider
- 1 cup orange juice
- 1 cup cranberry or pineapple juice
- ½ cup brandy (optional)
- 6 allspice berries
- 2 cinnamon sticks
- 1 teaspoon grated nutmeg
- Dash of ground cinnamon and ginger before serving (optional)

Use a melon baller to scoop the cores out of the small apples. Set the apples on cookie a sheet and fill each one with approximately 1 tablespoon brown sugar. Bake for 40 minutes.

Pour apple cider, juices, and optional brandy into a stock pot and warm over medium-low heat. Cut a square of cheesecloth or muslin and place the spices on top. Tie it closed with cotton twine and float it in the mixture until it warms. Do not let the brew boil.

When ready to serve, remove the spice bundle and float the baked apples. You may also add a dash of cinnamon and ginger to the bowl.

Chapter 3
Herbs of January

January finds us at the threshold of a new year, and the herbs I have chosen reflect the dreams we conjure during the winter. They are herbs of visions, strength, promise, and new beginnings. They are herbs that remind us that greener days are ahead, and the signs of hope lie just outside our own back door.

Birch (*Betula* spp.)

Planet: Venus

Element: Water

Energy: Feminine

Deities: Lugh, Brighid, Arianrhod, Thor, Freya

Planted mainly for its beautiful paper-white bark and lovely foliage, the birch is a great addition to northern gardens. As a tree of new beginnings, birch teaches us to look at the possibilities that lie before us and be courageous in our undertakings. It is also a tree of protection, as it was said to be full of Lugh, and at one time baby cradles were carved from the wood of the birch to ensure no harm came to the child.

Birch can mark the threshold between worlds, and it is there you may come in contact with the Lady of the Woods, a faery being who is connected with clarity. Traditional Witch's besoms are made from birch twigs and can be used in ritual to "sweep" out the old year.

Use birch in magick for protection, new beginnings, purification, clarity, and exorcism.

Traditional Birch Besom

Traditional besoms were made with ash wood for the staff, birch branches for the bristles, and willow withes (young, flexible branches) for binding. Try to find an ash branch that has fallen or gently ask the tree for one of its branches. Birch branches are easily gathered from beneath a birch tree, and willow withes can be cut (with plenty of thanks) from the tree. All these materials can also be purchased online.

You will need:

- 1 dry ash branch, 30 to 35 inches long
- A good handful of birch twigs, 12 to 20 inches long
- Garden twine
- A few willow withes, soaked in water for 24 hours before use

Before putting your besom together, prepare your staff by peeling and sanding or decorating and polishing it in a way that suits you and your craft. When ready, lay your staff aside as you gather your birch branches into a bunch and bind it with twine. Plunge the staff into the middle of your birch bundle and secure it to the staff tightly with willow withes or more twine.

Use your besom to sweep away negative vibes. As you sweep in a deosil direction, say something like this:

We call upon the guardians of the birch
To sweep away negativity and bring us mirth
Forest spirits, we thank thee
For peace and protection, so mote it be

Crocus (*Crocus* spp.)

Planet: Venus

Element: Water

Energy: Feminine

Deities: Brighid, Venus

Just when we thought winter would never end, these beautiful little flowers are the first to raise their colorful heads and remind us that spring will come again. What I love about crocuses is that that they are basically no-maintenance plants that naturalize easily and brighten a dreary garden with spots of color. Plant spring-blooming crocus corms between September and October if you live in colder northern regions or in November if you live in the south.

There are several variations of a story in Greek myth that describe the origin of the crocus flower. One says that a young man named Crocus was rejected by the beautiful nymph, Smilax. Unable to bear the affront to his ego, he asked the gods for help, and they turned him into a crocus plant. Another has him the companion of Hermes, who accidently kills him while playing a game of discus, and from his blood grows a crocus flower.

In magick, use spring crocus for love, merriment, friendship, new beginnings, and visions.

Visions of the Future with Crocus

Place a few crocus blooms with an iolite stone in a bowl of water on your nightstand. Before going to sleep, focus on the flower and say something like this:

> Bring me visions, second sight
> Dreams of the future on this night

Dab your fingers in the water and draw a solar cross at your third eye.

Hellebore (*Helleborus*)

Planet: Saturn

Element: Water

Energy: Feminine

Deities: Hecate

Commonly known as the Christmas rose or Lenten rose, hellebore is a wonderful plant for any gardener who wants to add a bit of bewitchment to the late winter landscape. Hellebores boast 2-to-3-inch blooms of deep romantic colors of burgundy, purple, black, green, and amber atop leathery foliage that seems exotic compared to the more fragile snowdrops or crocus that grow in their midst.

Highly poisonous, hellebore was used in mediaeval times as a purgative for black bile, melancholy, and madness. Plant hellebore in shady areas around your house as a means of protection.

Use it in magick for protection and exorcism. Again, hellebore is highly poisonous—do not ingest any part of this plant!

Wreath of Protection

- Several hellebore flower stems
- Your choice of fresh or dried sprigs of other protective herbs, such as rosemary, marjoram, basil, fennel, or mint
- Grapevine wreath (premade from any craft store)

As you weave and tuck the hellebore stems and protective herbs around the vines of your wreath, invoke their protective powers by saying something like this:

By the power of herbs and vine and flower stems
Protect this home and all within

Hang the finished wreath above a doorway. Any fresh herbs and flowers will dry on the wreath.

Rosemary (*Salvia rosmarinus*)

Planet: Sun

Element: Fire

Energy: Masculine

Deities: Aphrodite, Mnemosyne

This Mediterranean herb is certainly one of my favorites. It is an evergreen, woody perennial shrub with heavily scented needle-like leaves that can grow up to 5 feet in height in warmer climates, zones 8 to 10.

Use rosemary in all your favorite Mediterranean recipes, including stews, grilled and roasted meat dishes, sauces, and breads. In magick, use rosemary for remembrance, purification, protection, love, dispelling nightmares, and fertility.

Rosemary has long been used in love spells and was worn in chaplets by medieval brides. And though now thought of as a masculine herb, it was once said, "Where rosemary grows, the woman rules," meaning the plant only flourished where the woman was the head of the household. Known also by the folk name "elf leaf," rosemary can be grown in the garden to attract elves. Burn it to purify your magickal space. And with its strong ties to the sea (*rosmarinus* means "dew of the sea"), use it in sea witchery.

Sea Goddess Love Spell

- 2 tokens that represent you and your lover
- Red tea candle
- Small shells and/or sea glass
- Sprig of rosemary
- Pretty bowl filled with a little salt water (If you do not live near a salty body of water, use tap water with some added sea salt.)

To put the spark back into a relationship that may be growing a little stale, place tokens representing you and your lover on either side of a red tea candle. Surround tokens and candle with your shells or sea glass. Dip the rosemary sprig in the bowl of salt water and sprinkle the water 3 times in a deosil (clockwise) manner around your setup, saying each time something like this:

I call upon the Goddess of the Sea
To bring back loving vibes for my love and me
Thrice around I sprinkle, thrice I ask of thee
Let love reside here, so mote it be

Light the candle and leave it (safely) until it burns itself out.

Snowdrop (*Galanthus* spp.)

Planet: Venus

Element: Air

Energy: Feminine

Deity: Brighid

Snowdrops are one of the first blooms to appear and a true sign of winter's end. They grow approximately 3 to 4 inches tall with small, white drooping flowers.

Though thought of as a "shy" flower because of their drooping blossoms, in reality the blossoms tilt downward to keep the pollen dry and sweet for the few pollinators out during the winter. British folklore dictates these sweet, happy blossoms brought into the home was bad luck, causing the cow's milk to become watery and affecting the color of the butter.

In magick, use snowdrops for hope, grief, friendship, triumph, strength, and new beginnings.

Meditation for Hope

Winter can be a dark time for many of us—affecting us both physically and emotionally and resulting in a disorder known as seasonal affective disorder (SAD) in some extreme cases. If you are feeling a little blue or defeated by what feels like an endless winter, try meditating with snowdrops.

You will need a small pot of snowdrops available at any home and garden center.

Create an incense blend using the following:

- 1 part frankincense
- ½ part lavender
- ¼ part thyme

When you are ready, find a nice, comfortable place to sit where you won't be bothered and place your pot of snowdrops where you can see them. Play some calming music and light your incense on a charcoal tab in a fire-safe container. Take some deep, cleansing breaths as you focus on those beautiful flowers who remind us that greener times are ahead—both physically and figuratively. Take as much time as you need until you feel your spirit rise (even a little).

Around the Garden
To-Do List for January

January is the time to do your research. Check out garden books, magazines, and seed catalogs to get ideas for the coming year. If you're already a seasoned gardener, January is a great time to make sure leftover seeds are still viable. Most unused seeds will last, on average, two to three years after the expiration date if stored in a cool, dry place, but I have planted some that were over fifty years old, and they came up beautifully. A few garden centers will start putting seeds out (usually cool-weather crops like lettuce, onions, and spinach) in January.

If you already own garden tools, make sure they are cleaned, sharpened, and ready to go for the upcoming gardening season. My favorites for the gardening shed include a garden rake, a trowel, a digging shovel, loppers, pruners, a hori hori knife, and a digging fork.

Vines, fruit trees, and shrubs are best pruned while they are dormant. If the weather isn't too unpleasant, January is the time to get started. Trim fruit-bearing shrubs such as blueberries, currents, gooseberries, and the like of their old growth to maintain productivity.

January is a good month to purchase any bare-root plants, such as strawberries, fruit trees, roses, and asparagus, that may be planted early in the growing season. Trim all old stems and foliage from perennials and ornamental grasses, being careful not to cut any new growth that may be emerging. In colder climates, brush snow from branches of ornamental trees and shrubs to minimize damage. Add a layer of mulch to cover root crops during freezing weather. Trim yellowing leaves from winter greens. Pinch fading blooms from winter-blooming flowers, such as pansies, to stop seed from setting.

Grow Your Magickal Knowledge

January is a good time to start your own magickal garden Book of Shadows. List plants that you would like to grow along with their correspondences, planting requirements, and moon phase (see more about lunar gardening on page 58). You may also want to consider purchasing a lunar calendar if you plan on trying your hand at this age-old practice.

Combine pruning activities or celebrate the purchase of your first bare-root shrubs or trees with a wassail ritual. You can try the one on page 22 or create your own meaningful ritual.

FEBRUARY

They hold the power of light in the palm of their hand—their soul feeds on the seeds of the Divine.

FEBRUARY CORRESPONDENCES

Nature Spirits: Frau Welt, Baba Yaga

Colors: Light blue, violet, pale yellow

Herbs and Flowers: Primrose, coltsfoot, marjoram

Scent: Balm of Gilead

Stones: Amethyst, bloodstone

Trees: Poplar, rowan

Animals: Otter, lamb

Birds: Eagle, chickadee

Deities: Brighid, Februus, Aradia

Zodiac: Aquarius, Pisces

Work spells for purification, healing, fertility, self-love, accepting responsibility, self-forgiveness, growth, soul flight, banishing, new beginnings, and empowerment.

Chapter 4
Seeds of a New Dawn

Like most Witches who tend a garden, I pay close attention to the seasonal placement of the sun and moon as they ride across the sky. I can tell you the exact location and time the moon will rise on a sultry night in June when the hummingbird moth flits among the honeysuckle, or deep in December, when her light is so bright, silky strands of moonlight reach through my windows. I can even tell you the exact moment I begin to lose precious sunlight beginning in late August, when lengthening shadows lie across my rows of raspberries, whose used canes have already begun to grow weary of the season. It is during the dim of winter, when in Washington state our gray light decreases to just over eight hours a day, that my waiting becomes impatient. But then it happens…the wheel turns and suddenly it is February.

It is in February when we can truly see the light increase, day by day, minute by minute, and we rejoice in the little things—streams of lemony sunlight touching our face, the first green shoots poking through the snow, swelling buds on the trees, and the magick of seeds.

"Every seed is synonymous with life," my dear friend Stella, an herbalist and Witch, used to tell me. "For growth to happen, there must be deconstruction," she would say, as we planted flats of onion seeds on particularly cold February days in front of her wood cook stove. "Just as every seed must lose its protective casing in order to sprout, we too need to break down in order for transformation to occur."

Her words rang true to me. There is power in each and every seed—the power to heal, to nurture, to sustain, and to transform. To hold a seed is to hold a living connection with the earth. Yes, every time we plant a seed, we are taken on a mythical journey of the God, harrowed into the soil, only to rise up from the earth green and vigorous, and finally, harvested (sacrificed) for our use as food and medicine. Many of our myths and folktales too reflect the power of seeds. Most of us are familiar with the story of Persephone, daughter of Demeter, who was taken by Hades into the underworld. There, she is tricked by her suitor into eating six pomegranate seeds, which bind her fate. For the pomegranate represents not only fertility but the persistence of life. So it is in the underworld she must stay for half the year, leaving the earth to persist even as Demeter mourns, until Persephone's return in the spring. As this story illustrates, nothing perishes: life is a continuous circle of life, death, and rebirth. And the seeds we hold in the palm of our hand are the promise of that never-ending circle.

It's no surprise that planting seeds has been accompanied by story, ritual, and blessing for thousands of years. In the past, dancing, songs, charms, and sometimes sacrifice were employed to unleash the power of the vegetative spirit from the womb of the Mother. Even now, blessings and ceremony can be found connected to the seed. In late January or early February, the Hopi still call spirits, the *kachina*, for blessings of rain for their crops in a ceremony called a *powamu*, also known as the bean dance.[3] The bean sprouts represent fertility, growth for the crops, and good luck for the people. Other traditions, such wassailing, maypole dancing, Morris dancing, and well dressing, are all rooted in ancient traditions that were thought to bring fertility to the crops.

In the modern world, the importance of the seed has been all but forgotten by most of us. We go the grocery store or order premeasured meal boxes online without much thought about where or how the food was grown. And what about those magickal herbs that can be found in metaphysical stores or online? Who knows how old they are or how they were grown—and that, dear Witches, can affect your magick. But by picking up just one pack of seeds and plunging our witchy hands into the soil (be it a single pot on a balcony or a backyard plot), we are making connections: to

3. Tom Lowenstein and Piers Vitebsky, *Native American Myths and Beliefs* (New York: Rosen Publishing, 2012), 121.

the Earth Mother, whose womb is where all life regenerates; to our ancestors, whose lives depended on a good harvest; and to the old ways of life, where the cycles of the moon and sun were revered. It's an empowering feeling knowing you grew the herbs used in your magick or the greens you put into your body. And it's easier than you think. Let's get started.

It's All about Zoning

I am writing this book as a Witch who calls Pacific Northwest Washington home. We say we have the traditional four seasons, but sometimes it feels more like two: light rain season, for the misty spring and summer rain that frizzes our hair and beckons the slugs and snails into the garden, and heavy rain season, for the deluges of autumn and winter that can last for weeks and cover everything we own with moss. I'm exaggerating, of course, but as a resident of a narrow valley that's tucked up against tall, rain-trapping mountain peaks, my gardening differs from my that of neighbors to the east of the Cascades or along the coast. My gardening also differs from that of my closer neighbors, as my microclimate keeps me in the shadows longer than my neighbors ten miles from me. That's the thing about gardening—it's not a one-size-fits-all skill. It's about making connections and learning to work with *your* land and its special needs.

To help you get started, you will need to determine your plant hardiness zone. A plant hardiness zone map helps determine which plants might flourish in your area. Zones are determined by the minimum winter temperature in any particular area and help you select the best time to sow your seeds. You can access a map easily on the web or find one in just about any gardening magazine or seed catalog.

Next, you may want to consider your microclimate. I live tightly tucked against a bluff that traps precipitation, meaning I get more snow, more rain, and more shade than most people in my area. Microclimates are determined by your property's exposure to sun, wind, light, and water. If you live in an urban area, surrounding buildings can affect your garden, as they reflect and generate heat. If you live on a high hill, you may have more wind than your neighbors below you. The great thing about understanding your property's microclimates (yes, you can have several in one area) is that it can really increase your garden's potential.

Let's Get Dirty: Starting Your Seeds Indoors

It is during those long, dark months of winter that we dream of our enchanted gardens. Imagine with me moonflowers tangled around an arbor, the delicate tendrils reaching through the trellising and grasping at the aconite, whose purple blooms exude dark magick. And just beneath the foxglove we spy the mystical mandrake, whose roots offer protection to those who awaken its spirit. But stop. Hold on. What if you're in hardiness zone 5? That mandrake plant is not happening without some real garden know-how. If you're new to gardening, you might be disappointed to discover some plants won't grow well in your region, which can make picking out seeds (or plants) a daunting experience. Once you've established your hardiness zone, look for plants that will thrive in your area. My number-one rule has always been to start simple and grow with your garden. Relish in the small successes and learn from your mistakes.

A well-written seed packet is going to give you all the information you need to be successful. This will include hardiness zone, light and water needs, a basic overview of the plant (botanical and folk names, traits, and characteristics), and whether the seed should be sown directly into the soil after your last frost or sown indoors six weeks before your hardiness zone's last frost date.

Vegetables that perform well when sown indoors include tomatoes, peppers, brassicas, peas, onions, and squash. Veggies like carrots, beets, and spinach prefer to be directly sown. Herbs that require a longer germination period, such as rosemary, lavender, thyme, sage, and tarragon, are great for starting indoors. But other herbs, such as parsley and dill, can practically be tossed as an afterthought and still come up. Sunflowers, impatiens, alyssum, and marigolds are several flowers that start well indoors. Cosmos, calendula, and bachelor's buttons like to be scattered and look lovely growing in wild clumps around your tamer garden fare.

Seeds 101

The most important thing to consider when starting your new seeds is lighting and heat. You are going to need to find a place in your home, like a sunny south-facing window, that can give your seedlings twelve hours of light per day. Small grow lights are an inexpensive solution to unsuitable lighting. You also need to consider that for seeds to germinate, they need temperatures of 65 to 75 degrees Fahrenheit. Placing your seeds in a warm location or near a heat source will work. But you can also purchase small seed-starting heat mats to set your trays on.

You can use just about anything to sprout your seeds, including recycled containers (such as yogurt or discarded party cups) with holes poked through the bottoms, egg cartons, newspaper pots, peat pots, or seed-starting flats, which can be purchased and used year after year. Whatever you use, make sure they're washed and placed in leak-proof trays. The last thing you will need is a good seed-starting mix available at any garden center.

Transfer the seed-starting mix to a bucket and dampen it with a little water (do not saturate it). Fill your container within a half inch of the top. Follow the instructions on the backs of your seed packets for depth of planting. Cover the seeds with soil and press ever so gently. Label your containers and mist the surface of the soil with water. Check your seeds daily and continue to mist with water. If you're using grow lights, keep them within two inches of the tops of the seedlings.

Once the seedlings have grown their second set of leaves (true leaves), thin the pots down to one plant per pot by snipping weaker seedlings at the soil line. You will need to start your seedlings on an organic seed-starter fertilizer regimen. These fertilizers are available in any garden supply center or online and come with easy instructions.

Here is a simple seed blessing to perform before you plant your seeds: lay your hands over your seeds and say,

> Bless the seeds, for they are a promise of life's continuous cycle

Lay hands over your soil and say,

Bless the soil, for it is the womb where all life regenerates

Raise hands, palms up, and say,

Bless my hands, as they hold the secret of rebirth
Blessed be

Chapter 5
Sunwise Circles

The growing fingers of light of the young sun draw the Cailleach from her mountaintop, and she is transformed into the Fair Woman of February. Sunwise she walks the awakening landscape; sunwise we follow behind her. For even though winter's grasp is still very much present in many regions, the signs of spring ignite us with hope. It is the sun that dictates the Wheel of the Year. And as a Witch who keeps a garden, I watch with a steady eye as the newborn sun rises from its eastern realm every morning throughout its awakening. Higher and higher it rises until the shadows shrink back and we are once again bathed in sunlight.

In the early hours of a February morning, when the air is chilly and mist hangs low along the river, I walk deosil (sunwise) around my garden, planning, listening, checking the soil, and most importantly, connecting with the natural rhythm of the earth's yearly cycle. In doing so I am also sharing my own energy with the land. For to be successful gardeners, we must work hand in hand with the earth. As you walk your own sunwise circles around your garden, this is the time to check your soil. Nutrients make all the difference; therefore, you must care for it. This is the time to add compost or manure to give your plants their best start. Remember, dear Witch, if done right, with every little garden, we are restoring a piece of the earth. It's a spiritual connectedness with the green spirits of the land who challenge us to step back outside. So as you turn the soil or plant those first greens, be present in the moment—indulge in the ritual of transformation.

The Community Garden

It was a dark, rainy January evening when a coven member contacted me and said that she felt compelled to adopt a couple of beds at the local community garden to raise fresh vegetables for the local food bank and wanted to know if I would help.

"Really?" I asked. "We both have big gardens. I don't mind growing a bit more and donating from my home garden."

"I know. I just feel that in doing so, we are not only helping by giving fresh vegetables to food-insecure families but we're supporting the community too. Hardly anyone uses the garden."

She was right. The garden, with the lovely picket fence adorned with birdhouses made by elementary school children, had seemed all but abandoned in the last few years. We invited another coven member and the three of us went to check it out.

We stood under the protective covering of a small gazebo and looked out over the boxes lined up and numbered. A few still had the tell-tale signs of use—hand-painted signs, kitschy garden art, and decaying stalks—but most of the boxes were barren.

"Those two over there," my friend said, pointing to two four-by-ten-foot boxes on the southern side of the garden.

We all agreed, and within a couple days, the boxes were officially ours to nurture.

We spent the rest of month of January drawing up plans and discussing types of vegetables we could grow vertically to maximize the space and flowering companion plants to draw pollinators and to add beauty. The next step was to enrich the soil that was full of pebbles and leached of all nutrients, so we added copious amounts of compost to each box.

We had decided to bless the garden as a coven on Imbolc, which marks the halfway point between winter and spring. We walked sunwise circles around our boxes and asked for blessings upon the garden, all the while placing stones we had painted with our own sigils for growth, peace, beauty, and community. When we were finished, we tapped our own kitschy sign that read "Magick Grows Here" into the soil.

I like to believe that it was our blessing that brought upon the revitalization of the community garden that year. More people than ever rented boxes, we got to meet new people and exchange ideas with other gardeners, I was asked to teach a class to a group of elementary students who adopted their own plots, and our garden thrived, producing boxes of food to go out to families in need.

Community gardens began popping up in the United States in the late nineteenth century in response to a growing separation between people and their food source, as more and more people had to abandon their farms and moved to industrialized cities to make ends meet. Nowadays, community gardens can be found in most neighborhoods (even in small towns like my own). I recommend, whether as a family, a coven, a group of friends, or an individual, you check out what your local community garden has to offer. Boxes are typically inexpensive to rent, and you might be surprised by the community events and learning opportunities offered.

Community gardens do far more for the environment than just provide a green space. They help improve the air and soil quality, increase biodiversity, improve our own mental health, provide easy access to fresh fruits and vegetables, improve water filtration, and reduce neighborhood waste through composting. On top of that, by putting hand to soil, we are fueling a deep connection with the earth. It can be felt as we nurture the plants, who in turn nurture our souls.

Community Garden Blessing with Brighid

This should be done as the sun rises (if possible) and can be done with a group or alone. You can also perform this blessing at your own home garden.

You will need 4 stones painted with symbols of the elements or with sigils or symbols that reflect the qualities you would like to imbue in your personal garden space. You'll also need your own kitschy garden sign or ornamentation to set as a permanent marker. Because you are in a public space, you can say your ritual words aloud or quietly to protect yourself, your coven, or your family.

Start at the east end of your box and place your first stone. Say something like this:

> Blessed Brighid, I/we invite you to breathe life into my/our garden so that it may feed and nurture my/our soul(s).

Move sunwise to the southern point. Place your stone and say,

> Blessed Brighid, I/we ask for your light to bring me/us growth in both the garden and my life/our lives.

Move to the western point of your box. Place your stone and say,

> Blessed Brighid, I/we ask you to bless my/our soul(s) through the tranquility offered in this space.

Move to the northern point. Place your stone and say,

> Blessed Brighid, I/we ask you to bless this garden with abundance. May the food I/we produce bring pleasure and nutrients to my/our body/bodies.

Place your permanent sign or garden décor in its place and thank the Goddess in your own way.

Chapter 6
Herbs of February

February finds us with our hearts open to transformation. The signs of spring are at hand as the days continue to grow longer and the first green shoots appear. I have chosen herbs that represent the power of change, love, protection, and healing to guide us from darkness and into the light.

Basil (*Ocimum basilicum*)

Planet: Mars

Element: Fire

Energy: Masculine

Deities: Vishnu, Ra

There are some herbs that just make me feel witchy. Basil happens to be one of them. Easy to grow, this herb of the mint family is popular in Mediterranean, Italian, Thai, and Vietnamese cooking. Basil is an annual, native throughout southwest Asia to central Africa. A versatile magickal herb, basil can be used in spells to draw prosperity, passion, cleansing, protection, peace, courage, strength, purification, and love.

Basil Negativity Cleansing Wash

To rid your home of negativity, fill a quart jar with water and a black tourmaline. Add a couple sprigs of basil and allow it to infuse for 48 hours. Remove the sprigs and stone and add the water to your mop water. Clean your floors as usual following the path of the sun (clockwise).

Cottonwood (*Populus* sect. *Aigeiros*)

Planet: Saturn

Element: Water

Energy: Feminine

Deities: Pluto, Hercules

I like to think of cottonwood as a gateway tree, as it straddles the line between earth and water. It is one of many species in the *Populus* genus, which includes poplar and aspen, that call riparian zones home. Known for its resinous buds that have been extracted for centuries for use in medicine (sometimes called balm of Gilead), it is antibacterial, antifungal, and mildly analgesic. In magick, it is used in spells to attract money, hope, healing, encouragement, transformation, and soul flight.

Balm of Gilead Anointing Oil

Use as an anointing oil for spellwork, for meditation, or to dab on scrapes and bruises.

You will need:

- Mason jar
- Cottonwood buds
- Olive oil
- Coffee filter
- Rubber band
- Cheesecloth

Fill a mason jar halfway with cottonwood buds. Pour olive oil over the buds to within 1 inch of the top. Cover with a coffee filter and secure with a rubber band. Allow the oil to steep for at least 6 weeks. When ready, use a cheesecloth to filter out the buds, and store the infused oil in dark bottles for up to 6 months.

Marjoram (*Origanum majorana*)

Planet: Mercury

Element: Air

Energy: Masculine

Deities: Venus, Aphrodite

Used to enhance the flavor of soups, stews, and sauces, marjoram is a great magickal herb to enchant your meals to strengthen health and bring love and happiness.

Similar in flavor (slightly sweeter) to oregano, this member of the mint family is easy to grow and spreads prolifically. Plant in full sun to part shade in well-drained soil. Marjoram grows up to 2 feet in height and has clusters of white or lavender flowers atop stems of gray-green leaves. When grown in the garden, this plant is said to protect the homeowner against evil. Hang bunches of dried marjoram in your home as a way of protecting loved ones. Or use it in charm bags for money spells. In magick, use marjoram for love, happiness, money, protection, and health.

Money Charm Bag

- Coin
- Citrine stone
- 1 to 2 pinches of dried marjoram
- Green drawstring bag

During the full moon phase, place the coin, stone, and dried marjoram in a bowl. Using your fingers, roll the coin and stone around in the marjoram. As you do this, focus on your intention and say 3 times,

Stone and coin and powerful herb
Fill my pockets as I speak these words
Herb and coin and stone divine
Fill my pockets—the power is mine

Place all ingredients in your green drawstring bag and hang it where you can see it every day for 1 full moon cycle.

Primrose (*Primula vulgaris*)

Planet: Venus

Element: Earth

Energy: Feminine

Deities: Freya, Brighid

This sweet flowering plant in the family Primulaceae is native to western and southern Europe, northwest Africa, and parts of southwest Asia. These compact perennials grow 6 to 18 inches tall and are perfect for tucking into shady nooks or adding a spot of color in your woodland garden. Having primroses in your garden is said to encourage faery activity. Primrose contains high amounts of vitamin C, and both flowers and leaves can be added to salads or soups. The blooms also have been used in wine making. In magick, use primrose in spells to connect with the faery world, new beginnings, protection, beauty, and love.

Plant a Primrose for New Beginnings

I always get so excited in late winter when I start seeing the small pots of bright primroses at my local DIY and garden centers. Because they are so inexpensive, I always buy several to plant in pots that I set in my kitchen and on my front porch, and as spring unfurls, I transfer them to the garden so I can continue to enjoy them year after year. Try this simple primrose ritual for Imbolc.

You will need:

- Permanent marker
- Small terra cotta pot 1 to 2 inches larger in diameter than the original primrose container
- Container of bright yellow primroses

- ½ cup drainage gravel
- 2 cups of good potting soil (more or less, depending on the pot)

On the morning of Imbolc, make yourself a cup of tea and get comfortable. Use the permanent marker to draw sun symbols, sigils, words of power, or whatever symbols you connect to new beginnings on the terra cotta pot. As you focus on your new venture or outlook, channel that focus into the bright yellow blooms of the primrose. Treat the act of repotting your primrose as ritual. Add a layer of drainage gravel in the bottom of your new pot, followed by potting soil, up to approximately 2½ inches from the top of the pot.

Lightly squeeze the side of the primrose's container before gently pulling the primrose from its confines. Place in the new pot and fill the remainder of the pot with potting soil. Water your plant and place it somewhere in your home as a focal point to remind you new beginnings are what you make of them.

Witch Hazel (*Hamamelis virginiana*)

Planet: Sun

Element: Fire

Energy: Masculine

Deities: Mercury, Lugh

While other flowers are still dormant, witch hazel unfurls starry yellow blooms that brighten our hopes for spring's return. This small flowering shrub of North America and Asia has been used to soothe skin irritations and ease redness and inflammation for centuries. It is one of the few plants that have been approved by the FDA as an ingredient for over-the-counter medications. Use it in magick for healing after loss, for protection, and for finding lost objects.

Divining with Witch Hazel

Witch hazel is plant well known for its ability to divine (or dowse) for water, metal, or lost objects. Before taking a branch for divining, please remember to establish a relationship with the spirit of the tree. Spend time with it, meditate near it, and communicate with it in your own way. Ask the tree if it is okay to take a branch for magickal use. Then, while the tree is dormant, when its buds are still tight and the form of the tree is easily seen, select a branch that is naturally forked and trim it to form a Y shape. Make sure your "tines" are relatively equal in length for balance. Decorate and bless your new dowsing rod.

For divining lost objects, hold the forks at arm's length with the rod pointed upward at a 45-degree angle. Take a few deep, cleansing breaths and visualize the lost object. Channel your focus to the divining rod. Ask the rod to lead you to your lost object and then walk slowly, feeling for tugs or pulling. When the divining rod has come to its destination, you should feel a sharp downward pull.

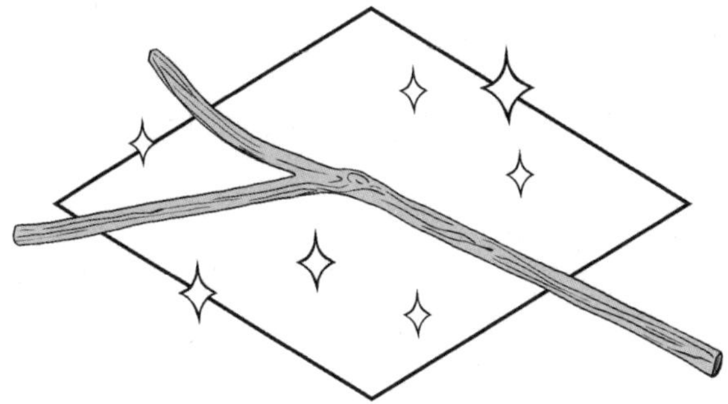

Around the Garden
To-Do List for February

This is a great time to start adding compost to your garden beds. There are many types of compost available at your local gardening center, including composted manure, mushroom compost, or vermiculture. You can also directly dig in kitchen scraps (no dairy or meat) or make your own compost.

You will need:

- 3 parts brown material, which may include dead leaves, shredded paper, straw, wood chips, or sawdust (supplies carbon)
- 1 part green material, which may include grass clippings, coffee grounds, eggshells, or vegetable and fruit scraps (supplies nitrogen)

Use a compost bin or tumbler and follow instructions for your bin for moisture content and aeration.

If you live in zones 7 to 10, you can most likely begin to direct sow cool-season crops such as beets, peas, kale, and carrots, as well as plant your bare-root trees, shrubs, and vines.

In zones 9 to 11 you can start planting crops such as corn, cucumbers, and squash—but always be prepared for a surprise frost.

In colder zones, you may want to start seeds for crops such as tomatoes, peppers, eggplant, and onions. Continue pruning dormant trees and shrubs.

Grow Your Magickal Knowledge

Use your garden BOS to expand your growing knowledge on magickal and medicinal herbs. Remember, as Witches, we never cease to learn. Nature always has lessons to share. Imbolc is a great time to get together with your coven or witchy friends to share and swap seeds and do a group seed-blessing ceremony.

MARCH

The Maiden awakens slowly, alluring our senses with swollen buds and tendrils of green. Spring can't come soon enough.

MARCH CORRESPONDENCES

Nature Spirits: Satyr, nymph

Colors: Light green, yellow, lavender

Herbs and Flowers: Daffodil, violet, wood betony

Scents: Apple, sandalwood

Stone: Aquamarine

Trees: Dogwood, ash

Animals: Hare, lamb, salamander

Birds: Swallow, sea eagle

Deities: Ostara, Persephone, Ares, Jarilo

Zodiac: Pisces, Aries

Work spells for rebirth, renewal, transition, fertility, and balance.

Chapter 7
The Awakening

The earth is warming, and the Maiden awakens with a green fire that ignites the surroundings with new growth. Like all Witches who are deeply rooted in the earth, I am acutely aware of the subtle changes that occur as the Cailleach hurls her staff at the base of the holly, releasing winter's reign. The shift of light enlivens my spirit, and winter begins to feel like a long-lost, dark dream. Birds begin to sing as the sun reaches golden fingers above the eastern hills, drawing me to the garden, where steam rises from my beds, carrying the scent of rich humus.

I am far too excited to share my enthusiasm for the Maiden's awakening. And I am always surprised by my mundane friends' reactions to my enthusiastic rambles. I remember running into such a friend a couple of years back as we both carried groceries out of our local grocery store. March released a chilly, pelting rain that stung our cheeks.

"It's cold." She motioned toward the dark, gray clouds that pressed against the surrounding hills.

"Sure is," I said, then quickly added, "but you can definitely smell spring unfurling in the air."

"What?" She furrowed her brows.

"You know, cottonwood on the breeze and the rising scent of the warming soil."

"What's a cottonwood?"

I tried my best to not look completely shocked. "You've lived here your whole life." I chuckled. "You know, the trees that release the fluffy seed heads in June. They grow near the river."

She laughed. "All I know is that those trees send my allergies out of control. And I hate cleaning up the fluff. In fact, I don't think I like those trees at all."

I stood mouth agape as I processed her blasphemy, then finally said, "How can you not like faery clouds?"

"You're weird. But that's why I love you." She winked. "Let's get together for coffee sometime."

I suppose I can't help coming across as a wee bit peculiar about it, because of all the seasonal changes, but it is the Maiden's awakening that fills me with the most emotion. Maybe it's because winter can sometimes feel too dreary, too long without my hands plunged into the soil. So, on that first day in March when a breeze tangles my hair with the scent of green, I stand and cry tears of happiness and thank the earth for the promise of spring.

Lunar Planting

Depending on where you're located, March may find you knee-deep in compost with spring gardening in full swing or still organizing seeds as you dream of greener days to come. In my area of the Pacific Northwest, March is a fickle month. There have been many a March when I prepped and planted beds during the first week under the buttery light of a young sun. But there have been many times too when I could be found standing in six inches of snow as I begged the Crone to release her icy grip. For the most part, much like the old adage says, March comes into my region like a lion and goes out like a lamb. By the end of the month of equal light and the promise of greener days, I have cleaned my greenhouses, raspberries are tied, beds are prepped, and seedlings are ready for transplant.

One thing I always like to do in early March is pull out my lunar calendar so I can get an idea of what my planting schedule will look like. If you've read my other books, you know that I consider myself a true child of the moon. Her gentle glow has guided me throughout my life. Her lovely full face lit the way home when, as a child, I would ride my horse too far down the forested trails that spoke of faery realms and adventure. Her thin, curved smile was the catalyst of my early spells when as a teen, I divined of her what my future might hold. And as an adult, I instinctively work with her gentle rhythms in both my magickal and mundane life, harnessing her energy as she waxes and wanes across the night sky. If you're not already working with moon energy, the garden is a good place to begin.

Planting in rhythm with the moon's cycle was used by our agricultural ancestors, who governed their lives and their livelihood by the placement of the closest celestial bodies. Done correctly, it encourages growth and water flow in new seedlings, and it also aids in growing more vigorous plants, adding a special touch of bewitchment to your garden. Why does it work? Because we are working with the moon's gravitational pull.

We know the moon's influence on the tides, but it also influences other bodies of water as well, including the moisture in the soil. In its simplest form, lunar planting (or moon gardening) is working with the moon's phases and timing your planting, harvesting, and maintenance accordingly. The moon's monthly cycle is approximately 29.5 days, with each phase lasting approximately 7.38 days. It is within these windows that we plan what time is optimum for planting our leafy greens and flowering plants, which days will best harness the moon's energy for working with vining plants or root crops, or when the best time for weeding or harvesting might be.

Sound complicated? It's really not. But's that's why I recommend a lunar calendar (try *The Old Farmer's Almanac* or *Llewellyn's Moon Sign Book*) that lays out favorable dates for sowing, planting, harvesting, and so on to make it easier for busy people like us to plan out what our gardening season might look like.

But for those of you who want a no-fuss guide to working with the moon's phases or astrological timing, don't worry—I've got you covered.

Simple Moon Gardening

This might be the simplest and least restrictive way to work with the moon's gravitational pull, and it's a great place to start if you're new to lunar gardening:

New Moon to Full Moon: As the shining face of the moon grows, she pulls moisture upward, encouraging leaf and stem growth. This is the time to plant your annual flowers, leafy greens, and fruits and vegetables that bear crops above ground (such as pumpkins, tomatoes, herbs, and peppers).

Full Moon to Dark Moon: As the moonlight decreases night by night, her energy focuses on root development. Plant flowering bulbs, biennial and perennial flowers, and vegetables that bear crops below ground (such as beets, onions, and carrots).

Gardening through the Moon's Phases

If you feel you're ready, let's take lunar gardening to the next level. Remember, as the moon shifts through her phases, not only is the gravitational pull manipulating moisture in the soil, but it also is helping create a higher sap run in plants as the moon waxes. As the moon wanes, the energy goes directly to the roots. Working with each moon phase grants us the ideal timing for encouraging the growth of our many and varied precious plants.

First Quarter (New Moon): Her sickle smile reminds us of the magick of new beginnings. During this time of promise, plant flowering annuals that produce their seeds on the outside: grains such as quinoa, wheat, or barley, and leafy crops such as chard, lettuce, and kale, as all the energy goes to the leaves.

Second Quarter (Waxing Moon): Her growing glow presents us with a time of increased energy. Plant flowering plants that produce their seeds on the inside, such as pumpkins, tomatoes, and legumes; and cane plants, such as raspberries, blackberries, and loganberries, that will benefit as growth and liquid absorption begin to peak.

Full Moon: At her shining peak, we take advantage of her full power: plant your corn and vining plants—pole beans, peas, and sweet peas will benefit from the full moon's extra light. This is also a great time to gather your magickal herbs and charge moon water to add a little extra power to those magickal plants.

Third Quarter (Waning Moon): The moon's transformative power plays softly on the landscape. During this time when the energy goes to the roots, plant root crops such as turnips, carrots, or beets; plants that grow on stalks rather than vines, such as brussels sprouts, asparagus, and strawberries; trees; and shrubs.

Fourth Quarter (Dark Moon): This time of darkness, when the stars are the brightest and magick takes us inward, is a rest period. Time to work on other gardening chores, such as weeding, pruning, thinning out plants, or turning compost.

Astrological Timing

If you want to add a twist to your lunar gardening, another way to utilize the moon's power is by using astrological timing. Like gardening by the moon, astrological lunar planting is based on the moon. However, instead of depending only on the moon's phase, astrological planting takes into account the moon's position in the astrological zodiac. As the moon travels through the sky, it passes through a different astrological sign every two to three days. We plant as the moon passes through fruitful signs (earth or water signs) and cultivate, harvest, or weed during semibarren or barren signs (fire and air). In the past, I have used the moon's phases for my fruits and vegetables and astrological timing for magickal herbs and flowers and have experienced wonderful results.

Earth Signs (Taurus, Virgo, and Capricorn): These are fertile signs and great for planting (especially root crops) and transplanting your seedlings.

Air Signs (Libra, Gemini, and Aquarius): Air signs are considered semibarren and mark a good time to harvest and to cultivate.

Fire Signs (Aries, Leo, and Sagittarius): Considered barren times, these signs are typically the best time for weeding, pest removal, and harvesting.

Water Signs (Cancer, Pisces, and Scorpio): Water signs are the most fertile of all the signs and are great for planting anything (especially flowering and leafy green plants).

Moon Water

During the growing season, it's nice to set aside specially moon-charged water for your magickal herbs. I find that it adds a little more enchantment to my spell crafting. I usually start with March's Ash Moon by setting out a bowl to reflect the full moon as she rides high above my garden, and I continue the process with every full moon until the end of the growing season.

You will need:

- Large cauldron (or bowl) that can hold approximately 1 gallon of liquid
- 1 gallon of water (nonchlorinated)
- Crystals of your choice (optional)

On the night of the full moon, place your bowl of water outside, on your balcony, or near a window. Just make sure you can see the moon's reflection in the water. If you'd like to add a clear quartz crystal, moonstone, or other stone associated with the moon, place it in the water. Lift the container toward the moon (or place your hands over it if the container is too heavy) and say something like this:

Mother Moon, Mother of the Seed, Mother of the Corn
In my cauldron may this water transform
For leaf and root and bud and flower divine
May your power help my garden shine

Leave the bowl overnight to absorb the moon's energy. The next day transfer the water into a watering can and use a bit while watering your magickal plants.

Chapter 8
Nature's First Blush

The small farm where I grew up, wild and free to roam the miles of woodland that surrounded us, has turned into a three-acre parkland of sorts, complete with trails winding through luscious English cottage garden favorites and a greenspace that features ponds and sitting areas tucked in shady nooks. It's one of those places you might find while flipping through the pages of a magazine—a place where weddings and holiday events have on occasion been held. Only shadows of what I remember of our humble farm remain.

You see, gardening was a simple utilitarian practice for my parents when I was kid. The breathtaking perennial beds that now weave a tapestry of color throughout their property were a hobby saved for after my sisters and I grew up and began lives of our own. So, oddly enough, most of what I learned about flower gardening as a child was taught to me by the man I knew as my grandfather. He was a peculiar creature who talked with a thick Carolina accent and whispered stories of haints and boo hags and had a Bible verse for every situation. My mother called him a superstitious old fool—I thought he was pure magick. For he was the one who taught me how to garden by the phases of the moon and how to save seeds that could be passed down to my children and my children's children. He shared with me folk beliefs concerning the weather and the plants that he grew and could quickly stir up a healing salve from the weeds that invaded his flower beds.

One of my favorite times to explore his garden was in March, just as the first spring bulbs poked through the soil and the first flowering shrubs blushed sweetly from the forest's edge.

We made a game of counting how many tulips, daffodils, and other flowering bulbs were coming up. It was akin to an Easter egg hunt for me. "Seventy-six, seventy-seven, seventy-eight," I would call out as I poked around the periwinkle that grew along the fence.

It was when I got to the bottle tree that my grandfather became playful. You see, the practice of hanging bottles upside down in trees to capture evil spirits was brought to the South by enslaved Africans in the seventeenth century. The hope was that by hanging the bottles in a tree, evil spirits would find their way into the bottles and become stuck. As the morning sun rose, it would destroy the trapped spirit. And my grandfather, well, he always wanted to spook me. Little did he know, I was unspookable (in hindsight, I think he did know).

"Listen." He'd mischievously shush me. "Can you hear the bottle's hum?"

I'd tilt my head toward the bright cobalt bottles and smile as I tried desperately to keep count.

"Another evil spirit trapped." He'd smile. "I sure hope it doesn't escape and mess up your counting."

"One hundred and two, one hundred and three, one hundred and four," I would count louder, then laugh.

When we were done with our game, my grandmother would have lunch ready, and a collection of prechilled spring bulbs, potting soil, and a terra cotta pot was waiting for me to put together my own tiny spring garden. As I planted, my grandfather told me stories of Narcissus, who fell in love with his own reflection, and of the stonemason who took his own life for love. And before I'd leave for home, my grandfather would remind to keep tulips on the nightstand by my bed for protection. I did (and still do). These were the moments that sparked my love for the magick of growing things.

The Bewitching Tulip

Once upon a time, there was a Persian princess named Shirin who fell deeply in love with Farhad, a simple stonemason. He too loved the princess with all his heart, but the princess's father did not approve of the match.

For his daughter was of royal blood and was not allowed to marry one of such a lowly position. For some time, the lovers met in secret, where they held each other and whispered to one another their plans of running away together. But as happens in tragic tales of love, Shirin's father found out about their affair and devised a plan that would put a stop to it. He summoned Farhad and ordered him to complete a complex task at the edge of the city.

While the stonemason was off doing as he was instructed, Shirin's father sent a messenger to him saying that the princess was dead. Overcome by grief, Farhad took his own life by throwing himself from a cliff. As for Shirin, upon discovering his lifeless body, she too took her own life. On that ground, for every droplet of their blood, a red tulip rose up.

This is one of many variations of the tragic tale of Shirin and Farhad. Reminiscent of Romeo and Juliet, the story represents both heart-wrenching love and rebirth. In Turkey, the tulip is considered a charm against evil. And in magick today, the tulip is used for spells for protection, love, and rebirth.

There are about 100 species of this bulbous herb in the Liliaceae (lily) family. It produces two or three thick bluish-green leaves at the base, and though there is tremendous variation in color and color patterns, the relatively basic bell-shaped flower form of the tulip remains the same.

The tulip (*Tulipa* spp.) is native to Central Asia and Turkey. Cultivation of this favorite likely began in Persia (Iran) in the tenth century, and it was soon a symbol of the Ottoman Empire. Tulips were introduced to the Western world by Augier Ghislain de Busbecq, the Viennese ambassador to Turkey, who boasted of the plant in letters and around 1551 sent seeds to Austria. But it's French botanist Carolus Clusius, an avid bulb grower in the late 1500s, who is most often credited with introducing spring bulbs across Europe.

The bulbs of the tulip are edible, but the core must be removed, as it is toxic. They were eaten during times of war as a substitute for onions or potatoes. The petals are also edible and make a colorful addition to salads or desserts.

Magickally, the tulip is one of the most versatile herbs in the Witch's springtime arsenal. Why? Because of the huge array of colors tulips come in, tulips can be used in a variety of spells and rituals. Of course, the simplest way to use tulips in magick is by planting them in a pot by your door or in grouping them around your home as a symbol of protection. The very act of presenting your partner with tulips acts as a love charm, and planting them near a grave or placing a pot of them on your spring altar is a visible symbol of rebirth. The bulbs too can be used in magick (especially for love). Gently write your intent on the papery bulb before planting during the appropriate moon phase. Connected to the planet Venus and the element of earth, tulips can be used in spells for protection and love.

Tulip Magick and the Moon

"Just like the moon, I go through phases." This is a very relatable saying that reminds me of the tulip in many ways. Its form is probably one of the most recognizable in the flower world, but its variations in color can subtly change the energy in your garden. I thought it might be nice to dedicate the month of March to utilizing the power of the tulip with moon energy in your magick. The following examples are just a starting point.

The New Moon

A time of new beginnings. The new moon reminds us that it's never too late to start again. We are never too old, too broken, or too set in our ways to make powerful changes that can impact us in a positive way. Plant the bulb of a bright yellow tulip with your intention written lightly on its papery skin and watch it grow.

Use these varieties with new moon magick:

***Tulipa* 'Moonlight Girl':** How suited this lily-flowered tulip is for new moon magick with a lemony yellow hue that becomes creamier as she matures!

***Tulipa* 'Gold Fever':** A double yellow tulip that is pure sunshine for the soul.

The Waxing Moon

A time for visualization. The waxing moon invites us to grow, to draw in, to attract, and to encourage. Float the petals of bright orange tulips in an invigorating ritual bath or use green petals in prosperity magick.

Use these varieties with waxing moon magick:

***Tulipa* 'Princess Irene':** Sunrise orange with splashes of bright pink, this tulip is a happy reminder that anything is attainable.

***Tulipa* 'Spring Green':** Creamy white with lovely green central veins, a striking addition for any magickal gardener.

The Full Moon

A time for power, the full moon is some potent magick. Lie on a bed of satiny petals of red tulips and use the power of the orgasm (alone or with a partner) to manifest your desires. Float a couple of white or lavender petals in a cup of psychic tea before divination.

Use these varieties with full moon magick:

***Tulipa* 'Kingsblood':** A late-blooming fiery red tulip that is truly bewitching.

***Tulipa* 'Purissima':** The white of this tulip positively glows and would make a great addition to a moon garden.

***Tulipa* 'Magic Lavender':** The name says it all. A true lavender variety with cup-shaped flowers.

The Waning Moon

A time for healing and banishing. As the moon wanes, we draw inward. Use brown tulips in spells when feeling a disconnect in your life and blue in spells for healing matters of the soul.

Use these varieties with waning moon magick:

***Tulipa* 'Brown Sugar':** This earthy tulip offers reddish-brown petals with just a hint of apricot. When one feels a disconnect from Mama Gaia, this is the tulip to work with.

***Tulipa* 'Blue Parrot':** As close as you're going to get to true blue, this frilly tulip has lavender-blue petals with streaks of true blue.

The Dark Moon

A time for introspection. At the dark of the moon, we meet (literally or figuratively) at the crossroads to face our shadows. Use pots of velvety black tulips to guard your rites.

Use these varieties in dark moon magick:

***Tulipa* 'Queen of the Night':** The perfect dark moon tulip whose deep purple (black) petals fill the air with mystery.

***Tulipa* 'Black Parrot':** This frilly deep maroon (black) tulip exudes dark magick. One of my favorites.

Planting Spring Bulbs

Did you know that most spring-flowering bulbs, including tulips, daffodils, and hyacinths, need a prolonged period of cold temperatures to grow and bloom properly? If you live in zones 3 to 8, this cold period is provided naturally by a winter spent in the ground. But bulbs planted in warmer zones 9 to 11 do not get the cold they need. To perform well, they must be placed in a refrigerator (not a freezer) at 35 to 45 degrees Fahrenheit for 10 to 16 weeks before planting. Exposing bulbs to these cold temperatures stimulates a biochemical response that switches on flower formation and initiates root growth. Crocus, daffodils, hyacinth, and snowdrops need approximately 12 to 15 weeks. Tulips can go a little less, 10 to 14 weeks. This is why in cooler climates we plant spring bulbs in the autumn.

But what if you live in a warmer climate and you're not ready to attempt (or even interested in attempting) prechilling bulbs for spring? I get it. It takes a lot of forethought. Well, it just so happens that prechilled bulbs are easily attainable online or at your local garden center during the spring months,

January through April, depending on your zone. Whether you prechilled the bulbs yourself or purchased prechilled bulbs, they need to be planted in partial shade or in pots for your porch, balcony, or window boxes as soon as they are brought out. Plant them outside in well-aerated soil or with a good potting soil mix in containers 2 to 4 inches deep. Planted in cooler climates, spring bulbs will continue to come back year after year. In warmer climates, they can be treated as an annual or dug up in the autumn and chilled in the refrigerator for approximately 3 months before replanting in late winter.

Use these popular spring bulbs in magick:

Daffodil: Love, abundance, fertility, luck (see page 75)

Hyacinth: Protection, love, happiness

Crocus: Psychic powers, love, strength, wisdom (see page 27)

Snowdrop: Hope, grief, friendship (see page 31)

Fritillaria: Love, healing, wisdom

Ostara Ritual for Renewal

Ostara, or the vernal equinox, which typically falls between March 20 and 21, marks the day when night and day are equal and the promise of brighter days ahead is fulfilled. On this day, we honor all that is burgeoning with new growth. We honor the fertility of the earth, and most importantly, we honor the budding possibilities within ourselves.

For this spell, we will give thanks to the four directions by planting eggs at the cardinal points of our garden space or property or in small pots in our home or apartment.

You will need:

- 4 eggs
- Natural egg dye (see page 71) or commercial egg dye
- Scribe or sharp tool for lightly scratching (nail or darning needle works great)
- 4 small pots filled with potting soil (if doing this in your home)

Dye each egg to represent the qualities of each of the cardinal directions: yellow for east, red for south, blue for west, and brown for north. When the eggs are cool, use your scribe to scratch personal sigils, symbols, or words of power to correspond with each egg. Make sure you have plotted out the cardinal directions before performing the ritual.

Starting in the east, raise your yellow egg to the direction of the rising sun and say,

> I call upon the power of air and give thanks for a new dawn. May this season of hope bring balance and joy.

Plant your egg. Move to the direction of south, raise your red egg, and say,

> I call upon the power of fire and give thanks for renewed strength. May this season of hope bring celebration and love.

Plant your egg. Move to the direction of west, raise your blue egg, and say,

> I call upon the power of water and give thanks for your constant healing flow. May this season be one of dreams and possibility.

Plant your egg. Move to the direction of north, raise your brown egg, and say,

> I call upon the power of earth and give thanks for renewal. May this season bring abundance and stability.

Plant your egg.

Thank the elements in your own way for their continued protection over the growing season.

Natural Egg Dye

- White vinegar
- Natural ingredients for color:
  - 2 to 3 tablespoons turmeric for yellow shades (east, air)
  - 1 cup chopped beets or red onion skins for red shades (south, fire)
  - 1 cup chopped purple cabbage or blueberries for blue shades (west, water)
  - 1 cup onion skins or 3 black tea bags for brown shades (north, earth)
- Eggs

In a saucepan, add 4 to 6 tablespoons of white vinegar to 1 quart of water. Bring to a boil and add your dye ingredients for the desired color. Lower the heat and allow to simmer for approximately 30 minutes. Turn off heat and add your egg(s). Allow them to soak for a minimum of 30 minutes or until you have achieved the color you want.

Chapter 9
Herbs of March

The hours of day and night are once again equal as we prepare ourselves to come out of dormancy. The herbs I have chosen are those of clarity, mirth, luck, and dreams, for this is the time of preparation and focus on those things that enliven the soul.

Bleeding Heart (*Dicentra* spp.)

Planet: Venus

Element: Water

Energy: Feminine

In the Pacific Northwest forests where I live, the delicate lacy green leaves of the wild bleeding heart poking through the humus are a true indicator that spring has finally arrived and all is right with the world. Native North American varieties include the Pacific Coastal *Dicentra formosa* in my region, as well as the Appalachian *D. eximia*, sometimes called turkey corn. They feature dangling, heart-shaped blooms in shades of pink and fern-like foliage.

A popular garden choice, *D. spectabilis* is a larger perennial variety that blooms in spring and was introduced to the West from Southeast Asia in the nineteenth century. The blooms have a broader range of colors, including white, red, purple, and yellow. Use bleeding hearts in magick for love, unrequited love, self-love, and healing.

A Love Chain for Self-Love

Bleeding hearts grow along a stem that is very reminiscent of a "chain" of hearts.

With this spell, we will hearken back to the child in all of us who sits among the flowers and dreams. It is best to do this in a place that gives you comfort. Outside in the garden or in your favorite pajamas while sitting on your bed—it's up to you.

You will need:

- Small vase with bleeding heart blooms, a potted bleeding heart plant, or just a botanical illustration of this old-fashioned favorite bloom
- Colorful strips of construction paper in your choice of colors
- Pen or pencil
- Glue stick or tape

Do you remember making paper chains as a child? Well, that's what we're going to do. Start by placing the bleeding heart flowers, illustration, or plant where you can see it. Play some music, burn some incense, and so on to help you relax. Once you're relaxed, cut strips of construction paper (length and how many is up to you) and begin to write one thing on each strip that makes you unique, special, and positively powerful. You can add future goals and more.

When you're done, tape or glue the ends of one strip together to make a loop. Insert a second strip of paper into the loop and tape or glue strip to make an interconnected loop. Continue the process until your paper chain is as long as you want it. Hang the chain in a place where you can see it on a daily basis as a reminder of how special you are.

Daffodil (*Narcissus* spp.)

Planet: Venus

Element: Water

Energy: Feminine

Deities: Freya, Artemis

The sunny daffodil is my absolute favorite of the spring flowering bulbs. It is an iconic harbinger of spring with cheery blooms in shades of yellow, white, and orange. In cooler zones, plant the bulbs in the autumn for splashes of color in late winter to spring, or in warmer zones, purchase pre-chilled bulbs in spring to add color to containers or garden beds.

The daffodil's botanical name comes from the Greek myth of Narcissus, who had been given the gift of beauty by the gods. Echo, a sweet woodland nymph, saw him and instantly fell in love. But he was so self-absorbed that he paid her no attention, and soon Echo wasted away from loneliness until nothing was left of her but her voice. While out hunting one day, Narcissus bent over a stream to drink and became infatuated with his own reflection, forgetting to eat or sleep. The flower that bears his name sprang up where he died. Use the daffodil in magick for luck, fertility, love, and abundance.

Good Luck Poppet

Save spent daffodil blooms to add to a good luck poppet. Keep in your bag or in a pocket so good luck will follow you wherever you go.

You will need:

- Rabbit cookie cutter
- Scraps of green fabric
- Needle and thread
- 1 part dried moss
- ½ part dried daffodil blooms
- ½ part dried violet flowers and leaves
- Pinch of allspice to activate attraction
- Small piece of pyrite, agate, or other favorite lucky stone(s)

Trace 2 rabbits with the cookie cutter on the green fabric scraps. If you're using a patterned fabric, flip the fabric over for 1 of the pieces. Sew with right (patterned or outward-facing) sides together, leaving a section open for stuffing. Turn the bunny inside out and fill it with the herbal mixture and stone, focusing on your intent. Hand-stitch the opening closed.

Periwinkle (*Vinca minor*)

Planet: Venus

Element: Water

Energy: Feminine

Also known as creeping myrtle, this hardy trailing evergreen ground cover boasts lovely blue, lavender, or white flowers that bloom throughout spring. It's perfect for shady areas, slopes, or hard-to-mow areas. Though lovely, periwinkle can become invasive under the right conditions, so it's important to trim it back from year to year.

One of my favorite folk names for this trailing plant is sorcerer's violet, in connection to its use in both love charms and protection against evil spirits. In Italy, periwinkle is called *fiore di morte*, which translates to "flower of death," as it was customary to lay periwinkle wreaths on the graves of deceased infants. It was thought that to gather periwinkle, one must be cleansed of all impurities, and then it could only be done on the first, ninth, eleventh, or thirteenth day in the moon's cycle. It was believed that those who carried the plant were protected from the devil and safe from the bites of rabid dogs and venomous serpents.

In Scotland, periwinkle was called joy-of-the-ground, as it was believed that if a cutting from the vine was placed under the marital bed, fidelity would keep.

Use periwinkle in magick for resetting a situation, protection, mental clarity, love, lust, fidelity, happiness, or funerary rituals.

Though *Vinca minor* is not poisonous, it may be mildly irritating for some people. Wash your hands after handling it.

Periwinkle Love Potion

Sometimes our love life needs for someone to hit the reset button. Place this bewitching potion under your bed before making love and see if it doesn't help do the trick. Make sure your partner is in on this one.

You will need:

- Incense or garden sage
- Equal parts of these herbs:
  - Dried or fresh periwinkle
  - Rose buds
  - Catnip
- Small cauldron or pretty glass bowl
- Carnelian
- Pinch of ginger powder to make it hot
- Pinch of sugar for sweetness

On the first day of the moon, gather your supplies. If you are growing periwinkle, this would be the time to snip a small section of the vine containing both flowers and leaves. Wash your hands after gathering. Set all the herbs and tools out and cleanse them with your favorite incense or garden sage smoke while focusing on your intention. Set a bowl of water outside with a carnelian to charge it with new moon energy. Bring it in the next day, set it aside, and cover it with plastic wrap to avoid evaporation.

On the ninth day of the moon, with your partner, mix the herbs, ginger, and sugar together while focusing on your intention and say,

> By flower and by vine, for love we combine.

Set the mix aside.

On the eleventh day of the moon, holding a single spoon together with your partner, stir your herbs in a clockwise direction 3 times while saying,

> By vine and by flower, give our love power.

On the thirteenth day of the moon, set the stage for love—candles, your favorite music, and so on. Pour the charged water and carnelian into a small cauldron or glass bowl. Stirring clockwise, add the herbal mixture to the charged water, place it under your bed, and say together,

> Blessings of the moon, of vine, and of flower. Blessing to our bodies, hearts, and to our bower.

Enjoy your evening.

Violet (*Viola odorata*)

Planet: Venus

Element: Water

Energy: Feminine

Deity: Venus

Sweet violets cover shady areas of the garden with bursts of purple light to ease our hearts and lend assurance of spring's return. These tiny woodland flowers grow in clumps that spread both by their roots and by seed, quickly carpeting those cool, moist areas where other plants refuse to grow. Violet's blossoms and leaves are edible and have been used in both sweet and savory dishes. They are rich in both vitamins A and C. Collecting violet blossoms has become a favorite springtime tradition for many of us who like to add the candied blossoms to baked sweets or make the fanciful blue syrup to add to tea or favorite recipes.

According to folklore, when picking violets, it's best to gather a handful or more, because bringing a single blossom into your home is bad luck. Other folklore includes dreaming of violets indicates change in one's life; putting violets under your pillow will enhance prophetic dreams; and, my favorite, for the blessing of the fae, leave violets and a bowl of milk outside your door. Use violets in magick for working with the fae, prophetic dreams, friendship, love, luck, healing, lust, and wishes.

To Dream of a Faery Lover

A dream pillow made with violets is said to bring visions of a faery lover.

You will need:

- 4 parts violet flowers
- 2 parts lavender
- 2 parts rose petals
- 1 part thyme
- 1 part mugwort

- Small tumbled amethyst
- Muslin drawstring bag

Mix the herbs and amethyst together in a large bowl. As you do this, say,

I call upon the secrets that the faeries hold
To sweeten my dreams with a love that I'm told
Is waiting for me beyond the veil of night
And fill my sleeping with visions of delight

Fill the drawstring bag with your dream mix and tuck it under your pillow or lay it on your nightstand.

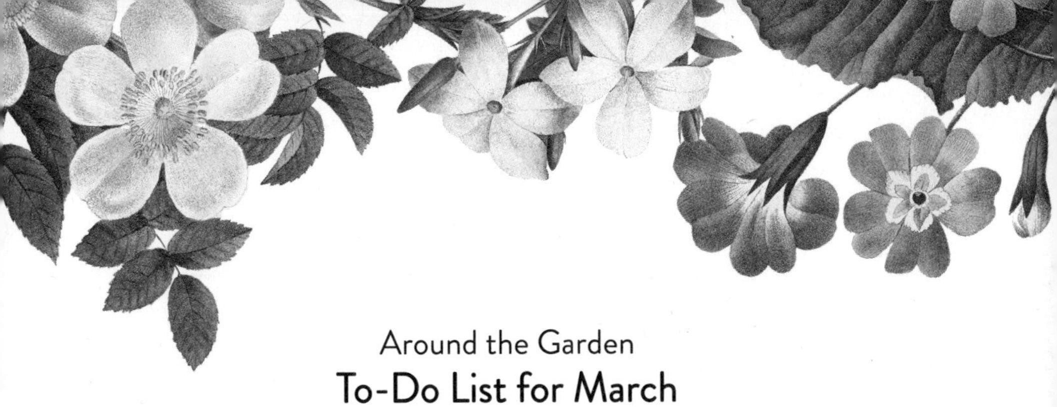

Around the Garden
To-Do List for March

Once the ground has thawed, this is a great time to plant bare-root vines, shrubs, and trees.

Plant lovely hardy primroses, pansies, and prechilled spring bulbs in pots or window boxes. If you haven't started seeds for crops such as tomatoes, peppers, and eggplants, you still have time. Plant cool-weather crops such as peas, leafy greens, and radishes. You can also get potatoes, asparagus, and cabbages into the ground.

For those of you in warmer zones, add mulch to perennial beds and deadhead spent blooms from winter-blooming annuals. Fertilize citrus trees, rosebushes, palms, and camellias.

Plant summer-blooming bulbs and warm-season crops, such as beans, peppers, squash, corn, tomatoes, and eggplants.

Grow Your Magickal Knowledge

Familiarize yourself with the cardinal directions in your yard or garden space for outdoor ritual as the weather warms. You can start by creating simple illustrations of magickal plants for your garden BOS. How about tulips? This is also the time to give lunar planting a try. Start out simply by planting according to the waxing and waning moon phases.

Add a touch of folklore or magickal symbolism to your garden space. Pennsylvania hex symbols, bottle trees, gazing (or Witch) balls, deity statuary, Green Man or Green Woman plaques, and faery houses are among a few selections.

APRIL

Dancing spirals in the rain—their magick woos the sprouts from the soil. The earth sings a song of green.

APRIL CORRESPONDENCES

Nature Spirits: Hyades, flower faeries

Colors: Green, pale yellow, pink

Herbs and Flowers: Sweet peas, comfrey, daisy, fennel

Scents: Bergamot, bay, patchouli

Stones: Diamond, white sapphire, emerald, quartz crystal

Trees: Willow, hazel

Animals: Wolf, bear

Birds: Cuckoo, magpie

Deities: Aphrodite, Ceres, Venus

Zodiac: Aries, Taurus

Work spells for balance, opportunity, growth, self-reliance, and prosperity.

Chapter 10
Earth Song

The Pacific Northwest has many types of rain. There is winter rain that falls as cold icy pellets that chill one to the bone and drenching rain that can come down in sheets nonstop for days, testing one's spirit and the integrity of any boot that claims to be waterproof. The rain of summer storms brings with it the scent of earth renewed and tempts even the stodgiest among us to dance under threatening skies. Autumn brings with it a saturating rain that grows moss on anything standing still and swells rivers beyond their capacity.

But of all the rain Western Washington offers up, it is April's showers I like best, a misty rain that frizzes your hair and plumps your cheeks. It is the rain that encourages the last of the buds to open and leaves every leaf covered with drops that glisten in the bright spring light. It's the rain that draws out the bees and encourages the chirring of insects. It is also, most definitely, the rain that brings on the blooms.

In April, the bleeding hearts have already begun to flourish—they take up residence in the moist soil under trees where few other flowers dare to bloom. Flowering currant, dogwood, wild cherry, and hazelnut trees blossom, releasing their magick perfume into the air, easing my spirit. In my region, the hellebores, witch hazel, primrose, daffodils, tulips, and dead nettle are already in full bloom, and the columbine, meadowsweet, bellflower, and sweet cicely are among the beauties reaching up to take center stage. We are steeped in green magick in April, so follow me down a stony path and let's see what the Witch's garden has to offer up.

Garden Foolery: What's in a Name?

In April, one should be suspicious of Witches disguised as hares—at least that's what I've been told. If you are wandering near the garden's edge as spring unfolds and spy a rabbit nibbling on a toe of frog or the Englishman's foot that is tangled in flowers of death, you should probably . . . Well, just wiggle your toes in the loamy soil and allow the lemony light of spring to caress your cheek, for there is nothing to fear.

A hare in the garden is an auspicious sign (though you may want to shoo them away from your veggies). And if you're lucky enough to see the long-eared creature shape-shift back into its witchy form, you could inquire of them about moon rites and messages from your dearly departed. As far as "toe of frog" is concerned, it's an old folk name for buttercup (*Ranunculus* spp.), and "Englishman's foot" is common plantain (*Plantago major*). "Flower of the dead" is another name for periwinkle (*Vinca minor*).

Our gardens are steeped in the memory and folklore of those ancient cunning folk who came before us. They were the healers, midwives, and herbalists who knew the secrets of both cure and curse held within the plants that grew along the hedgerows, within the cover of the forests, and in the garden. It was the humble door of the herbalist, both respected and feared, that would be tapped upon when one needed "seed of the bird's nest" (Queen Anne's lace) for contraception or the berries from the "waythorn" (buckthorn) to purge oneself of foul humors. Where did these names come from?

Throughout history, and specifically before binomial classification was invented, commonly used plants and herbs had been given different names based on certain attributes of the plant, its growth habits, or even specific reasons it was used. Our ancestors knew *Digitalis purpurea* by folk (or common) names such as foxglove, fairy gloves, fairy caps, fairy thimbles, fairy herb, fairy bells, fairy fingers, goblin gloves, and fairy weed to reflect its connection with the fae. It has also been called dead man's bells, giving an insight to its poisonous nature. Less commonly known are names like flop-dock, pop-dock, cowflop, flop-poppy, and rabbit's flowers in reference to its large, downy leaves.

Depending on where you live, you may call *Centaurea cyanus* a bachelor's button, or you may refer to it as a cornflower or blue caps. But did you know that *Cichorium intybus* is also sometimes referred to by the same folk names? You may also know it by its most common name of chicory, but you can see how it can become confusing.

It wasn't until the mid-1700s that Carolus Linnaeus gave us the binomial (two-name) system of classification, which grouped plants according to similarities. The first name (genus) is a capitalized noun that denotes related groups of organisms. The second name (species) is always written in lowercase and describes one kind of plant within a genus. Combined, the genus and species provide a unique botanical classification for each individual plant. You will notice that scientific names for plants are in Latin or Greek, which helps prevent confusion caused by multiple, and often contradictory, common names. As you grow your magickal garden know-how, remember it is important to know the scientific names of your plants. The last thing you want to do is go to a garden center asking for flop-poppy when wanting *Digitalis purpurea*. It wouldn't be wrong, mind you, but you might be led to the *Papaver* (poppy) section.

Though I always use a plant's scientific name when researching or purchasing plants, and I adore the old-fashioned folk names like foxglove, hollyhock, and lily-of-the-valley that inspire one to dream of an English cottage garden, I think my favorite names for herbs are the grislier folk names associated with Witchcraft. There is no evidence to prove it, but if you read enough books on plant folklore, you'll find it suggested that cunning folk were specifically careful to guard their herbal secrets and would come up with odd and grisly-sounding folk names for the plants they regularly used so their herbal secrets could not be copied. A more logical reason is that it's hard to forget a plant called "devil's apple" or "five fingers," which made remembering and passing on plant knowledge much easier.

Sometimes body parts were used as code for the part of the plant used in a spell or herbal remedy. For example, "hair of..." could refer to dried roots or herbs or stringy stems. But "guts" too referred to both roots and stem. "Blood" could refer to sap, and the "eye" could refer to a seed.

Eye: Inner part of a blossom or seed

Guts: Roots or stalks

Hair: Dried or stringy herbs or roots

Head: Flower

Heart: Bud or seed

Genitalia: Seed

Tail: Stem

Toe, Leg, Wing, or Paw: Leaf

Tongue: Petal

Animals too were used to reference the herbs that filled a Witch's larder. Examples follow (and may vary depending on region):

Bat: Holly

Cat: Catnip

Dog: Grasses

Eagle: Garlic or fenugreek

Frog: Cinquefoil

Lamb: Lettuce

Nightingale: Hops

Rat: Valerian

Toad: Toadflax or sage

Woodpecker: Peony

Weasel: Rue

Now let's combine the two. Say you need a peony petal for a protection spell. You could write it in your BOS as "tongue of a woodpecker." A little valerian root for aiding sleep might be called "hair of a rat."

As the Witchcraft hysteria settled over Europe during the Middle Ages, the village wisewomen, midwives, and healers were seen as being in league with Satan, and therefore, the plants they used must, of course, be of the devil. Many common herbs that were used in medicine and magick took on demonic names.

Devil's Apple: Datura
Devil's Cherries: Belladonna
Devil's Eye: Henbane or periwinkle
Devil's Flower: Bachelor's button
Devil's Oatmeal: Parsley
Devil's Guts: Bindweed
Devil's Milk: Celandine
Devil's Nettle: Yarrow

Folk names give us a surprisingly accurate insight into the magickal and medicinal nature of the herbs that grace our surroundings, and I hope my simplified look into the quaint and sometimes grisly history of our plant's names piques your interest enough that you continue to research plant lore on your own.

Hedgewitch Protection Jar

As your magickal garden begins to produce the herbs you will need for spells, tinctures, balms, charms, and all your other witchy needs, it's important to find a cool, dark area of your home to store your dried herbs, tinctures, tea blends, and the like. Because I know many Witches are still broom closeted, I channeled my inner Shakespeare to come up with this protection jar to shield your Witch's pantry from the prying eyes of the mundane. May they see only herbs for cooking.

As with any of the herbs used in the spells of this book, the following herbs may be replaced with plants that resonate with you or that are more easily accessible. Have fun researching their grislier folk names and using them in spellwork.

You will need:

- Eye of newt (mustard seed)
- Toe of frog (buttercup)
- Wool of bat (moss)
- Tongue of dog (houndstooth)
- Adder's fork (violet)
- Howlet's wing (garlic clove)
- Devil's bush (fern)
- Blind worm's sting (knotweed)
- Pint canning jar and lid
- Black candle
- Scribe (nail or darning needle will do)

As you place your ingredients into a pint canning jar, repeat something like the following:

> Bubble, bubble, this Witch is trouble—let's stir up magick on the double
> Eye of newt and toe of frog, wool of bat and tongue of dog
> Adder's fork to make it sweet, add howlet's wing—that's nice and neat
> Throw a devil's bush in that thing and tie it up with blind worm's sting
> Now this spell has been spun. As I will it, what's done is done

Secure the lid and drip wax from a black candle over the top. While the wax is still soft, use a scribe to draw a hexafoil or protection symbol of your choice into it. Place it in your Witch's pantry.

Green Medicine: You Just Might Be a Hedgewitch ...

The woman who called the edge of the forest home could be seen, once upon a time, wandering the hedgerows where the bramble tangled with the May bush and witchbane. If you passed by, you might have heard her as she muttered her charms while plucking a bit of leaf here or a few berries there and chuckled at the sight. She may have looked to be a bit ridiculous in your eyes. But this woman knew exactly the amount she needed of every herb she touched—never taking more and always thanking her plant allies in her own way. She was the one you went to when winter set in and sickness was on your breath. She was the one you watched eagerly as she brewed a decoction to ease a broken heart. And she was the one who, under the glow of firelight, stirred up poultices made to help mend broken bones.

To call oneself a hedgewitch is to pay homage to those who called the outskirts home. You might consider a modern hedgewitch to be a midwife or a doula, an herbalist, or someone who practices green magick in some capacity.

It's important to know, with any kind of green witchery, that you educate yourself about the herbs you are working with—not by the label on the packet or because another practitioner told you it was a specific plant, so it must be so. You must know your plant ally by sight, scent, touch, and taste (if not toxic). And most importantly by sound. Yes, I said that. Meditate near the herbs, trees, and bushes in your region and listen. Talk to your plants and get to know them on a vibrational level. What are their messages for you?

My challenge for you is to get to know one plant per month that grows in your neighborhood. Learn its uses in medicine. Learn its folklore. And if it's edible, use it in a recipe. The backyard is a good place to start, especially during the spring months when fresh greens are plentiful. To start you off, I have listed herbs that are easy to identify and can be found growing in most regions. All of them are edible, medicinal, and (of course) magickal. They are also great starter herbs for your Witch's pantry.

The following are some of nature's healing greens you may find growing in the backyard. Always remember to harvest from chemical-free environments and only where permissible.

Chickweed (Stellaria media)

Folk Names: Mouse ear, chicken wort, starweed, and winterweed

Oh, those tiny pinpricks of white blooms that seem to rest on soft clouds of green foliage can be seen almost anywhere we go. Chickweed is able to thrive in the strangest of places, between cracks in sidewalks and on top of compost heaps. It can be found creeping along the disheveled remains of a cottage or in the most beautifully cultivated garden. Sometimes referred to as nature's microgreen, this delicate plant grows low to the ground with pairs of opposite leaves and tiny white, five-petaled flowers.

It's a cold-hardy creeper that can grow year-round in milder climates and contains many nutritional benefits, including riboflavin, potassium, flavonoids, beta-carotene, and vitamins B, C, and D. Eat chickweed in salads, sauté it, or puree it for pesto or smoothies. And because chickweed contains omega-6 fatty acids, it's not only good for us but also a great supplement for backyard chickens, boosting their health and helping them produce nutrient-rich eggs.

Infuse chickweed in oil for salves to ease burns and soothe itchy, dry, or chapped skin. Teas made with this herb aid in digestion and may help with constipation.

The flowers of this plant are reminiscent of the five-pointed star, which makes them a seemingly appropriate plant for Witches. This watery plant connected to the moon can be used in magick for love, attraction, rebirth, and fidelity.

Dandelion (Taraxacum officinale)

Folk Names: Piss-in-bed, swine's snout, bitterwort, blowball, lion's tooth

For many of us, dandelion was our first magickal tool (and we didn't even realize it). How many of you made a wish as you blew at the downy head of this common herb? Known as a very adaptable plant, the dandelion can be seen growing everywhere, from the cracks in a sidewalk in the burbs to cracks in rocky, mountainous landscapes (up to ten thousand feet). Though despised by many a weekend garden warrior, its existence in one's garden should be praised, as it loosens compacted soil with a long tap root, drawing earthworms who in turn change and rejuvenate the soil. They also provide bees and other insects with both pollen and nectar when other plants cannot bloom.

With only one flower per stem, dandelions are one of the most recognized of common garden weeds. Leaves and stems grow directly from the rootstock, with leaves having toothed edges that give the plant its French name, *dent de lion*. Individual seeds are carried away by parachute-like hairs with the slightest breeze and have been known to travel on the wind as far as five miles.

All parts of the dandelion are edible and pack a nutritious punch. They are a great source of calcium, folate, potassium, and vitamins A, C, and K, and they may aid in controlling blood sugar, lowering cholesterol, and reducing inflammation. The leaves, which are best eaten in the spring, as they become more bitter throughout the growing season, have a spicy kick comparable to arugula. They can be used as a salad green or sautéed. Use it in recipes as you would spinach or kale. Flowers can be used fresh to give color to a spring salad, sautéed or dried for use in tea blends, infused in oil or alcohol for salves and tinctures, or used in winemaking. Roots can be dried or roasted and used as a coffee replacement. Connected to both the sun and Jupiter and the element of air, use dandelion in magick for adaptably, transformation, wishes, strength, and release.

Lamb's-Quarter (Chenopodium album)

Folk Names: Wild spinach, fat-hen, goosefoot, pigweed

Lamb's-quarter seems able to fill a garden space overnight, but instead of angrily ripping it from between your neatly prepared beds and tossing into the compost heap, why not eat it instead? This common garden weed also helps restore healthy nutrients to poor quality soil. And because it's not picky about soil conditions, this small, dusty-looking annual spreads easily and quickly. It produces tiny green flowers that form in clusters on top of spikes, typically growing 1 to 2 feet in height. The leaves have been thought to look like a goose foot, hence the folk name goosefoot.

Lamb's-quarters can be eaten both raw and cooked and are highly nutritious, offering fiber, protein, vitamins A and C, manganese, calcium, and omega-3 fatty acids. The leaves break down easily when cooked, so a quick sauté or steam works best. Use it like spinach in your favorite recipes. It can be pureed and frozen for continuous use.

The seeds can be harvested in the fall and ground into cereal, used as flour for bread, or sprouted for use in sandwiches or salads.

Medicinally, the leaves can be made into a poultice for insect bites, minor scrapes, and sunburns. Infuse lamb's-quarter leaves in oil to make a salve to ease arthritic joint pain and reduce inflammation. Teas made with lamb's-quarter can aid in stomach irritation and be used in the bath to support healthy skin. The roots contain a significant amount of saponin and can be used in making natural shampoo or body wash.

Connected to Saturn and the element of fire, lamb's-quarter is useful in magick for healing, invisibility, protection, and abundance.

Nettle (Urtica dioica)

Folk Names: Burn weed, burn hazel, burn nettle, devil's claw

If you've ever been walking near the forest and brushed up against the bright green foliage of a seemingly delicate plant, only to feel a sharp sting, you probably had an encounter with a stinging nettle. But don't let its fierce nip intimidate you. Nettle is one of the best backyard medicinal plants out there.

Not only does it contain essential vitamins and minerals including calcium, iron, fatty acids, and vitamins A and C, but it has also been used throughout history to treat allergies, eczema, arthritis, gout, and anemia. It has anti-inflammatory antimicrobial, antiulcer, astringent, and analgesic capabilities, and it is worth doing more research on if you're interested in its medicinal benefits.

Nettle can be found growing in many habitats, including along the hedgerows, in forests, in fields, and in backyard gardens. The plant grows between 2 and 4 feet high with bright heart-shaped leaves and yellow or purple blooms that blossom from June to September.

The stinging is caused by fine hairs on the leaves that contain the chemicals serotonin, histamine, and acetylcholine. If you are stung by a nettle, avoid scratching, as it just makes it worse. The best method of relief is to wash the affected area with soap and water to remove the fine hairs, which contain the chemicals. You can also use crushed herbs such as dock or sage to relieve the sting if you are in the garden or a woodland setting.

When gathering nettles in the spring, I find it easiest to wear gardening gloves and use scissors to snip the young leaves into a basket. All parts of this plant are edible, but you do not want to eat it raw—always dry or cook nettles to avoid the sting.

Use dried leaves in tea blends alone or with other herbs. The leaves can be steamed and cooked much like spinach. Make a nettle soup or add it to other soups and stews. It can also be puréed and used in recipes like pesto or polenta, and it's great in smoothies. Nettle leaves can also be used in beer making, and the seeds can be gathered in late summer or fall and then eaten raw or dried or used in hot or cold recipes, teas, or tinctures. And if you're feeling crafty, try making rope or spinning them into fiber. Make yellow dye from the roots and a green-yellow dye from the leaves. In magick, this fiery Mars herb is great in spells for binding, protection, exorcism, lust, and healing.

Yellow Wood Sorrel (Oxalis stricta)

Folk Names: Cuckoo's bread, cuckoo's meat, sourgrass, bird's bread, fairy bells

It was my grandfather who handed me my first wood sorrel leaves and invited me to chew on them. I was surprised by the bright, tart flavor and have been a fan ever since. This common weed found in woodlands, fields, and gardens is full of vitamin C and beta-carotene.

Though it looks similar to clover, it has no nitrogen-fixing capabilities, so I try to keep it out of my working beds. It boasts three heart-shaped leaves and small, yellow five-petaled flowers. Its leaves, flowers, and stems have a tangy flavor that makes an excellent iced tea reminiscent of lemonade, hence the name "sourgrass." Infused in oil, wood sorrel makes a wonderful salve for soothing and cooling irritated skin. Throughout history, it has been used in treating scurvy, for urinary tract infections, as a mouthwash, and to treat nausea and sore throats.

Wood sorrel can be used in cooking to flavor soups, stews, and salads and adds a lovely lemony flavor to vinaigrette. The seed pods are also edible and may be ground as a spice and added to recipes. The flowers are a historical source of orange-yellow dye.

In English folklore, it was said the magickal cuckoo had to eat wood sorrel to find its voice in spring. Connected to Venus and the element of earth, wood sorrel can be used in magick for healing, health, love, and communication with the faery realm.

Round about the Cauldron Go: Simple Infusions, Tinctures, and Salves

Using your herbs is the best way to learn about them. All these recipes are simple and chosen to help you succeed and inspire you to learn more by taking classes through local community education programs, learn hands-on through a certified herbalist, or learn online.

Infusions, Teas, and Tisanes

Infusions are herbal extractions that use water as a menstruum (solvent). They are similar to teas and tisanes in that they typically use the aerial parts of plants that are steeped in boiling water. The only difference between an infusion and a tea (or tisane) is the amount of herb that is used and the time steeped.

But what's the difference between a tisane and tea, you ask? Well, not much. A tea is actually an herbal infusion using *Camellia sinensis* (tea plant), and a tisane is an infusion using herbs unrelated to the tea plant family.

To make a proper herbal infusion, partially fill a container with dried herbs. Pour boiling water over them and cover with a saucer to prevent the loss of active ingredients. Leave to steep. Times will vary depending on the herbs used. Then strain the infusion with a strainer.

Decoctions

Because bark, roots, twigs, and berries require a more forceful treatment, they can be simmered in hot water for up 30 minutes to produce a highly concentrated liquid known as a decoction.

A great way of using both infusions and decoctions topically is by making a compress: pour the liquid onto a clean, soft cloth and place it onto the affected area.

Poultices

Before antibiotics, poultices were used to draw out infection from abscesses, ease arthritic pain, and heal minor wounds or abrasions. Poultices, or cataplasms, were created by making a paste from herbs and other substances, like bread and milk, spread on a warm bandage, and applied to the affected area. Herbs great for poultices include comfrey, dandelion, horseradish root, ginger, garlic, onion, turmeric, and aloe vera.

A good basic recipe includes 2 to 3 parts fresh or dried herbs mixed with 1 to 2 parts bentonite clay. Mix with hot water for a thick paste. Apply directly to the wound and cover it with cheesecloth.

Oxymels

An oxymel is an infusion of medicinal herbs with vinegar and raw honey. This a great alternative to tinctures made with ethanol alcohol, both for children and for adults who want to avoid alcohol. Besides receiving the herbal benefits from the infusion, you will also receive digestive assistance provided by the apple cider vinegar. This herbal remedy can be taken on its own or added to beverages or your favorite recipes.

To create an oxymel, pack a glass jar ¼ full of your desired tincturing or infusion herbs. Fill the jar ½ full of raw apple cider vinegar. Fill the remainder of the jar with raw honey. Store in a cool, dark place for 2 to 3 weeks, shaking every 2 to 3 days. Strain and store in a sanitized jar. Oxymels last up to 6 months in a cool, dark environment.

Tinctures

Unlike an infusion or a decoction, tinctures take longer to make—anywhere from a couple of weeks to a couple of months to fully saturate the liquid with the plant medicine—but they're worth it. I have included instructions for the folk method, an intuitive method of making tinctures, unlike the modern standard method, which relies on basic weight and volume ratios.

By using ethanol alcohol as a menstruum, the extraction of the beneficial medicinal qualities is generally more concentrated than with water extracts. Because of this concentration, tinctures may also be faster acting than water extracts, and they can maintain their potency for three to five years.

Folk Method Tincture

This tincture recipe makes enough to fill approximately 8 2-ounce bottles.

You will need:

- Wide-mouth pint jar with lid
- Cheesecloth
- 2-ounce amber tincture bottles with glass pipettes (available online)
- 100-proof vodka or grain alcohol
- Plant material (dried or fresh):
  - For fresh leaves and flowers: Enough chopped fresh herbs to fill a pint jar ¾ full (pillow packed)
  - For dried herbs: Enough dried herbs to fill approximately ½ the jar
  - For dried roots, bark, and berries: Enough finely cut material to fill ¼ to ⅓ of the jar

Chop your fresh herbs or grind your dried herbs. Pour your menstruum over the herbs to the top of the jar (cover the plant material completely) and secure the lid. Shake well. Label your jar with the name of the plant (botanical and common) and the date. Set it aside in a warm place and shake once daily for 4 to 6 weeks. Using the cheesecloth, strain the liquid and transfer it to amber glass jars. Keep them in a cool, dark place.

Common Herbs for Tincturing

Dandelion (*Taraxacum officinale*): May ease indigestion and gout. Supports overall well-being. Use the roots, leaves, or flowers.

Feverfew (*Tanacetum parthenium*): Eases migraines or headaches. May reduce the effects of arthritis. Use the leaves or flowers.

Garlic (*Allium sativum*): Helps with circulatory disorders and may lower blood pressure. Has antibiotic properties. Use the cloves.

Ginger (*Zingiber officinale*): Reduces inflammation and relieves digestive problems. Has antibacterial properties. Use the root.

Goldenseal (*Hydrastis canadensis*): Eases inflammation and is astringent. Use the root.

Hawthorn (*Crataegus monogyna*): Increases blood flow and restores heartbeat. Use the berries.

Lavender (*Lavandula angustifolia*): Promotes restful sleep and offers stress relief. Use the flowers.

Lemon Balm (*Melissa officinalis*): Eases anxiety and depression. Aids sleep. Use the leaves.

Mullein (*Verbascum thapsus*): Eases coughs and congestion. Is an expectorant, stimulating coughing up phlegm. Use the leaves.

Nettle (*Urtica dioica*): May help support immune system and maintain energy and stamina. Use the leaves.

Onion (*Allium* spp.): Anti-bacterial and anti-inflammatory. Supports gut health. Use the bulb.

Peppermint (*Mentha ×piperita*): Eases digestion and relieves common stomach ailments. Use the leaves.

Raspberry Leaf (*Rubus idaeus*): Supports pregnancy and menstruation. Helps alleviate cold and flu symptoms. Use the leaves.

Rosemary (*Salvia rosmarinus*): Has antibacterial properties. Relieves stress. Use the leaves.

Sage (*Salvia officinalis*): Eases digestion. Relieves sore throat. Use the leaves.

Saint John's Wort (*Hypericum perforatum*): Eases anxiety and depression. Relieves inflammation. Use the flowers.

Self-Heal (*Prunella vulgaris*): A self-heal mouthwash eases bleeding gums and provides sore throat relief. Use the leaves, flowers, or stems.

Skullcap (*Scutellaria lateriflora*): Reduces stress and promotes restful sleep. Use the leaves or stems.

Thyme (*Thymus vulgaris*): Soothes cough or sore throat. Relieves muscle spasms. Use leaves or flowers.

Turmeric (*Curcuma longa*): Eases stomach pain and is anti-inflammatory. Use the root.

Valerian (*Valeriana officinalis*): Relaxes and promotes restful sleep. Use the root.

Willow (*Salix alba*): Reduces fever and is anti-inflammatory. Use the bark.

Yarrow (*Achillea millefolium*): Reduces fever and prevents cold and flu. Use the leaves or flowers.

Yellow Wood Sorrel (*Oxalis stricta*): May help support immune system and is antiseptic. Use the leaves or flowers.

Infused Oil

Herbal oils are renowned for their healing abilities. They can be used in massage oil, added to your bath, or used to make healing salves, balms, soaps, or lotions.

Prepare your jar, making sure it's clean and dry. Any water in the jar can lead to spoilage.

You will need:

- Glass jar (canning jars work nicely)
- Dried, coarsely chopped herbs
- Oil (such as olive oil or sunflower oil)
- Strainer and cheesecloth
- Amber bottles for storing finished oil

Fill the jar with herbs. Pour oil slowly over the herbs until they are completely covered. Place the lid on your jar and give it a few shakes, and then place it in a cool, dark place inside your home. Every couple of days, give your jar a shake. It will be ready to use in 3 to 6 weeks. When ready, strain the oil through a cloth-lined strainer and place it in into your storage bottles. Remember to label your bottles. The oil should last at room temperature for up to 1 year.

Common Herbs for Infused Oil

Black Cottonwood (*Populus trichocarpa*): Is antimicrobial and relieves muscle pain. Use the leaf buds.

Burdock (*Arctium lappa*): Smooths skin and eases irritated skin. Use the root.

Calendula (*Calendula officinalis*): Soothes diaper rash and chapped, itchy skin. Suitable for sensitive skin. Use the flowers.

Chamomile, German (*Matricaria chamomilla*): Great for minor cuts and scrapes. Use the flowers.

Chickweed (*Stellaria media*): Reduces inflammation, soothes irritated skin, and is antiseptic. Use the leaves or flowers.

Cleavers (*Galium aparine*): Great for skin irritation due to insect bites, sunburn, or abrasions. Use the leaves or flowers.

Comfrey (*Symphytum officinale*): Supports healing and relieves pain and swelling. Use the leaves or root.

Dandelion (*Taraxacum officinale*): Is anti-inflammatory, eases sore muscles, and relieves stress. Use the leaves, flowers, or roots.

Echinacea (*Echinacea purpurea*): Eases rashes, stings, and insect bites. Use the flowers, leaves, or roots.

Eucalyptus (*Eucalyptus globulus*): Is antiseptic, anti-inflammatory, and a natural insect repellent. Use the leaves.

Hops (*Humulus lupulus*): Is anti-inflammatory and antioxidant. Relieves dry, itchy skin. Use hop flowers (heads).

Lamb's-Quarter (*Chenopodium album*): Eases arthritic joint pain and reduces inflammation. Use the leaves.

Lavender (*Lavandula angustifolia*): Is calming, antiseptic, and antibacterial. Use the flowers.

Lemon Balm (*Melissa officinalis*): Eases chapped lips, insect bites, rashes, and cold sores. Use the leaves.

Nettle (*Urtica dioica*): Eases aching muscles. Soothes irritated skin and is anti-inflammatory. Use the leaves.

Plantain (*Plantago major*): Soothes itchy skin due to poison ivy, sunburn, or insect bites. Use the leaves.

Self-Heal (*Prunella vulgaris*): Is astringent, anti-inflammatory, and detoxifying. Use the leaves or flowers.

St. John's Wort (*Hypericum perforatum*): May help with acne. Soothes swelling and skin irritation. Use the flowers.

Thyme (*Thymus vulgaris*): Is antifungal and antibacterial. Use the leaves.

Yarrow (*Achillea millefolium*): Eases swelling and soothes abrasions. Use the flowers.

Easy Salve Recipe

- ¼ cup beeswax pastilles (or candelilla wax)
- 1 cup herbal infused oil
- 20 to 25 drops essential oil of choice (optional)

In a double boiler, melt the beeswax over low heat. Add infused oil and stir until well mixed. Remove from heat and add the essential oil(s). Pour the mixture into containers and allow it to cool completely. Makes approximately 4 1-ounce containers.

Lip Balm

Lip balm is a great beginner recipe and a wonderful way to introduce your kids to herbal medicine.

You will need:

- 6 tablespoons carrier oil (grapeseed, olive oil)
- 2 tablespoons beeswax (or candelilla wax)
- 2 tablespoons solid cocoa butter or shea butter
- 5 to 10 drops essential oil (optional)

In a double boiler, add oil, beeswax, and butter and heat over a low setting until melted. Add essential oils and carefully pour into ½-ounce refillable tins. My favorite blend includes a combination of peppermint and rosemary essential oils. It's both cooling and soothing for dry, chapped lips.

Chapter 11
Magick in the Green: Using Nature as Our Guide

I have said it many times: I am a Witch who teeters between what is wild and what is tame. The moss-laden trails that wind through old-growth cedar and hemlock trees guide me to the places where I commune with the fae and worship my deities near the river's edge. I am as comfortable in a forest setting as I am in my own backyard, so it is within the boundaries of my backyard that I attempt to duplicate many of the lessons I have learned in nature.

Nothing in nature is linear. It is the curves of leaves and ripples in waterways that wind their way to the ocean. It's spirals and arcs and twists and turns. Nature is not neat and tidy. It is layers of humus and decay that provide the perfect nourishment for both plant and animal life. It is a symbiotic circle of life, death, and rebirth. So why do we try so hard to create the perfect lawn, free of weeds or too many trees whose leafy canopies create a mess? As humans, we tend to try to tame that which is wild, and in doing so we inadvertently alter our environment in negative ways. When creating a garden space, we need to look to nature as our guide. By copying her systems and patterns, we can tailor our gardens to not only meet our own needs but also enhance the ecological systems already in play in the unique biomes where we reside.

Mimicking nature's systems is sometimes referred to as biomimicry. When it's used in the garden, we can enhance our soil, water, and air quality, as well as wildlife habitat. You may be familiar with the term *permaculture*, a biomimicry planting method that integrates plantings, structures, terrain, and human and animal needs into a symbiotic system, which has become widely used among many gardeners. But there are simpler measures that you can employ to mimic nature in your backyard or balcony or patio garden spaces.

Mimicking Nature

Have you noticed, or maybe you have been guilty of it yourself, the tendency to cut straight lines when creating garden borders or beds? To create a more natural look, design your beds and borders with flowing lines. Play with spirals, circles, and curves to create interest and mimic those forms in nature.

By using a diverse selection of plantings, you can make your backyard a natural ecosystem. Plant trees and shrubs to anchor the soil, provide shade and form habitats. Add native plants for their stability, resilience, relatively minimal maintenance, and ability draw beneficial pollinators. If you live in an apartment, planting native plants in containers will provide birds, butterflies, and other insects a place of respite in an urban environment. Remember, in nature, symbiosis is the key—our gardens should reflect that too.

Nature doesn't need someone to fertilize the trees, nor does it need anyone to weed around the shrubs. Wild spaces have their own system of recycling. Leaves and debris fall, break down, and eventually become nourishing humus. We can mimic this in our own gardens by allowing the natural composting process to take place in areas where deciduous trees and shrubs are incorporated in our borders and beds. Instead of raking up the leaves, allow them to break down in the beds, providing nutrients and acting as a natural weed barrier to surrounding plants. In vegetable or herb gardens, try using sheet mulching, also known as lasagna gardening, where organic materials are layered in proper proportions to break down into a rich growing medium.

By utilizing vertical gardening techniques, including tiered planters, trellises, and arbors, we can mimic how plants utilize their environment (think of tree trunks and cliff faces). For those who have very little space for growing plants, vertical gardens help maximize the use of limited space.

And for any gardener, adding this technique provides easy maintenance, pest and disease control, and visual interest and allows us to layer plants within a space, which in turn increases our yield.

Water is life. Birds, frogs, small animals, and beneficial insects are more likely to visit a garden that includes a water feature. Ponds are easier to install than you think, and by adding fish and aquatic plants that thrive in your region, they practically maintain themselves. Most DIY centers carry small kit ponds, complete with a waterfall, which can be installed even on the smallest of patios or decks. Not quite ready for the commitment? A simple birdbath will do. Don't forget to hang a few birdhouses or bee boxes too.

He Who Shapes: Morpheus, Greek God of Dreams

As I sit near the edge of our pond that serves as a gateway to my herb and vegetable garden, I am charmed by the creatures who call it home. There are toads whose appearance indicates a healthy garden and tells the story of its beautiful transformation. The koi glint under ripples that reflect the sunlight and remind me to relish the serenity only found in a garden setting. Birds of all kinds shake the branches of surrounding trees, shrubs, and vines, and near the forest's edge, I spy a deer or two—the shy creatures who remind me of my interconnectedness with nature. It's hard for me to believe sometimes that the very place my home and large garden sit was once an empty field. It took years of slowly planting and adding features, while also amending the sandy soil that so resisted our efforts. But all that shaping worked—the land was restored, and we have been rewarded with abundance.

I can't say it was easy, nor can I tell you I didn't doubt my efforts from time to time. It can sometimes feel like an impossible task to turn bare ground into something as bewitching as a garden. Even after a long day of moving soil was done and I had fallen into bed with the scent of green still clinging to my hands, I wondered if what I was envisioning was possible at all.

If this happens to you, you may choose to seek guidance from Morpheus, the Greek god formed of dreams, and allow him to bring to you the visions of what your garden one day may be if you work in tune with nature's rhythms and have patience—a lot of patience. For gardens are not made overnight; they are built upon, ever-shifting, ever-shaping. Morpheus too is a shape-shifter, who's sometimes depicted as having one winged ear to symbolize that he is listening.

Dedicate a small altar in your emerging garden to Morpheus. He is associated with poppies, so plant some near his altar or place a bowl of poppy seeds upon it. He is said to come to you through a gate made of horn. If you have any carvings made of horn or an old drinking horn, place that on the altar as well. To invoke him, drink some herbal tea to open your third eye before bed and envision this godly messenger coming to you as you fall asleep. Ask him to take you to your garden. Keep a journal near your bed so when you wake up you can quickly write down your vision. Did you feel inspired? How did the garden look? Was it different from what you had originally envisioned? If you can, draw a quick sketch of the layout of the garden you were presented.

Third Eye Blend

Here's a tea blend that opens the third eye, promotes peacefulness, and readies one for dreamwork.

You will need:

- 2 parts mugwort, for astral projection, inner journeys, and psychic awareness
- 2 parts peppermint, for unblocking your third eye, peacefulness, and prophetic dreams
- 1 part yarrow, for communication, psychic ability, vivid dreams

Steep the blend for 5 to 8 minutes in hot water and enjoy.

Hand to Soil

It is with dirt under my nails, twigs in my hair, and sweat trickling down the back of my neck that I feel the closest to the Goddess. For kneeling in the dirt feels like prayer, and planting seeds is my offering. There is something meditative about the repetitive aspects of gardening—weeding, hoeing, pinching off spent blooms, and trimming trees are the therapy that settle my restless mind. For me, the garden is a temple, my respite from what can feel like a harsh world.

In the garden I find the favor of the Divine—dirt on hands, a breeze to caress my face, the heat of the sun, rain on an April afternoon, and a soul at peace. I'd like to invite you to join me for a little dirt therapy as we sow the seeds for magick.

Before you run out to your plot of soil and start poking seeds into it, make sure you have done your research. Not all seeds are created equal—different plants have different soil and light requirements. Some seeds can be planted outdoors right after the last frost, while others require the soil to be warmer in order to germinate. There are seeds that prefer to be scattered on top of the soil, while others need to be planted beneath the soil. Most of this information can be found on the back of the seed's packet, but if you're new to gardening, it's worth it to glean as much information as you can about the seeds you have selected. You can go online, check out gardening books that specialize on the specific gardening requirements of your region, or best of all, talk with other gardeners in your neighborhood.

How to Direct Sow Seeds

Depth of planting and spacing really depends on the type of seeds you are planting, and this will be on the back of the seed packet. Typically, seeds will be planted anywhere from ⅛ to 1 inch beneath the soil, with some varieties, such as cosmos, California poppy, oregano, and thyme, preferring to be scattered. Once your seeds are planted, it is very important to keep them moist. Be gentle as you water and do not let them dry out. Make sure to mark your plots. I can't tell you how many times I've direct sowed seeds and thought I'd remember what I'd planted, then either planted over the top or had to wait until they came up to jar my memory.

I tend to overplant and go back and thin out crowded seedlings later. Once again, spacing depends on the plant variety, but the rule of thumb is the smaller the mature plant, the less space required between seeds. Thinning is a necessary step to ensure large, healthy plants. Instead of pulling the seedlings from the ground, I suggest using scissors and clipping them at ground level. This way you're not disturbing fragile root systems, and depending on the seedlings, the trimmed microgreens may be used in recipes.

Bewitching Container Gardens

Whether you have a sprawling garden, a simple backyard, or even a small patio or balcony, planted containers add instant color and appeal to any space. One of the prettiest gardens I've visited was small, cozy, and completely made up of planted containers. Everything from vining plants, dwarf fruit trees, shrubs, herbs, flowers, and veggies grew in my friend's garden. And with a small corner kit pond that drew in frogs, hummingbirds that darted between feeders and flowers, and fairy lights that twinkled as evening approached, you would never know you were in the middle of town.

The sky's the limit with container gardening. You can plant anything from a bold single species to awe-inspiring color combos. Houseleeks in old shoes to dwarf trees in a whisky barrel, container gardens make it possible for any space to be truly enchanting.

An important question to ask yourself when picking out your containers is will the container support the root system of my chosen plant? Consider the size and shape of the root system. Are you planting a shrub or tree? Perennials or annuals? Succulents? Or maybe a combination. If your container is too small, it will dry out easier and you will run into the problem of your plants becoming root bound, which stunts their growth.

Because anything that holds dirt can be used as a planter, it's important to make sure your container has good drainage. If there are no drainage holes in the bottom of the container, you will have to drill them. Containers need to have good drainage to keep your precious plants from becoming waterlogged and possibly dying.

Now that you have picked the perfect container, it's time to get planting. Large containers can be very heavy to move around, so before filling with soil, place your container where you want it located. Dirt from the backyard is far too dense for containers, so purchase a good potting soil from your local nursery or DIY store. It's best to premoisten (or dampen) your planting medium. I like to moisten my soil in five-gallon buckets before transferring to my containers, but you can also open the bag and use a spray setting on your hose and spray a little bit directly into the bag.

To release your plants from their nursery containers, give a good squeeze around the base of the container to loosen its roots, turn the plant upside down, and gently pull it from its confines from the base of the stock. Gently loosen the roots and trim off a couple inches if needed. Make sure the hole you dig is large enough to support your plant's root system. When deciding how many pants to plant per container, here's a good rule of thumb:

- 3 to 4 plants to a 10-to-12-inch container
- 5 to 7 plants to a 14-to-16-inch container
- 6 to 9 plants to a 16-to-20-inch container

Magickal Container Combinations

To the mundane, these lovely container gardens are just pretty flowers or culinary herbs, but we know better. Try one of my bewitching combinations or get creative and conjure up a few of your own.

Healing and Peace

This group of healing herbs can be made into incense, smudge bundles, and teas or used in spells to promote healing, peace, and tranquility. This combination is designed to have single planted containers that might be grouped around a comfortable seating area to promote peace and relaxation.

Bee Balm (*Monarda* spp.): The scent alone can put you in a meditative state. Bee balm is associated with Mercury and the element of air and can be used in spells for prosperity, peace, and clarity, as well as useful in banishing negative energy.

Floribunda Rose (*Rosa multiflora*): These smaller rose varieties bloom in beautiful clusters that are no less alluring than the larger hybrid varieties. Associated with Venus and the element of water, rose petals can be made into healing brews, used in love spells, and used for divination, purification, peace, friendship, and happiness.

Lavender (*Lavandula angustifolia*): One of my favorite calming herbs, lavender is associated with Mercury and the element of air. Use it in purification rituals and in spells for tranquility, peace, dreamwork, divination, love, happiness, and protection.

Lemon Balm (*Melissa officinalis*): Ruled by the moon and the element of water, this prolific herb can be used in spells for healing, happiness, spirituality, and peace; in love charms; and as part a soothing ritual bath.

Spellcasting

If you're a Witch who likes to work with herbs, it makes sense to have the ingredients you use in spellcasting close at hand. These are some of the herbs I find I use a lot of, but I encourage you to put together your own container overflowing with the herbs of your craft. I designed this to be planted in one large container with bay laurel taking center stage and surrounding it with dwarf or trailing varieties of spell-crafting favorites.

Bay Laurel (*Laurus nobilis*): Associated with fire and the power of the sun, bay leaves can be used in a multitude of spells, including those for divination, creativity, wisdom, protection, strength, and prosperity. Bay laurel is a small tree that can grow up to 50 feet tall. In a 24-inch container, if kept pruned, it will average only 4 to 5 feet tall and can be easily moved indoors in colder climates.

Creeping Thyme (*Thymus serpyllum*): Associated with Venus and the element of water, sweet, simple thyme carries a magickal punch. Use in rituals for purification, reversing harmful energies, healing spells, love charms, dreamwork, courage, sleep, and psychic powers.

Dwarf Sage (*Salvia officinalis* 'Minimus'): This tiny but mighty variety of sage can be used in smoke-cleansing bundles and incense blends to clear a space, self, or object of negative energy just as well as its larger cousin. Associated with Jupiter and the element of air, sage can be used for cleansing and spells for protection, wisdom, longevity, and communication.

Yerba Buena (*Clinopodium douglasii*): A trailing variety of mint, this herb can be used in healing tea blends or substituted in any spell that calls for peppermint. Associated with Mercury and the element of fire, yerba buena can be used in purification rituals, in spells for clarity and focus, in love charms, and for sleep.

Kitchen Witch

When these herbs are planted in lovely terra cotta pots in a sunny window or outside the kitchen door, no one will know they mean so much more than just ingredients for your dinner.

Rosemary (*Salvia rosmarinus*): Associated with fire and the power of the sun, this powerful herb purifies and rejuvenates stagnant energies. Use it in spells for clarity, protection, love, and lust and in sea witchery.

Garden Sage (*Salvia officinalis*): Popular for its cleansing properties, this herb is associated with Jupiter and the element of air and can be used in spells for wisdom, longevity, communication, and protection.

Thyme (*Thymus vulgaris*): Associated with Venus and the element of water, thyme is wonderful for spells for healing. Use it in magick for reversing harmful energies, purification, love charms, dreamwork, courage, sleep, and psychic powers.

Basil (*Ocimum basilicum*): Use this lovely herb, associated with Mars and the element of fire, in spells for love, lust, wealth, and protection.

Parsley (*Petroselinum crispum*): It's said that, when eaten, parsley provokes lust. Associated with Mercury and the element of air, parsley can be used in spells for lust, fertility, and protection.

Protection

It's nice to have a few garden guardians standing vigil at the front door to keep negative energies at bay. The plants I chose are both beautiful and powerful. All these plants should be grown in large containers with the addition of an inexpensive trellis panel to include with the honeysuckle.

Angelica (*Angelica archangelica*): This lovely plant, associated with Venus and the element of fire, keeps nasty spirits at bay. Also use it in spells for visions, and healing.

Honeysuckle (*Lonicera periclymenum*): Plant this prolific climber near your front door to keep illness and bad vibes away. Associated with Jupiter and the element of earth, it also attracts luck to your home. Use it in magick for attracting money and psychic powers.

Rue (*Ruta graveolens*): Associated with Mars and the element of fire, this beautiful plant will stand guard to keep toxic people and negative energy at bay. Also use it in spells for love, clarity, and healing.

Psychic

These herbs can help you with your divinatory practices or developing your intuition. Plant them in a large pot and keep it close at hand. Combine them for a powerful tea to activate psychic sight.

Calendula (*Calendula officinalis*): This bright and smiling herb is associated with the sun and the element of fire. Its petals can be used for a tea to trigger prophetic dreaming. Use it in protection spells, for psychic powers, and for strength and courage.

Mugwort (*Artemisia vulgaris*): Magickal mugwort is associated with the planet Venus and the element of earth. Use it to amplify psychic sight and induce astral travel. Also use it in spells for protection, healing, and dreamwork.

Yarrow (*Achillea millefolium*): Use this beauty to aid in astral travel and to induce psychic visions. Associated with Venus and the element of water, it can be used in spells for courage and love. Yarrow is also (for me) a wonderful go-to substitution herb in my magickal practice.

Chapter 12
Herbs of April

The herbs I chose for April represent renewal, prosperity, protection, and courage. April is a joyous time of renewal, and it takes great courage in order for growth to occur. Protect those seeds of the soul, dear Witches, and prosperity will be at hand.

Peony (*Paeonia* spp.)

Planet: Sun

Element: Fire

Energy: Masculine

Did you know that the peony is one of the most protective plants in your garden? Imagine a ritual circle surrounded by the luscious blooms of this herbaceous perennial. But throughout history, this showstopper has meant different things to different cultures. For ancient Greeks, the plant symbolized healing, as it was named after Paeon, a student of the god of medicine. In Japan, the flower was a symbol of a healthy marriage. The peony was a symbol of China during the Tang Dynasty, representing prosperity, elegance, and solemnity. Subject of many paintings for nineteenth-century impressionists, it was said to be deeply appreciated by the likes of Renoir, Manet, and Delacroix. But Victorians also thought if you brought peonies into the home, you'd be cursed by the faeries.

Peonies are edible, and the petals can be used to flavor summertime drinks, in jams and jellies, or as a garnish. Medicinally, the dried root was suggested to relieve menstrual discomfort and was also used for symptoms of gout, upper respiratory illness, and fever. Use peonies in protection magick as well as magick for elegance, prosperity, and healing.

Peony Seed Amulet

Amulets are charms that protect one from bad luck, negativity, or disease. As magickal wards, they can be worn on your person, hung on a wall, or tucked just about anywhere. Amulets made of seeds have been crafted by people of many cultures for thousands of years. You can use one seed variety or several to combine their energies. I recommend using dental floss for its strength because the seeds can have rough edges and cut thin thread, though a heavy thread will work too. Here are some basic instructions, but feel free to take it further by inscribing your seeds with symbols or combining them with other beads or charms.

You will need:

- Peony seeds
- 1-inch-thick board
- Needle-nose pliers
- Drill with 1⁄16-inch drill bit
- Dental floss
- Sewing needle

If you're harvesting your seeds, cut the seed pods from the peony plant in the fall when they are brown and leathery and have begun to crack open. Or you can purchase a packet of peony seeds from your local garden center or online. Drilling seeds can be tricky, so do this in a place that offers plenty of light.

Place your board on your work area and place a seed on the board. Hold the seed securely with your pliers and drill a hole through each seed. Thread dental floss through your sewing needle and tie the floss off at one end. Thread each seed onto the floss. As always, do this with intention, imbuing your amulet with your personal power. When you're finished, you can tie the ends together to make it wearable or tie the end off and hang the seeds as garland. String only a few seeds so it can be slipped into your bag or hung on a keychain. It's your amulet. Use it how you will.

Radish (*Raphanus sativus*)

Planet: Mars

Element: Fire

Energy: Masculine

There's nothing like the crisp, spicy flavor of a fresh radish, one of the earliest producers in my spring garden. They are a great plant for first-time gardeners or as introductory plants for your little Witchlings, as they are easy to sow and are ready for harvest within 3 to 5 weeks. They are a cool-weather crop, so I sow them in the spring and once again in the fall to enjoy with harvest meals. A powerhouse of vitamins and minerals, both the roots and leaves are edible and can be used in a variety of recipes. Radish is said to stimulate digestion and may help lower blood pressure.

In magick, radishes are considered protective and were once carried to protect oneself against the evil eye. Added to meals, their spicy nature can invoke lust. They can also be used in magick for strength or courage.

Radish Protection Ward

If radishes are left to mature in the garden too long, they get tough, woody, and unpalatable. If this happens, they don't all have to be tossed into the compost. You can carve a few (as you would a turnip) and use them in protection spells or mojo bags or just tuck them around the garden as tiny protection wards.

You will need:

- A few mature radishes
- Sharp kitchen paring knife

On a Mars day (Tuesday) or any day during a full moon phase, prepare your radish by rinsing off any dirt and removing the green tops. Use your paring knife to carefully carve a frightening face or protection symbol of your choice (or both) into your radish. When you're finished carving, place your hands over your radishes and say,

> I invoke the power of the root
> I invoke the power of fire
> I invoke the power of protection
> To charge my ward with magick I require
> Blessed be

You can tuck your radish wards around your garden and allow them to stand guard until they decompose, or dry them out in a cool, dark place to be used later in your in spells or mojo bags for protection.

Rhubarb (*Rheum rhabarbarum*)

Planet: Venus

Element: Earth

Energy: Feminine

For those of us who live in zones 3 to 8, rhubarb is one of the true old-fashioned delights of spring. I have two varieties that grace my spring garden—one is an old-fashioned variety known as 'Linnaeus', with green stalks that blush red toward the base. This rhubarb originated in the garden of one my great-great-grandmothers, and the rhizomes from the plant have been passed down through generations of family gardeners. I also have a scarlet red variety known as 'Ruby'. And though there is very little difference in taste between my two varieties, the bright red cultivar is more aesthetically pleasing in tarts or pies.

Rhubarb is a perennial vegetable that grows from rhizomes, but because of its tart, bright flavor, it is used as a fruit. The whole plant contains oxalic acid, but only the leaves have enough of it to make them toxic to humans. Instead, clip the leaves and use them in your compost. Because rhubarb leaves can grow 2 to 3 feet in width, they are perfect for using as molds for bird baths or garden altar tables.

In magick, rhubarb is connected to love, sex, fidelity, and protection. It is said if your lover is having problems with their libido, make them a rhubarb pie and see where the night takes you. Or if your lover is being unfaithful, stuff a poppet with rhubarb leaves and tie it up with the string from the stalk to keep them from straying. Personally, I use the leaves to cast everything from garden altars (larger leaves), birdbaths, and stepping stones to smoke cleansing bowls (smaller leaves). Not only are they beautiful, and fitting for a Witch who spends most of her time in the garden, but because they're made with intention, they're imbued with your own personal power.

Creating a Garden Altar with Rhubarb

Large rhubarb leaves make excellent casting material for a lovely leaf-shaped altar that can be tucked under a tree and dedicated to the fae or placed on a garden table to adorn with your magickal tools and dedicated to your favorite deity. You can even make stepping stones to lead the way to your "secret garden." If you don't have rhubarb, no worries. Any large veiny leaf will do. Try pumpkin, elephant ear, or Japanese butterbur. Smaller altar bowls can be made from hosta, cucumber, or even cabbage leaves. They make great Yule gifts too.

You will need:

- Plastic sheeting
- Leaf
- Enough playground sand to support the size of your leaf
- Bucket for mixing
- Vinyl concrete patch
- Water
- Disposable gloves
- Acrylic craft paint (optional)
- Concrete sealer

This project is best done outdoors. Lay plastic sheeting in an area you will be able to leave your casts to cure. Pick your leaf. Make sure it has a nice veiny structure free of tears and holes.

Dampen your sand and create a mound on top of the plastic. For a rounded bowl shape, make your mound high and round. Flatten the sand for an altar or stepping stone. Place more plastic sheeting over the sand and place leaf vein side up on the plastic.

Mix the vinyl concrete patch with water as instructed on the container. It will be smooth, with a brownie batter–like consistency. With gloves on, press the concrete over the entire leaf. Allow it to cure for 48 hours. Peel off the leaf. If you want to add color, use watered-down acrylic craft paint and spray with concrete sealer.

Sweet Pea (*Lathyrus* spp.)

Planet: Venus

Element: Water

Energy: Feminine

This cottage garden favorite is definitely a favorite in my Witch's garden. Scratch sweet pea's hard casing or presoak the seeds for 24 hours before sowing them in early spring. You will have a climbing vine with sweetly scented blossoms that will bloom all summer long.

Sweet peas are an ornamental flowering plant that are not edible and should not be confused with green peas (*Pisum* spp.). As they are both legumes, they do share a lot of the same characteristics, but there are a few key differences. Sweet pea blooms come in a wider range of colors and are very fragrant. And unlike the rounded succulent stems of edible peas, sweet peas are generally smaller leaved with slightly flattened, rough stems.

The magick they are associated with is as sweet as their name, as they can be used in magick for friendship, protecting children, chastity, and courage.

Witchling Garden Protection Arbor

If you have children who like to garden, an arbor at the entrance of their garden covered with fragrant sweet peas will be the magickal pièce de résistance.

Have your Witchlings help by starting seeds indoors about a month before planting in the garden. Before planting the seedlings in their permanent bed, harden them off to prevent shock (see page 127), then plant on either side of an inexpensive metal arbor that can be purchased at any DIY store or garden center. You may also consider bamboo or willow teepee plant supports at the corners of the garden in colors that represent the cardinal directions.

Once your sweet peas are planted, have the kids invoke the protective power of the sweet pea by saying,

Sweet pea of the moon, of the water and the earth
Draw only friends to this space of abundance and mirth
Watch over our play as we harvest and learn
And protect this garden until winter's return

Willow (*Salix* spp.)

Planet: Moon

Element: Water

Energy: Feminine

Deities: Hecate, Persephone

The most graceful of trees who root themselves betwixt and between, willows are seen growing along waterways with elegant branches that bend toward the pools and ripples. This deciduous tree thrives in cooler climates where there is plenty of moisture. Willows have elongated leaves and produce catkins in the early spring. With a high concentration level of indolebutyric acid (a hormone that stimulates root growth), willow trees can be easily planted just by poking cuttings into the ground. You can place a small stem of willow in water and use it as a rooting hormone for other plant cuttings too. Willow trees grow quickly and have durable root systems, which makes them perfect trees for areas prone to erosion.

Medicinally, white willow bark has been used for thousands of years as a pain reliever, as it contains a chemical called salicin, which is similar to the active ingredient in aspirin.

Sometimes connected to death, the willow was thought to guide those who'd passed on to Summerland. Planted on a grave, it was said that the roots would take up the spirit of the deceased so they could live on in the tree. The willow is connected to many goddesses as well, including Hecate, the powerful Greek goddess of witchcraft and sorcery; Helice, associated with water magick; Persephone, queen of the underworld; and Demeter, the powerful Greek goddess of the earth.

A favorite of many Witches who practice moon magick, the wood from the willow makes an excellent wand. Use it in magick for divination, protection, love, and healing; to work with the element of water; and in female rites of passage.

Gift of a Wand

If you practice moon or water magick, you are probably familiar with the magickal properties of willow. Having a wand made of this gracefully bewitching tree makes sense.

A magick wand is an extension of the Witch's power hand. It helps us focus and direct our energy. You can buy a wand that has been expertly turned on a lathe, polished, and bejeweled. I've seen many and they're absolutely beautiful. But in my opinion, if you can make your own magickal tools, they will be imbued with your personal energy, making them that much more powerful.

To find your perfect wand in nature is truly a gift. It may be a piece of driftwood or a broken branch that fits comfortably in your hand. If you require the energy of a specific tree, never just break off a branch and be on your merry way. Ask the tree for a small branch and use hand clippers to neatly snip the branch you desire. Remember to leave a small offering as a thank-you.

I used a wood-burning tool to decorate a lovely alder wand I was gifted on a walk. My elder wand is simply rubbed with a little beeswax and set with a crystal at its tip, and my apple and willow wands were only rubbed with the beeswax to protect their wood. But you can decorate your wand as you like to represent your craft. I like to charge my new tools under a full moon before I use them. Here is a list of a few common trees used to make wands and their associations:

Alder: Communication with spirits, protection, strength

Apple: Love, healing, abundance, fertility

Beech: Open communication with deity

Birch: Rebirth, fertility, cleansing, inspiration

Cedar: Protection, purification, clarity, wisdom

Elder: Wisdom, communication with the Otherworld

Hazel: Psychic powers, wisdom, water

Holly: Courage, strength, luck

Maple: Power, protection, strength, vitality

Oak: Wisdom, power, truth, protection

Rowan: Protection, faery magick, clarity, psychic powers

Willow: Moon, water, healing, divination, love

Around the Garden
To-Do List for April

Depending on your location, you might still be working on spring cleanup. Till under cover crops (read more on page 253), add compost to existing beds, and prepare soil for direct sowing. For colder zones 3 to 5, start warm-weather seeds indoors.

For zones 6 to 8, if you're ready to plant the seedlings you started in March, it's time to slowly acclimate your seedlings to their new environment through a process called "hardening off." This will prevent your delicate plants from going into transplant shock.

How to Harden Off Seedlings

It is important to gradually expose your seedlings that were started indoors to the elements. Once the outside temperatures are over 45 degrees Fahrenheit, you can take your seedlings to a protected location outside for 1 hour for the first day. Add 1 hour for each day for a full 7 days. This is enough exposure to safely transplant your plants.

For warmer zones 9 to 11, prune spent blooms from flowering shrubs, add mulch to minimize weeds, and conserve moisture during dry weather. Continue planting warm-season crops, such as beans, sweet corn, and squash.

Grow Your Magickal Knowledge

Continue to use the moon's energy in your gardening practices. Charge water with the power of the full moon. Plant by her cycles. Walk barefoot under her gentle glow. Practice ritual outdoors (if possible). Get to know your local weeds by both folk and botanical names, and use them to create tinctures, balms, and soaps. Plant magickal containers to keep favorite herbs for spell crafting close at hand.

MAY

I will follow the path that leads just past the woodbine. My faery lover waits for me wrapped in a cloak of leaves.

MAY CORRESPONDENCES

Nature Spirits: Aos sí, Jack-in-the-Green

Colors: Green, brown, pink

Herbs and Flowers: Sweet woodruff, apple blossom, rose

Scents: Sandalwood, rose, vanilla

Stones: Emerald, fluorite, fire agate

Trees: Hawthorn, birch, rowan

Animals: Frog, bees, goat

Birds: Swallow, owl

Deities: Flora, Cernunnos, Venus, Bel

Zodiac: Taurus, Gemini

Work spells for fertility, growth, love, passion, abundance, and good fortune.

Chapter 13
I'll Be in the Garden All Night

As the sun falls gently behind the hills to the west, I walk out to the garden where giant conifers began their shadow play and the brighter colored flowers that rule the day, like phlox, rose, hollyhock, and foxglove, recede as darkness encroaches. Their glory is replaced by the brilliant white blooms of the honeysuckle, moonflower, liatris, foxglove, and daisy, whose brightness becomes a beacon that signals to creatures both magickal and mundane that it is twilight time—come out and play.

It is at this liminal time, neither night nor day, that my magickal juices begin to flow. It is a current that prickles under my skin and raises the hair on my arms. My children too inherited a love for the twilight hours and, when they were young, could be found outdoors exploring the shadows and talking to those magickal creatures that make up this realm. It is during this time when I typically like to gather the ingredients for spellwork as I chant into the wind to call faeries near.

At twilight, bats begin to flit and swoop; tree frogs chirp; a large owl with glowing eyes sometimes calls out, haunting the shadows; and a small rabbit sometimes appears to nibble at the grass. But I am partial to the toads that can be found lumbering around my home. For I have had known them since childhood, when their presence spoke to me of fairytale cottages and Witch's gardens—you know, the kind with belladonna and wolfsbane growing just beyond the prying eyes of neighbors. Now that I live in a cottage of my own, complete with my very own Witch's garden, toads are held with the highest regard. And as they lumber from beneath rotting stumps or crawl from the leaf mulch, they seem to look up at me to say, "Welcome, friend, to the twilight hour," the very time that seems to whisper the secrets of transformation to anyone who wants to listen. And listen we should: as any Witch knows, the most potent magick can be found when we are neither here nor there.

Neither Here nor There

Liminal or between times are when the veil between this world and the Otherworld thins and one can more easily reach through the threshold and connect with the silky threads of communication with the fae and the spirit world. Shadows of the future lighten, and it is said that magick during these times takes on a deeper connotation.

The status of liminal space and time has been noted, celebrated, and revered as sacred space for thousands of years. In mythology, heroes such as Lleu could only be killed in a 'tween place and time. In Hinduism, the god Vishnu appears as a liminal being (half man, half lion) to destroy a demon who can never be killed during day nor night, in the air nor on the ground.

Between spaces can include borders such as tree lines (marking the border between tame and wild), shorelines or other watery edges (which designate the space between land and sea, river, or stream), bridges, thresholds, windows, cemeteries, crossroads, marshes, and volcanic craters. In modern times, places such as hospitals, hotels, airports, and train and bus stations may all be considered between spaces because they are passed through but never lived in.

Time can be liminal. Dawn is not quite morning nor still night, noon is between morning and evening, dusk is neither day nor night, and midnight is not light nor shadow. As the Wheel of the Year turns slowly round, we have many "between times" that are celebrated. The most noted for their thinning veil are Beltane (between winter and summer for the ancient Celts) and Samhain (between summer and winter), but the equinoxes and solstices are between times as well. And what about New Year's Eve? At this time between the new and the old, superstitions abound. Ghost stories were told, and rituals were conducted to ensure your luck for the coming year.

Humankind shares many between-time experiences: coming-of-age celebrations; new beginnings such as births, new homes, or handfastings;

and endings that include handpartings, death, or retirement. These liminal passages have been dealt with by ritual or ceremony since ancient times.

The most widely recognized 'tween place in folklore and superstition, in many countries, is probably the crossroads. Hecate is goddess of the three-way crossroads and was said to walk the roads of Greece with her sacred dogs, carrying a torch. But of all liminal places, it is in the garden at dusk I am drawn to, that time when day fades and moths flit about my porchlight. The corners of my garden are swallowed by shadow, and I can feel the presence of the Otherworld. That is when I go outside and step gently through the veil.

Flower Favorites for a Twilight Garden

There are some plants who prefer to open just as the sun dips behind the western hills. Cool evening air prevents delicate blooms from drying out as they hold a luminous vigil until a new dawn returns. And their seductive scent not only casts a spell on the one lucky enough to have them in their garden but draws in pollinating moths, who are attracted to the flowers primarily by scent.

Here is a list of a few you may want to add to your magickal twilight garden:

Evening Primrose (*Oenothera biennis*): This lovely plant, whose flowers begin to bloom in the evening and fade by the next afternoon, is connected to the moon and the element of water. It can be used in ritual spells that explore family trauma, creating boundaries, healing, and self-love.

Four o'Clocks (*Mirabilis jalapa*): These lovely Venus plants, with heart-shaped leaves and colorful blossoms, open in the late afternoon and continue to bloom throughout the night. Connected to the element of water, these charming flowers can be used in magick for dreams, sleep, and love and to add sweetness to your spells.

Angel's Trumpet (*Brugmansia suaveolens*): "Beautiful and baneful" best describes this stunning plant. Growing up to 15 feet tall with

8-to-10-inch trumpet-shaped blooms, it has an intoxicating scent that has been said to induce nightmares. *Brugmansia* has been used in some cultures for its trance-inducing effects. Connected to Venus and the element of water, it can be used in spells for seduction, working with the Dark Goddess, divination, communication with the dead, and protection.

'Red Flare' Water Lily (*Nymphaea* 'Red Flare'): Often used as ornamental plants for ponds, these stunning red waterlilies are associated with the moon and the element of water and can be used in magick for clarity, direction, and the creative process.

Evening Rain Lilies (*Zephyranthes drummondii*): Typically open a day or two after the rain, these dainty lilies open in the evenings and last only a few days. Connected to Neptune and the element of water, they can be used in spells for protection, familial love, and working with ancestors.

Night Phlox (*Zaluzianskya capensis*): Night phlox is a sweetly fragranced flower that only unfurls its pinwheeled-shaped flowers after dusk. Associated with Mercury and the element of air, it can be used in spells for harmony, productivity, communication, and love. It may also be used in magick for spring rites or handfastings.

Garden Animal Allies of Dusk

As evening seeps inky hues across the landscape, be on the lookout for those magickal creatures who are most active as twilight approaches. Be it a lumbering toad, the moth that flits near windows and porch lights, or the bat that swoops seemingly too close for comfort—be quiet and respectful in their presence, for they all have wisdom to share.

Bats

These misunderstood creatures of darkness have been given a bad rap and are more loathed than loved by many homeowners. But bats play an important role in the garden, as they consume insects, including many pest species.

As magickal creatures, bats in your life symbolize change and transformation. They signify the promise of rebirth and power gained through transition.

To attract bats to your garden, try adding these:

Flower Power: Plant plenty of fragrant and evening-blooming plants that entice nocturnal insects, which in turn attract the bats.

Shelter: Buy a small bat house (online or at any garden center). Mount their new home on the side of your house at least 15 feet high. Never mount on fence posts or trees, as these can be easily accessed by predators.

Water: Bats can lose up to 50 percent of their body weight in water per day, so having a water source nearby is a very important aspect of enticing bats to your garden space. A bird bath or fountain will do.

Toads and Frogs

Seeing a toad in the dusky light of twilight reminds us that transition must happen in order for us to grow. A toad begins its life in the water. Its eggs are gelatinous clumps, but once hatched, an amazing metamorphosis begins that is all at once complex and beautiful.

As magickal creatures, toads and frogs are symbols of metamorphosis and reminders of our own creative power.

Toads in the garden are beneficial, as they eat thousands of pesky insects and provide you with the pleasure of hearing their soothing, throaty song as evening approaches. To encourage toads (and frogs) into your garden, consider the following:

Water: Both toads and frogs are amphibians and need a water source to lay their eggs and for their transition from tadpoles to toads to take place.

Shelter: Provide leaf litter under shrubs, a small hollow piece of log, or an upturned terra cotta pot with an opening large enough for them to enter to protect themselves from the elements and from predators.

Avoid Chemicals: Using chemical pesticides or fertilizers in your garden will kill beneficial frogs and toads. Use organic mulch and let the toads and frogs take care of the pests.

Luna Moths

I have never encountered a luna moth, as they are not indigenous to my region. But if you live anywhere in southern Canada or throughout the eastern half of the United States, you're in luck, as these magickal creatures of twilight call the hardwood forests of these regions home. The bug cocoons for two to three weeks before emerging as an adult moth. As they have no mouth or digestive system, they do not eat but spend their approximately seven-day lifespan seeking a mate and laying their eggs.

As magickal creatures, moths are masters of the mysterious realm of shadow. They teach us to have courage in change and to always seek the light.

In their larval stage, they eat from the leaves of many fruit and nut trees. To attract them to your garden, consider planting trees such as chestnut, black cherry, sweet gum, or hickory. And not to worry, the caterpillars pose no harm to the trees.

Owls

One of my favorite sounds to hear as I stroll through my garden at twilight is the hoot of an owl from the forest that borders my property. Owls are not a common backyard bird and require more than a handful of seeds to entice them to call your yard home. Most of these mysterious raptors are not active during daylight hours but hunt at night. They are excellent for rodent control, but that being said, they will also eat other birds or small mammals. Smaller owl breeds are excellent for insect control. As magickal creatures, owls are harbingers of magickal wisdom, omens, and visions.

To attract owls to your garden, consider the following:

Nesting Boxes: Owls prefer to nest in hollow trees, but nesting boxes, which can be purchased or made, hung in trees 10 to 20 feet high are a great substitution.

Provide Perches: Leave a "naturalistic" untouched section of your yard or garden, including leaving a couple of trees unpruned to provide perches.

Water: Owls obtain most of their water from their prey, but if you live in a hot climate, provide a water source in a secluded part of your garden.

Switch Off the Lights: Many owls hunt more effectively in darkness. Keep exterior light limited.

Most importantly, if you have cats or small dogs, make sure and bring them in during the evening when owls are hunting.

Fireflies (Lightning Bugs)

As magickal as the area I live in is, fireflies are not a part of my landscape, as this species of beetle in the Lampyridae family who lights up is typically not seen west of Kansas. The truth of the matter is I have never seen a firefly. My parents took a long road trip that led them across the US to the east and then down south along the coast a few years ago. My mother sent me beautiful pictures of an evening landscape that seemed lit up by thousands of tiny faeries. Her message was "I thought of you." I was smitten.

These magickal creatures show us illumination when we are feeling lost, are a powerful vehicle in faery magick, and are associated with fire magick.

To attract fireflies to the garden, consider these:

Water: Fireflies like to gather in moist areas such as marshes, near ponds or pools, or near standing water. By adding a fountain or other water feature, you can better entice them to your yard or garden.

Naturalization: Encourage fireflies to your garden by choosing native trees and shrubs to add to your landscape, leaving leaf litter or conifer needles under trees to provide nest material, and adding a downed log or stack of firewood for nesting and attracting soft-bodied invertebrates to provide a food source for larvae.

Honoring the Fae

Twilight in the garden brings out nocturnal creatures, but this is also a time for the fae. These spirit beings are very connected to the land. When they are called upon to empower our personal sacred spaces, the results are nothing but extraordinary.

Dedicating a space in your garden to the fae during the dusky light of evening is a great way to connect with these fickle beings of the Otherworld. Remember, working with any new energy, be it plant, animal, spirit being, guide, or deity, takes easing into. Like any relationship, mutual trust must be established before jumping into a magickal working relationship.

Set up a flat stone (or make the leaf altar cast on page 124) and set it in a pretty section of your garden. Set out a little honey and a few shiny objects or a pretty crystal. If you are introducing your children to the fae, string some bells and invite them to shake and dance about as you ask the faeries to enchant and enliven your outdoor space. After setting up your altar, you might say something like this:

> We ask of you, nature spirits, as do merry we meet
> To tread your magick well with softness of beat
> As day gives to night and we are neither here nor there
> Please enter our garden and honor it with your care
> In turn, we honor your arrival and thank thee well
> Blessed be and bright blessings wherever you dwell

It is at dusk, within the protective boundaries of my garden, as a breeze tinged with the scent of earth tangles itself around me, that I am able to cross that thinly threaded veil and reach to those guides who help me better understand my connection to both worlds. It is there that I know change is possible. It is there that I know I am a walker between the worlds.

So go ahead, plant a magickal twilight garden. Listen to the messages of our animal allies of twilight as they speak to you of the beauty of metamorphosis or guide you in your rites. Remember to create sacred space for the fae, and don't forget to dance, chant, or sing as day becomes night, with bells on your feet and magick in your heart.

Beltane Twilight Tryst

It is at Beltane that the earth's energies are most active and life is bursting all around us. The Goddess, in her maiden form, has reached her fullness and takes the young God in a Greenwood marriage. Together, they are a symbol of fertility and growth. They represent sexuality, vitality, passion, and the joy of true freedom.

This act has been played out throughout the centuries in springtime rites. The most recognizable Beltane image is that of the maypole. A maypole, often made of birch, is a phallic symbol that is inserted into the earth and represents the potency of the God. The flowered crown represents the fertility of the Goddess. Colorful streamers that are plaited as dancers weave in and out and around the pole represent the coming together of male and female energy.

Modern practices may also include ritually joining the chalice and the athame (ritual knife), representing the coming together of the masculine and feminine in either a group or solitary rites, or sacred sex between consenting adults. Other practices may include eggs as symbols of fertility or flower baskets to represent the earth's vitality and fullness. Do remember that, no matter what your practice, Beltane is a great time to promote sex and body positivity and a great opportunity to talk to your own Witchlings about the subject.

Spontaneous sexual encounters in the forest have often been a part of my own Beltane rites, but I realize not everyone has access to a private woodland setting. If you do, I highly recommend it. As with any of my rituals, I suggest an outdoor setting, but this can be done in any location you feel comfortable.

This ritual is to be performed with your partner or another consenting adult. It is meant to be playful, so enjoy the freedom this "'tween time" offers. For Beltane is between winter and summer, and with the addition of a twilight setting, magick is definitely at hand.

You and your partner will be reenacting centuries-old spring rites as consorts of the Greenwood.

You will need:

- Candles (as many as you like)
- Greenwood masks or flower chaplets (optional)
- Beltane incense blend (see next page)
- Bell
- Sensuous food or drink, such as chocolate, figs, berries, avocados, oysters, and of course, mead

If you're outdoors, light your candles and place them safely about the garden, yard, patio, or forest setting. Definitely have a bonfire lit if permittable. Indoors, light candles in firesafe containers, lanterns, and the like.

Before you begin, don your masks or chaplets (optional) and light the Beltane incense. When you're ready, ring the bell as you call upon the fae (or your spirits of the land) to bless your rite.

You may say,

Spirits of the land, we call upon you this night.

Ring the bell.

As we revel in spring's ripeness, bestow your blessing on our rite.

Ring the bell.

May joy reign throughout this season of growth and vitality.

Ring the bell.

And may we continuously seek the magick that dwells in liminality.
Blessed be.

Use this time in the Greenwood to play a flirty version of hide and seek within the garden. Eat sumptuous food and drink plenty of your favorite beverage. Take in the twilight hues and embrace the encroaching darkness. If lovemaking outdoors is possible, do it. If not, take the fun inside. Remember, there is power in orgasm, so use it to your advantage. As you climax, focus on your magickal intentions. At the conclusion of your evening, remember to thank the spirits of the land in your own way.

Beltane Incense Blend

- 2 parts birch bark
- 1 part rose petals
- 1 part sweet woodruff
- 2 to 3 drops vanilla extract

Grind the ingredients using mortar and pestle and burn the blend over a charcoal tab in a firesafe container.

Chapter 14
The Enchanted Lunar Garden

There is something ethereal and mysterious about the garden at dusk, but with the addition of white flowers and silvery tinted leaves, it becomes magickal. The first recorded all-white garden (or lunar garden) in the United States was designed by Benjamin Poore in 1833. Not only did he fill two 700-by-14-foot borders with an amazing array of white flowers, but he added a small herd of white cattle, white pigeons, and a white dog. Okay, so that might be a little overkill, but I would have loved to see it.

When planning a lunar garden, don't stress if when researching plants, you are unable to find plants that are completely white. The plants in my list will have green leaves or yellow centers, or even a stain of pink that lightly tinges the petals, but that's okay—it will help set off the white that much more. For a whimsical touch, add luminaries and white garden statuary.

When designing your lunar garden, remember that it doesn't require a lot of space. All the plants listed can be planted in containers to create an enchanted environment on a deck or patio. To help encourage growth and water flow, use moon phases or astrological timing to plant your flowers.

Here's a list of plants to get you started:

Pearly Everlasting (*Anaphalis margaritacea*): This beauty grows 1 to 2 feet tall and features clusters of white flowers with tiny yellow centers atop gray leaves. Also known as life everlasting because it dries and keeps easily, this plant can be used in spells to improve health and longevity. Zones 3 to 8.

Shasta Daisy 'Alaska' (*Leucanthemum ×superbum* 'Alaska'): These lovely bright white daisies with yellow centers grow 2 to 3 feet tall. Use daisies in magick for protection, dreams, love, and connecting with the element of earth. Zones 4 to 8.

White Foxglove (*Digitalis purpurea* 'Alba'): A faery favorite, this biennial boasts long 3-to-4-foot spikes with white tubular flowers. Use foxglove in magick for protection, working with the fae, and divination. Zones 4 to 9.

Lily of the Valley (*Convallaria majalis*): Another great faery flower, this plant prefers shade, grows approximately 8 inches in height, and has fragrant bell-shaped flowers. Use it in magick for connecting to the fae, intuition, and creating. Zones 2 to 9.

Yarrow (*Achillea millefolium*): This all-purpose Witch's herb is lovely in an all-white garden with its clusters of white flowers over mats of hairy gray-green leaves. Use it in tea to improve your psychic abilities. Zones 3 to 9.

Lamb's Ear (*Stachys byzantina*): Sometimes called woolly hedgenettle, this perennial in the mint family has fuzzy, silvery-green foliage. Use it in magick for healing and protection. Zones 4 to 8.

Moon Flower (*Ipomoea alba*): A moon garden wouldn't seem complete without this favorite evening vining plant. The moon flower has amazing, creamy trumpet flowers that open as the light begins to fade, releasing a lovely lemony scent. Use it in magick for dreams, psychic abilities, and women's mysteries. Zones 3 to 9 (annual), zones 10 to 12 (perennial).

'Rocket White' Snapdragon (*Antirrhinum majus* 'Rocket White'): This plant has spires of white flowers and 3-foot green stems. Use it in magick for protection, hex breaking, bravery, and passion. Zones 3 to 9.

'Royal Wedding' Sweet Pea (*Lathyrus odoratus* 'Royal Wedding'): This sweet pea cultivar has fragrant white flowers on vining stems.

Use it in magick for loyalty, friendship, and communication. Zones 3 to 9.

'White Shooting Star' Flowering Tobacco (*Nicotiana* 'White Shooting Star'): This plant is a tropical perennial and an annual in colder climates. With pretty, white, lightly scented flowers, use in magick for dreams, cleansing, protection, connecting with animal guides, and psychic abilities. Zones 9 to 11.

Sweet Alyssum (*Lobularia maritima*): Tiny clusters of sweetly scented flowers cover this 4-inch plant that is perfect for borders or containers. Use it in magick for calm, protection, peace, and faery magick. Zones 5 to 9.

Under the Light of the Moon

As moonlight slips over the garden, we watch the shifting shadows and find strength in her gentle glow. The energy and feeling of the lunar garden changes as the moon transitions through her phases, and we can take advantage of those subtleties of light and vibration with simple ritual.

Waxing Moon

With great clarity and courage, we enter the phase of the waxing moon. This is the time to get our creative juices flowing and focus our intentions on our potential and possibilities that are within our grasp. Let the delicate blossoms and bright scent of sweet orange (*Citrus ×sinensis*) or mock orange (*Philadelphus coronarius*) motivate your magick for new beginnings, focus, and clarity.

Invigorating Waxing Moon Bath Salts

Use this wonderfully bright bath salt before working waxing moon magick.

You will need:

- 3 cups Epsom salts
- ½ cup baking soda
- 1½ cups pink Himalayan salt

- 25 drops sweet orange essential oil
- 10 drops ylang-ylang essential oil
- 2 tablespoons dried orange blossom

Mix the ingredients in a large glass bowl and store the salts in glass containers in a cool, dark place. This recipe makes 5 cups and should be used within 6 months.

Full Moon

As the potent energy of the full moon spreads a milky glow across the garden, honor your own light and embrace the energy manifested through self-love and acceptance. The beautiful glowing face of the white rose in moonlight reminds us to trust in our own power. Try planting *Rosa* 'Alba Maxima' or *Rosa* 'French Lace'. Use the petals in ritual to honor self-love and in spells for emotional balance and trust.

Rose Water

Use rose water on your skin as an act of self-love before ritual or add it to your favorite recipes.

You will need:

- 4 cups distilled water
- Petals from 4 pesticide-free roses
- 2 teaspoons vodka

Simmer all ingredients in a saucepan for approximately 30 minutes. Let cool and strain through a cheesecloth. Bottle and store the rose water in your refrigerator for up to 6 months.

Waning Moon

The waning light of the moon invites us to surrender our fears and release those things that no longer serve us. White lavender in the garden is both soothing and mystical under moonlight—try 'Nana Alba' lavender

(*Lavandula angustifolia* 'Nana Alba') or 'Crystal Lights' lavender (*L. angustifolia* 'Crystal Lights') to promote peace as we learn to let go.

Incense Sticks for Release

Use lavender and sandalwood incense sticks during your meditation practice for release.

You will need:

- Incense stick blanks (can be purchased online or at your local metaphysical shop)
- 2 parts lavender essential oil
- 1 part sandalwood essential oil

Mix your essential oils according to how many incense sticks you plan on making (20 drops per stick) in a glass bowl. Lay your incense stick blanks on a sheet of aluminum foil and use a dropper to evenly distribute the essential oil. Let dry for 24 hours before use.

Honoring the Triple Goddess

The multiple facets of femininity were believed to be associated with the phases of the moon. Though there are many manifestations of the Triple Goddess the world over, I am using the archetypes from popular Roman and Greek mythology. This manifestation of the Goddess is considered the Three-in-One, whose triple nature reflects not only the moon's cycle but also our own.

The Triple Goddess's three aspects reflect the three phases of the moon. The waxing moon has been associated with Roman goddess Diana (Greek Artemis), always new, virginal, reborn. She is a goddess of fertility, nature, and the hunt. She is the Maiden who reflects beauty, curiosity, and new beginnings. The full moon has been associated with the Roman goddess Luna (Greek Selene). Pregnant with life, the Mother Goddess is a light in the darkness. She is nurturer and healer and reminds us of our full potential. The waning moon has been associated with Roman goddess Trivia

(Greek Hecate), the Crone who rules the underworld and has the power to transform. She is profound wisdom and holds the secrets of the dark arts.

With this simple garden ritual, we will honor the Triple Goddess under the light of the full moon.

You will need:

- 3 candles:
  - White to represent the Maiden
  - Red to represent the Mother
  - Black to represent the Crone

Have your 3 candles set up in a pleasing way on a small altar or table under the light of the full moon. Light the Maiden's candle and say,

> With the power to give flame to my desires, Maiden, I celebrate you who sparks joy and reminds me that rebirth is always possible.

Light the Mother's candle and say,

> With the power to nurture possibility, Mother, I celebrate you who guides me along the spiral path and reminds me that I am in charge of my own destiny.

Light the Crone's candle and say,

> With the power to transform that which feels broken, Crone, I celebrate you whose divine wisdom leads me through the darkness and reminds me that true power is within myself.

Outstretch your hands to the moon and say,

> I honor this night, Goddess of the moon whose divine light reminds
> me that magick is there for those who seek it.
> Blessed be the Goddess in all her forms.

Chapter 15
Herbs of May

May brings with it a raucous energy that leads us outdoors and draws upon our frivolous nature. The veil is thin during this time of year, and faery activity is evident to those who know where to look. The herbs I chose reflect May's frolicsome qualities.

Foxglove (*Digitalis purpurea*)

Planet: Venus

Element: Water or earth

Energy: Feminine

Deities: Juno, Flora

This cottage garden favorite is a must for any magickal gardener who works with faery energy. A biennial that grows on spiked stems up to 5 feet in height, every bit of this plant is poisonous, so be careful if you have small children or pets. With distinctive bell-shaped flowers, the wild variety blooms in shades of purple and white. Modern cultivars offer bright shades of pink, yellow, apricot, and cream.

Many of the folk names attached to this plant reflect its connection to the fae, including fairy fingers, fairy bells, fairy weed, and fairy petticoats, to name a few. One of the saddest and most fascinating legends that connect foxglove with the fae comes from Ireland, where it was said if one suspected their baby to be changeling, they were to squeeze the juice of the foxglove into a bowl. Then they were to place three drops of the toxic liquid on the child's tongue and three in each ear. It was believed if the child died, it was surely a changeling. Do not try this—foxglove is extremely toxic.

In Wales, a black dye was made from the leaves of foxglove and used to mark crosses as a means of protection on the stone floors of dwellings.

Medicinally, foxglove is the source of cardiac glycosides, used in medication for congestive heart failure. Use it in faery magick, women's magick, protection, and divination.

Foxglove Protection Circle

Foxglove planted in a circle around your garden altar is perfect for protecting your magickal space. Whether you dedicate it to the Triple Goddess for magick concerning women's mysteries or you're working with faery energy, these lovely varieties will truly bewitch your space.

For magick concerning the Triple Goddess, moon goddesses, or moon magick, try planting these:

'Camelot White' Foxglove (*Digitalis purpurea* 'Camelot White'): With large white bells, this variety is magickal under moonglow.

'Dalmatian White' Foxglove (*D. purpurea* 'Dalmatian White'): This white beauty features deep purple speckled throats that add a touch of mystery to your setting.

'Snow Thimble' Foxglove (*D. purpurea* 'Snow Thimble'): This variety is absolutely luminescent under the light of the moon.

For faery magick, try planting these:

Rusty Foxglove (*D. ferruginea*): Rusty foxglove is a whimsical, creamy variety that looks to be cultivated by elves.

'Apricot Beauty' Foxglove (*D. purpurea* 'Apricot Beauty'): This is one of my favorites, whose blossoms fade from apricot to a lovely cream.

'Illumination Flame' Hybrid Foxglove (*Digiplexis* 'Illumination Flame'): This hybrid has fanciful blossoms splashed in hues of sunset. Perfect for twilight.

Maidenhair Fern (*Adiantum* spp.)

Planet: Mercury

Element: Air

Energy: Masculine

Deities: Puck, Laka

The fern is the mysterious plant of magickal groves where the moss is thick and the Horned One can be seen hidden among the trunks of trees. Ferns are a member of one of the oldest plant groups, and their vibration reflects ancient knowledge. There are approximately 200 species of *Adiantum* worldwide. These delicate ferns can be distinguished by their graceful, fan-like pattern. Our Western maidenhair fern (*Adiantum aleuticum*) is a favorite of mine as I walk the shadowy, moist areas of our temperate rainforests. It is said that if you carry a fern frond, it will guide you to treasure. Other folklore tells that biting the first fern frond in spring will take away a toothache, and breaking the first frond in spring will bring good luck.

Medicinally, it has been used as a decongestant and to soothe coughs and sore throats. Magickally, use fern in spells for rain, healing, renewal, protection, luck, and invisibility.

Cloak of Invisibility Spray

To keep the unwanted eyes of the mundane from noticing your spellwork, this fern, sage, and cedar spray spritzed on yourself and around your space should do the trick.

You will need:

- Small fern frond
- Small green calcite crystal (optional)
- Filtered water
- 2 drops sage essential oil
- 2 drops cedarwood essential oil
- 4-ounce glass spray bottle

- 1 tablespoon witch hazel
- ¼ teaspoon sea salt

Place the fern frond and crystal in approximately ½ cup of filtered water. While that sits, add essential oils to the spray bottle. Add witch hazel and sea salt. Give the bottle a quick shake to mix the essential oils and witch hazel. Remove the fern frond and crystal and add them to bottle. Pour in filtered water until bottle is about ¾ full. Place the spray cap on the bottle and give the bottle another gentle shake to incorporate the essential oils.

Mayapple (*Podophyllum peltatum*)

Planet: Mercury

Element: Fire

Energy: Masculine

Deities: Circe, Hecate, Diana, Hathor, Saturn

Though unrelated to the mandrake (*Mandragora officinarum*), mayapple is sometimes referred to as American mandrake, as early colonists recognized the similarity in its usage as a purgative. Mayapple is a woodland plant that is widespread across most of eastern North America and south to Texas in zones 3 to 8. It prefers open deciduous areas and shady areas near riverbanks and roadsides. Each plant has 1 to 2 large, rounded, umbrella-like, deeply divided lobed leaves. White-to-rose-colored flowers appear in the spring, followed by a lemon-shaped berry in summer that can be used to make jams or jellies. The seeds are toxic.

Medicinally, mayapple was used to reduce fever, to expel worms, as a liver tonic, and topically to treat genital warts. Magickally, use it in spells for fertility, love, healing, protection, and prosperity. It is a wonderful substitution for mandrake root in spells.

Mayapple Root Amulet

When making this amulet, your choice of crystals, dried herbs, and sealing wax will depend on your magickal intention. Love, for example, may include dried rose petals and rose quartz chips with red sealing wax.

You will need:

- Fillable corked glass bottle pendant (can be found in any craft store)
- Small piece of dried mayapple root
- Small crystals (or crystal chips)
- Dried ground herbs
- Sealing wax (your choice of color)

As you fill your bottle, focus on your intent. Use sealing wax to secure the cork and hold the magick. Wear the pendant against your skin.

These make great gifts for magickal practitioners in your circle or coven.

Hawthorn (*Crataegus monogyna*)

Planet: Mars

Element: Fire

Energy: Masculine

Deities: Olwen, Blodeuwedd, Hymen, Hera

If you were to ask me what plant symbolizes both Beltane and Samhain best, I would answer hawthorn, as it serves as a gateway between worlds when the veil thins and the tendrils of the Otherworld are present. Hawthorn is one of the three trees that make up the triad—the oak, the ash, and the thorn—and where the three grow, one may see faeries. A small tree in the rose family, it can be seen in hedgerows or as a single tree along roadsides and on farmland. They have deeply lobed leaves and lovely white five-petaled blossoms that typically bloom in May. The fruit, called a haw, is an important food source for wintering birds and can be used in healthful recipes for humans too.

Both berry and flower were used in medicine including issues concerning the heart, to lower blood pressure, and treating insomnia. Magickally, hawthorn is used to communicate with the fae, in Beltane rites, and for fertility, happiness, and protection.

Hawthorn Protection Wreath

At Beltane, the veil thins and the spirit world is a whisper away. If you are highly sensitive to spirit activity and would like to keep them at bay, a simple hawthorn protection wreath hung above your door may help.

You will need:

- Floral foam wreath form (available at any craft store)
- Around 25 3-to-4-inch clipped hawthorn branches with blooms intact (please be respectful of the tree—always ask permission)

Soak your floral wreath form in water until completely saturated. At an angle, gently push flowers into foam. Repeat until you are happy with the results. Hang the wreath above your front entrance. As you hang the wreath, say something like this:

All spirits who malevolent may be
Pass by in peace upon seeing this tree

Sweet Woodruff (*Galium odoratum*)

Planet: Mars

Element: Fire

Energy: Masculine

Deities: Herne, Pan

Sweet are the secrets of this common ground cover that gently scents the air in spring. When dried, the scent becomes magickal as it intensifies to that of fresh cut hay with a hint of vanilla. A common strewing herb in medieval times, it was stuffed into pillows and sachets to ward off evil. It was also a popular herb used to enhance the flavor of tarts and cakes.

Native to central Europe and Asia, it prefers cooler climates and is the perfect ground cover for a faery-inspired woodland garden. In the right conditions, sweet woodruff can become invasive, so make sure to give it plenty of room. Use it in magick for protection, purification, prosperity, Midsummer or Beltane rites, and victory.

Maibowle

Maibowle, or May wine, is traditionally made in Germany and served on May 1. May wine is perfect for Beltane, weddings, or Midsummer rites. Collect the tiny woodruff stems just after they bloom and separate the leaves from the bitter stems. Dry your sweet woodruff leaves in the oven on a low setting (200 degrees Fahrenheit) for approximately 20 minutes or in a dehydrator set at 100 degrees for approximately 1 hour.

You will need:

- 25.4-ounce bottle of light white wine (like Riesling or Chablis)
- 1 cup dried sweet woodruff leaves
- Sparkling wine to taste
- Sliced strawberries

Pour the white wine into a large glass container and add dried sweet woodruff. Cover and place in the refrigerator to infuse for approximately 1 week.

Before serving, strain the sweet woodruff from the wine. Pour into a pretty glass pitcher along with sparkling wine (to taste). Add strawberry slices to individual glasses before serving.

Warning: Sweet woodruff contains certain chemicals that might slow blood clotting. Do not consume if you take blood thinners.

Around the Garden
To-Do List for May

If you live in an area where frost is still a threat, start seeds such as cucumbers and squash indoors or in a greenhouse. For some, it's your last chance to plant cool-weather crops such as peas, lettuce, and radishes (until fall). Remember, as soon as the soil temperature reaches 60 degrees Fahrenheit, it's okay to plant veggies such as tomatoes, peppers, cucumbers, and eggplants.

In warmer zones, if you haven't already, mulch your crops. This will help retain moisture as the temperatures become warmer. Stay on top of the weeds in your garden to avoid them taking over, and adequately water your plants to maintain their health and productivity.

Grow Your Magickal Knowledge

May is the perfect month to set up an altar for the fae. Get to know your garden at twilight: make notes on how it feels and what kinds of wildlife are present. Practice liminal magick.

Why not introduce yourself to the spirits of your land? This is easily done by remaining present while in nature—meditate, commune with trees, gather and make your own magickal tools from what you find on walks along the beach or in the garden. Leave trinkets or other offerings for the spirits that dwell in your garden.

JUNE

**The garden unfolds its magick to me.
Every leaf holds enchantment;
every bloom casts a spell.**

JUNE CORRESPONDENCES

Nature Spirits: Lady of the Lake, merfolk

Colors: Bright green, yellow, blue

Herbs and Flowers: St. John's wort, vervain, lemon balm

Scents: Honeysuckle, rose, lavender

Stones: Moonstone, alexandrite, blue lace agate

Trees: Oak, hawthorn

Animals: Fish, fox, snake

Birds: Robin, peacock

Deities: Bel, Freyr, Juno, Hera

Zodiac: Gemini, Cancer

Work spells for self-growth, love, prosperity, abundance, healing, and transformation.

Chapter 16
Kissed by the Sun

Where I'm from, June is a promise well kept. In this region, tucked deep within the cover of rainforest in the Pacific Northwest, gray skies that hang low around the chimney tops and the constant rain that batters one's spirit are the norm for most of the year. Even the toughest of souls struggle when in February it dawns on us that we have not seen the sun for several months. But in June our world brightens with a burst of green that seems to outshine the sun. Flowers bob colorful faces along roadsides and in fields, and cottonwood fluff floats like faery snow on a honey-fragranced breeze.

Because of June's exuberance, "There is always June" has been a common saying during hard times in my family, and it is that saying that percolates within me when winter's dreariness causes anxiety to rise in my chest as all that gray seems tinged with the scent of longing and missed opportunity. But I always pull through because I know one morning I will wake up and the clouds will have cleared to reveal a sky the color of sapphire, highlighting the fairy-tale setting of my home. It casts a spell on me as I wander through my garden, and I quickly forget about the rain that causes the moss to grow on my roofing and draws out the slugs, who nibble away at my tender greens. And for my patience and hard work, I am rewarded with a landscape that has truly been kissed by the Sun God.

This is the time to linger in the garden and begin to enjoy the fruits of your labor. Enjoy salads made with fresh greens or snack on peas or radishes as you stroll through your beds. Or maybe you're in a region where you're already plucking sweet, juicy tomatoes. Is there anything better than a fresh tomato straight off the vine? All the extra light June offers means you can get up early before work (or stay out late after work has ended) and enjoy nature at her zenith. Even if you don't have a sprawling garden in your backyard, stroll through your local park or community garden or just sit on your porch or balcony and take in the sun's radiant energy. Pick some flowers or treat yourself to a bouquet from a grower at your local farmer's market. These are the days, as the Sun God reigns, to truly take the time to stop and smell the roses.

That Which We Call a Rose

I have a secret to share with you: I have never been good at tending roses. In my cool, damp environment, the lovely hybrid tea roses with velvety blooms that seem at home in formal gardens where tea is served precisely at 4 p.m. tend to struggle here with black spot, powdery mildew, rust, and other diseases that weaken the plant's constitution. I don't have the patience or the time to give them the attention they deserve, so I end up with a leafless thorn bush by the end of the summer.

That being said, I do have several heirloom varieties, most of which were propagated from plants grown by my great-grandmother. They are at home in my cottage garden, where they can ramble freely over fence posts or dip gracefully near the pond. Hardier than hybrids, heirlooms do not require the fuss or care that their more high-maintenance cousins ask of me in climates such as my own. And if I'm being honest, it doesn't bother me. I have always been a bit wild. I'm the one you see in town with my hair piled sloppily atop my head with bits of moss or twigs attached. My nails are typically stained with soil or dye, and my favorite overalls are patched. I prefer that which is untamed. Why would my choice in roses be any different?

Roses are believed to be the oldest plant cultivated and used for decoration. It is suggested that rose gardens go back five thousand years in China and Japan, and it is thought that ancient Romans cultivated them on plantations for ornamentatal, medicinal, and culinary use. In fact, in Colorado in the late nineteenth century, Swiss botanist Léo Lesquereux found fossils (the Florissant Formation) that suggest roses have been in existence for more than 35 million years. Cultivated roses as we know them today were introduced into Europe from China in the eighteenth century. These repeat bloomers were easy to cross, and breeders began crossing them with native varieties for increased hardiness. Many of the popular tea roses are the result of these crosses. Victorians, who were fascinated by the language of flowers, sometimes demonstrated their feelings by giving flower bouquets, and the rose was prominent as the voice of friendship, sympathy, pride, and of course, love.

The rose's connection to love goes as far back as their history of cultivation. The Greeks associated the rose with Aphrodite, and in Rome, the rose was consecrated to Venus. Vishnu was said to have formed his bride, Lakshmi, from roses. A Persian folktale tells of a great love of a nightingale for a rose. As the tale goes, roses were once all white. But one evening, a nightingale came to a rose garden and fell in love with one of the roses, whose scent intoxicated the bird so much that it began to sing to it. Wanting to get closer, the nightingale pressed its breast up to the rose but hit a thorn. Despite the piercing pain, the bird continued to sing, and where the drops of blood fell, red roses appeared.

Maintaining Your Rose Bushes

For easier care, pick out disease-resistant varieties. Plant your new roses in the spring just after the last frost or in the fall at least a month before the first frost. Roses should be planted where they will have a minimum of six hours of sunlight per day.

Fertilize once a month with compost or an organic fertilizer. Water adequately and without wetting the foliage to avoid disease.

Deadhead back to first leaf below spent blooms every couple of days during growing season. Clean debris around the base of plant that may harbor disease or harmful insects.

Major pruning should be done in the spring. Remove dead or damaged canes. If a hard pruning is needed, cut back around a third of the previous year's growth.

The Magick of Red Roses

In magick, rose petals are a prominent ingredient in love spells, and depending on the color, they can be used to enhance the many nuances love has to offer.

Red roses are the quintessential love token and can be used in spells for true love, passion, and romance. Try 'Velvet Fragrance' (a hybrid tea rose, zones 5 to 10). With its large, classically shaped blooms and a lovely scent, it is great for bouquets.

Old-Fashioned Romance

Want to know a wonderful way to send loving vibes to your lover whether near or far? Write an old-fashioned love letter on pink paper and infuse it with a couple of drops of rose oil. Add a few red rose petals into the envelope and send in the mail to your romantic partner.

The Magick of Pink Roses

Pink roses can be used for love, especially platonic love, admiration, and self-love. Try 'Eden Climber' (a climbing rose, zones 5 to 10). With large, old-fashioned cupped blooms, this beauty is considered a short climber (10 feet) and looks lovely growing up a pilar or obelisk.

It's All about You

Impulsively treat yourself to a bouquet of beautiful pink roses. Place them in a pretty vase somewhere where you can just enjoy them—a magickal symbol that reminds us of how important self-love is.

The Magick of White Roses

White roses can be used in spells for faithfulness in love, as well as pure love and the sanctuaries attached to love (home, cathedrals, temples or churches, sacred sites, etc.). Try 'Tranquility' (an English shrub rose, zones 5 to 11). Heat tolerant, this lovely white rose will not droop under the midsummer sun. It produces beautiful double blooms on a shrubby bush with a light, fruity scent.

Sacred Garden

Treat your garden space, patio, deck, or porch as sacred space by planting a white rose as a proclamation of its divinity. After planting, declare something like this:

> This space is a place of love and peaceful energy
> I banish all that mean me/us harm or negativity

The Magick of Yellow Roses

Yellow roses are associated with friendly or familial love. Use them in connection to the ancestors. Try 'Persian Yellow' (a foetida rose, zones 3 to 9). Cold hardy, this bright yellow beauty is a shrub rose that bears healthful rose hips in the fall.

Honoring Ancestors

A vase of lovely yellow roses in honor of your ancestors is perfect for gravesites. Scatter yellow rose petals around your ancestral altar as an offering.

The Magick of Orange Roses

Orange roses may be used in spells for the fun or unconventional side of love. Try 'Apricot Clementine' (a dwarf rose, zones 5 to 10). Perfect for a container on the patio or balcony, this compact rose has lovely, long-lasting blooms.

Celebration Bath Bomb

Celebrate love with a tub full of glitter and the bright scent of rose and orange.

You will need:

- 1 cup baking soda
- ½ cup Epsom salts
- ½ cup citric acid
- 2 tablespoons dried orange rose petals
- 2 tablespoons carrier oil (coconut oil or sweet almond oil)

- 15 drops orange essential oil
- 20 drops rose essential oil
- ½ teaspoon water (if needed)
- Mica-based glitter in color of your choice
- Bath bomb molds

Mix the baking soda, Epsom salts, citric acid, and rose petals in a bowl. Add the carrier oil and essential oils and mix with your hand until it holds together when squeezed. Add up to ½ teaspoon of water if the mixture is too dry. Sprinkle a bit of glitter into both sides of your molds, and press in the mixture. Let the bath bombs dry for 24 hours before use. This recipe makes 8 to 10 bath bombs, depending on the size of your mold.

The Magick of Green Roses

Green roses are all about new love, as well as fertility and renewal and the freedom of love. There are no true green roses. A rose that is considered "green" typically starts out another color and then turns a greenish hue or has green-tipped petals. Try 'Greensleeves' (a floribunda rose, zones 4 to 10), whose semidouble pink blooms turn white and green as the flowers mature.

Love with Healthy Boundaries

Thinking of starting a new relationship or rekindling an old one? Sprinkle green-tinged rose petals and rose thorns around a small lit cauldron. Write "Love deserves healthy boundaries" on a piece of paper and toss it into the flames. Focus on a loving relationship with mutual respect as you watch the flames consume the paper.

The Magick of Purple Roses

Purple roses deal with sensuality and can be used to divine or dream of love. True deep purple roses do not exist. But there are a few varieties that are close, and 'Rhapsody in Blue' (a shrub rose, zones 5 to 9) is one of them. With pretty, cupped blooms and a bright citrusy scent, this rose is a showstopper.

To Dream of Your True Love

Tuck dried purple rose petals in a sachet along with equal parts mugwort and a small amethyst stone and sleep with it under your pillow to dream of your true love.

The Magick of Lavender Roses

Lavender shades of roses deal with the romantic side of love, including beauty, romance, and harmony. Try 'Sissi', also known as 'Blue Moon' (a hybrid tea rose, zones 5 to 10), a stunning rose with classically shaped lavender blooms that practically glow.

Harmonious Home

Place a mixture of dried lavender rose petals and lavender (*Lavandula angustifolia*) buds in bowls around your house or in the bedroom to calm anxious energy and restore loving vibes.

The Magick of Black Roses

Black roses can be used in spells that deal with the mysteries of love, including secret love and rebellion. There are no true black roses; blooms are typically a very deep shade of burgundy or red whose buds start out looking black or whose petals deepen to almost black as the plant matures. Try 'Black Velvet' (a hybrid tea rose, zones 6 to 9). This dramatic rose with deeply hued, classically shaped blossoms will take center stage in any garden.

Dark Moon Rose Water

Create rose water (see page 146) with the darkly hued rose petals to use in dark of the moon rituals or for the mysteries of love.

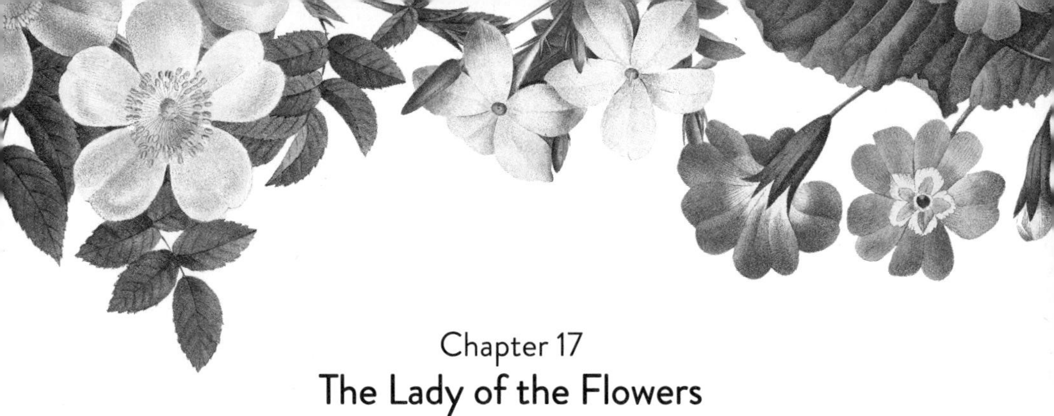

Chapter 17
The Lady of the Flowers

I was numb as I stood at the edge of the forest. It was the shushing of the wind that finally drew me into the Greenwood, where on a lovely June evening, when the moon hung low and reflected in silver ripples on the river, I learned that we are not alone as we walk between this world and the other.

This incident happened early in my marriage, when I was young and thought I had to please everyone (but myself). I had allowed my husband to talk me into a job he had heard about through a friend, which paid very well and, as he put it, "could really pad our bank account." I too had received an offer on a job that was closer to home and ideal for my quiet personality type. But because it didn't pay quite as much as the one my husband was excited about, I reluctantly turned it down. After starting my new job, I quickly figured out that though the money was good, the work environment was unsavory at best. Some days my boss made me feel small, and other days, he just pissed me off. But I always bit my tongue and reminded myself that I'm not a quitter, and on top of that, I didn't want to disappoint my husband.

But one day, after another patronizing comment from my boss, I cracked. I felt I could take no more, so I impulsively told my boss to fuck off and walked out. On one hand, I felt empowered by my act of rebellion. The chorus of Aretha Franklin's "Respect" played out in my head and a hint of a smile played at the corners of my mouth as I sauntered out the side entrance and got into my car. But as I drove the twisted road home that glowed under June's luminous light, guilt tugged at my ear—"Your decision is going to affect more than just you, selfish, selfish girl." But before I turned the car around and drove back to my boss, crying out, "Never mind,

I promise I will stay here until the abuse cripples my spirit," I took a breath and reminded myself that there was no amount of money that could make up for the destruction of one's self-worth.

I can't tell you that my husband took it well when I told him. Though he said he understood, the disappointment that reflected in his eyes told a different story. And, as I always do, I went to nature for consoling, for my heart was still heavy with guilt.

In June, the light in Washington state lingers until well after 9 p.m., but as darkness finally wrapped around my surroundings, I felt a presence walk with me and reassure my spirit that my fate was my own and I didn't have to give up my personal sovereignty in exchange for any amount of money, let alone to please another. The guilt suddenly lifted.

As I continued to walk with only moonlight as a guide, the story of Blodeuwedd filtered through my mind. In Welsh mythology, she was created by magicians, Math and Gwydion, from surrounding flora as a representation of the land and as a wife for Lleu to legitimize his kingship. She was called Blodeuwedd ("flower face" or "owl"). Trapped in an unhappy marriage she did not choose, Blodeuwedd made a hasty decision of her own in order to control her own fate. She, along with the man she chose to love, Gronw, plotted to kill Lleu. The only obstacle stopping them was that the king's life was protected by magick. Blodeuwedd feigned concern to persuade the king to show her what means it would take to kill him, which he did. But in the end, the attempted assassination failed, and the wounded king transformed into an eagle and flew off. The magician Gwydion healed Lleu, and they took revenge on the lovers. Lleu killed Gronw, but Blodeuwedd was punished by Gwydion with a fate, he reassured her, that was far worse than death. She would fly the night sky and all other birds would be hostile toward her. She was transformed into an owl.

I am not using Blodeuwedd's story as a comparison to my own. Just as an illustration of the importance of controlling one's own life. Me not taking that job would not have created a life-or-death situation in our household. We would not have lost our house, nor would we have starved. This was just me allowing another person to make a decision for me that I was uneasy about to begin with just to make another person happy. In other words, allowing someone else to control my fate. I found another job that I actually enjoyed and that offered me the quiet work environment my restless mind requires. As for my husband...he apologized and I've kept him around.

Blodeuwedd is a goddess of thresholds. She stands at the cusp of morning upon a lush field. She reigns as "Flower Face" where she is light, fertility, and passion. But she also keeps vigil as evening seeps inky hues across the land. She reigns as "Owl" where she is darkness, initiation, and rebirth. Her story represents many principles—seasonality, sovereignty of the land, sacred kingship, death, and rebirth, among others. She has been seen as an unfaithful wife, a manipulator, and as a betrayer. She has also been looked upon as a champion to those who feel manipulated, a liberator, and a trailblazer. I see her as a powerful representative of the wild feminine. She alights within in us a spark of assertiveness to help inflame our passion. She gives a voice to the meek and is the promise of spring when we face our darkest winters.

Blodeuwedd's story can be found in the fourth branch of the Mabinogion, and it is there where Math and Gwydion take up the blossoms that conjure the beautiful maiden. In the original text they use only the blooms of three sacred plants: oak, broom, and meadowsweet.

Work these herbs together to honor Blodeuwedd or to use in magick associated with her, including liminal magick, assertiveness, liberation, new beginnings, initiation rites, Beltane rites, rebirth, fertility, passion, and strength. To work with Blodeuwedd's energy, set up an altar in your garden with owl statuary and plenty of white and yellow blooms. As twilight beckons you to linger under its deepening hues, burn an incense made from any of the herbs listed below and invite Blodeuwedd to bless your garden.

The following are the three plants from the original Fourth Branch of the Mabinogion:

Broom (*Cytisus scoparius*): A very useful plant, broom was once used to thatch roofs and weave baskets. Its fibers were spun for cloth and, of course, as its name suggests, used to make brooms. In medieval literature, the blossoms of broom were sometimes used as a descriptor for beauty, specifically yellow (blonde) hair, and may give us a clue to Blodeuwedd's own hair color. Use broom in magick for cleansing, purification, protection, and divination.

Oak (*Quercus robur*): Associated with many solar deities, the oak tree shelters Lleu in his wounded eagle form. Oak has been used medicinally for its astringent and antiseptic abilities to treat wounds and reduce inflammation. Oak is long-lived and has offered protection, a place to gather for ritual, food, and medicine for thousands of years. Use it in magick for strength, healing, luck, working with solar deities, midsummer rites, health, and money.

Meadowsweet (*Filipendula ulmaria*): Sometimes referred to as bridewort, this sweet flower is one of liminal spaces. It grows along hedgerows, near riverbanks, and along roadsides. In ancient times, it had traditional use both in bridal bouquets and as a funerary herb. The transitional nature of this herb seems to coincide with Blodeuwedd's own liminal nature, as she is a goddess of both light and darkness. Use meadowsweet in magick for funerary rites, handfastings, liminal magick, love, divination, and happiness.

Color Magick in the Garden

Color in the garden sets the tone, be it the mystical ambiance of an all-white garden under moonlight or the raucous energy of a garden splashed with blooms in a bright palette of rainbow hues. Throughout this book, I have used examples of color magick working in partnership with the energy of specific blooms (roses or tulips, for example). Another way we see color and bloom symbology work hand-in-hand is within mythology and folklore, as seen in the story of Blodeuwedd, where the blooms and their colors paint a picture of who this powerful archetype was meant to be.

Color can have both a physical and a psychological effect upon the mind and help the practitioner tap into the vibrations associated with each color, which in turn can greatly enhance your spellwork. As a manifestation of vibration, colors vibrate at different speeds and allow changes in emotion, mood, and behavior. A high-vibrating color like red is considered stimulating, whereas lower-vibrating colors such as blue or purple are cooling and suggest vastness. Green gives off quiet and soothing vibes, and yellow produces joy. You can see why surrounding ourselves with the colors of nature is effective for our peace of mind.

The great thing about color magick in the garden is that it's so versatile. Say you're wanting to do a spell for passion, but you don't have any herbs you feel match your intention. Just find yourself a red bloom. It doesn't matter if the flower is a dahlia from your friend's garden or a carnation from the grocery store. Red is the color of passion and those high-vibrating blooms will help enhance your magick.

Here's a list of common garden bloom colors and their magickal associations:

Red: Passion, love courage, lust, protection, element of fire, root chakra

Orange: Attraction, success, goal setting, legal matters, business endeavors, ambition, real estate, invitation and welcome, drawing warmth, sacral chakra

Yellow: Blessings, joy, communication, balance, happiness, travel, intelligence, clarity, element of air, solar plexus chakra

Green (Foliage): Money, hope, tranquility, abundance, promise, achieving goals, environmental, fertility, element of earth, heart chakra

Blue: Cleansing, clarity, patience, messages, spiritual inspiration, calm, creativity, element of water, throat chakra, third eye chakra (deep indigo blooms)

Purple: Spirituality, higher self, awareness, power, third eye, inner knowledge, crown chakra

Lavender: Otherworld, divination, self-improvement, beauty, harmony, psychic growth, dreams

Pink: Friendship, romance, peace, healing, nurturing, femininity, caring, relaxation

White: All-purpose use, the Goddess, higher self, purification, protection, summoning

Black (Very Deep Maroon or Purple): Binding, protection, shapeshifting, removing negative influences

Gold (Deep Golden Yellow): The sun, radiance, higher self, healing, success, health, the God

Silver (Leafy Plants like Dusty Miller, Eucalyptus, or Artemisia): The moon, money, possibilities, open hearts, the Goddess

Celebration Ritual

June is Pride Month, so I thought I'd share a celebration ritual a friend of mine, who is part of the LGBTQ+ community, put together for our coven. This ritual is designed to be a celebration of individuality, gender and sexuality, diversity and inclusion, and love in all forms.

You will need:

- Blooms of any flower in colors of your choice (1 or more per person)
- Rainbow-colored pillar candle
- Tea lights in colors of your choice (1 per person)

Have each person bring favorite blooms in their favorite color. The color and variety of flower should hold symbolism to each individual. As a group, arrange the blooms on a table around a center rainbow-colored pillar candle. Around the flowers, place a tealight for each participant. Call the quarters in your own way and light the pillar candle. Everyone will gather around the table and, one by one, use the flame from the center candle to light their tealight. Use the time to talk about the symbolic choice of your bloom and how it pertains to you. Talk about your journey, talk about your gifts, talk about your courage. Remember to give positive feedback to others—this is about being joyous. When everyone has finished, release your circle and turn on the tunes. Dance, eat, and celebrate.

Chapter 18
Herbs of June

The sun has reached the height of its power, and we are thankful for the long, bright days of growth. The herbs of June reflect the joy, abundance, and strength of a garden at its pinnacle.

Daisy (*Bellis perennis*)

Planet: Sun

Element: Water

Energy: Masculine

Deities: Ra, Cernunnos, Lugh, Helios

It's funny how folklore and magick have followed us throughout the centuries. Even the most ardent of nonbelievers still blow out their candles on birthdays, knock on wood to ward off bad luck, or even wear a lucky shirt when watching a favorite sports team. Daisies were for many of us our first divination tool (and we didn't even know it). How many of us can remember sitting in the grass and pulling the petals from a daisy, one by one, as we chanted, "They love me, they love me not"?

The common daisy can be seen popping up in fields, yards, parks, and along the side of the road. They can grow up to 2 feet tall and are characterized by their white petals and bright yellow center. They are native to Europe but have become widespread and are now thought of as a weed in some areas in the United States. Medicinally, daisies have been used as an astringent; to relieve minor soreness and inflammation; and to treat bronchitis and coughs. Magickally, use daisies in spells for love, lust, joy, divination, abundance, and creativity.

Daisy Chaplet

For this easy chaplet, we will basically be creating a daisy chain and connecting the ends to form a crown. This can be worn for Beltane or Midsummer rites.

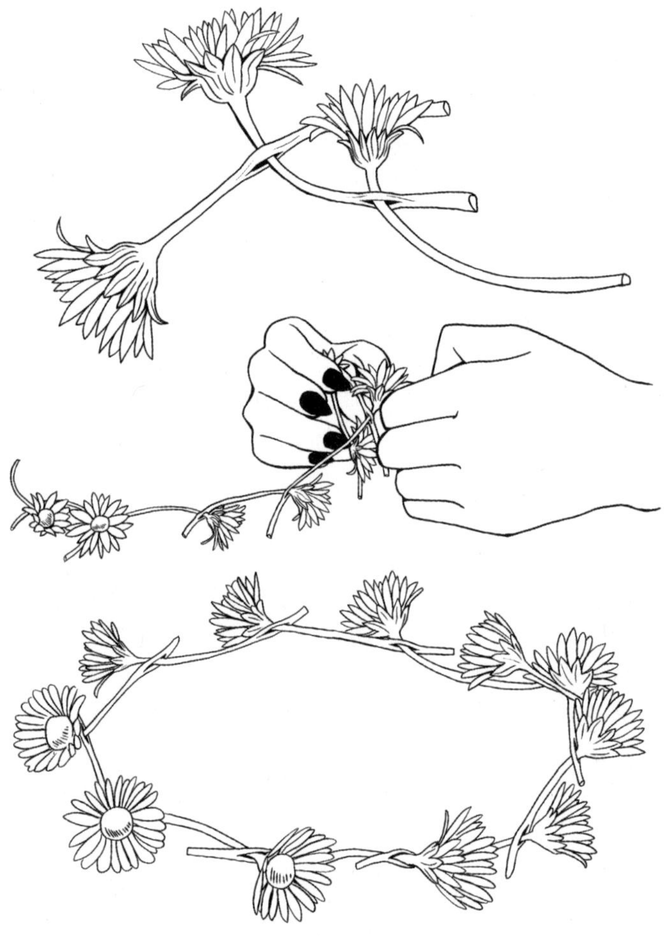

Gather as many daisies as you feel you will need, leaving approximately 2 to 3 inches of stem attached to the flower. Using your thumbnail, carve a ½-inch slit into the stem of the daisy. Once you have created a slit, take another daisy and thread its stem through the slit of the original daisy. This creates the chain-like effect. Repeat this step as many times as you please to achieve a desired length for your chaplet. Attach the ends in the same way to form a circle. As you do this, you may repeat,

A daisy for the Goddess
A daisy for mirth
A daisy for the God
A daisy for rebirth
A daisy for abundance, and one for creativity
By the power of petal, stem, and leaf
Blessed be

Oak (*Quercus* spp.)

Planet: Sun

Element: Fire

Energy: Masculine

Deities: The Dagda, Dianus, Jupiter, Thor, Zeus, Herne, Janus, Rhea, Cybele, and Pan

Associated with many gods of thunder and lightning across many cultures, the oak is a true symbol of strength and protection. These awe-inspiring trees can grow to an impressive 110 feet in height with girths up to 40 feet.

The oak (with over 400 species) can live up to 700 years and is an important feature in the regions it is native to. It provides food for wildlife, and its shade encourages the growth of wildflowers. And though many of the mighty oak forests have fallen victim to deforestation, the tree is truly still King of the Forest, as it remains a favorite for its deep cultural resonance and unconquerable spirit.

It was beneath the limbs of this mighty tree that the cycles of the year were celebrated by many people's ancient ancestors. Even today our modern Pagan practices still venerate this tree. During the solar celebrations of the solstices and equinoxes, the tree represents the God with strength, power, and protection, and during the cross-quarter celebrations, it imbues the feminine qualities of fertility, nurturing, and continuation of life. Use oak in magick for strength, protection, fertility, health, luck, working with solar deities, Midsummer rites, and money.

Acorn Amulet

It was traditional to place acorns on your windowsills to protect your home. But if you're facing a stressful situation outside of the home, why not take the protective power of the oak with you? Draw the runic symbols Thorn for protection and Ur for strength on an acorn (see next page).

Thorn and Ur runes

As you draw, you may say something like this:

I imbue thee with protection
I imbue thee with strength
As I carry this token, I take courage with me
Blessed be

Place the amulet in your pocket or keep it in your purse or bag.

St. John's Wort (*Hypericum perforatum*)

Planet: Sun

Element: Fire

Energy: Masculine

Deity: Baldur

One of my favorite memories while raising my little Witchlings was the first time I tinctured St. John's wort with them. As the bright yellow flowers made contact with the grain alcohol, the liquid turned red, and my children's eyes lit up. They had just witnessed some of nature's most potent magick. This happens because St. John's wort contains hypericin, which has been shown to have antibiotic and antiviral properties, and it will also stain your fingers red when you press the flower's buds between your fingers. This is a great indicator for first-time gatherers that they have the right herb.

There are around 490 species of plants in the genus *Hypericum*, but only *H. perforatum* is widely used in medicine. St. John's wort has been used for many years not only for its antiviral and antibiotic properties but also as an antidepressant, an antimicrobial, an anti-inflammatory, and a healing agent. For centuries before the Christian era, St. John's wort was an herb of fate whose golden flowers were a perfect representation of the sun. With Christianity, it became known as St. John's wort, as it bloomed near the time of his alleged birth. Use it in magick for protection, healing, Midsummer rites, luck, divination, happiness, and strength.

Midsummer Protection and Blessing Bundles

Gather St. John's wort on or around Midsummer and tie up two small bundles with other herbs such as fern fronds, mugwort, lavender, and elder. Keep one bundle to throw into a Midsummer rite's fire. Hang the other above your entry to bless your home and keep negative vibes away all summer long.

Strawberry (*Fragaria vesca*)

Planet: Venus

Element: Water

Energy: Feminine

Deity: Freya

When I taste the first strawberry of the season, I always get the chills. The sweet flavor takes me somewhere beyond the memories of my present life. It lasts for just a brief moment, and just when I think I can grasp that distant memory of another life, it fades.

A member of the Rosaceae family, strawberries are not a true berry but an aggregate fruit that produces many ovaries (what we think of as seeds) over a red, juicy receptacle. Strawberries don't necessarily rely on seeds but on daughter plants that grow off runners from the main plant until they can root themselves properly. Is it any wonder they have been connected to fertility in myth and folklore for centuries?

In Bavaria, strawberries were gathered and hung in baskets on the horns of cattle to pay the local nature spirits for healthy calves and abundant milk production for the year. To share a strawberry was said to produce love, and pregnant women were known to carry strawberry leaves to relieve pain due to their condition. Use strawberries in magick for love, fertility, success, luck, and healing.

Chocolate-Covered Strawberries

I can't help it. There is nothing like chocolate-covered strawberries to put one in the mood for magick. Especially with strawberries in season. Serve these at your Midsummer sabbat or to bewitch your lover.

You will need:

- 1 pound large, beautiful, ripe strawberries
- 12 ounces dark baking chocolate
- Chopped nuts, shredded coconut, or other toppings (optional)
- 3 ounces white chocolate (optional)

Wash and dry your strawberries. Do not remove the stems. Set out a parchment-lined baking tray to place the dipped strawberries on. Melt your chocolate using a double boiler or in the microwave.

Holding the stems, dip the strawberries in melted chocolate. Coat with desired toppings (optional). Lay them on the parchment and allow them to rest until the chocolate has set. Drizzle with melted white chocolate if desired.

Yarrow (*Achillea millefolium*)

Planet: Venus

Element: Water

Energy: Feminine

Deity: Achilles

I cannot seem to tame the yarrow that calls my garden home. Regardless of where I plant it, it tends to escape, preferring to spread into the grass where it thrives. But who am I to tame that which is wild? I've never appreciated it. With feathery fern-like leaves, yarrow grows abundantly along paths and roadsides. Long used in medicine for its cooling properties, it may help break a fever and stimulate sweating. With its antiseptic and anti-inflammatory properties, combined with the herb's ability to slow bleeding, yarrow was used on the battlefield for treating wounds.

Yarrow has a rich magickal history. It was once hung above doorways and baby cradles to keep negative spirits at bay. Placed in a wedding bouquet, it was thought to ensure a happy marriage, and carrying it guaranteed courage in any situation. The stalks of yarrow were used for the I Ching in China, and in Britain, women slept with yarrow under their pillows to dream of their true love. Use yarrow in magick for psychic abilities, divination, courage, protection, love, and dreams.

Yarrow Dream Pillow

Looking to dream of love?

You will need:

- 2 parts yarrow flowers and leaves
- 1 part mugwort
- ½ part lavender
- Lavender-colored drawstring bag

Mix your herbs and place them in a lavender drawstring bag. Place the bag under your pillow.

Around the Garden
To-Do List for June

If you are growing hardneck garlic, this is typically the time to harvest scapes (stalks that grow from the bulb that produce the flower). Not only does this allow for more energy to go directly to the bulb, but they're great in recipes too.

For colder zones, it's time to plant those tomatoes. Dig them in deep, and to avoid disease, never water tomatoes from the top; concentrate on a slow soak around the roots.

Cut back perennial flowers that are done blooming to maintain full plants and generate new growth. Use a garden spade or lawn edger to clean up the edges around your garden beds and to keep weeds from creeping in. If you have a compost pile, make sure summer temperatures aren't drying it out. Rewet the heap by watering it. You can also give it a boost by adding fresh material.

Grow Your Magickal Knowledge

Practice combining your knowledge of both herbal and color magick in your spellwork.

Start gathering herbs to dry (see more on pages 200–201 about drying and storing herbs) for spell crafting, tincturing, recipes, and so on.

As you walk through your own garden, the park, the community garden, or just down a country road or trail, continue to test your knowledge of the magickal and medicinal uses of plants in your surroundings. How many plants can you connect with stories in folklore and mythology?

Host a Midsummer sabbat gathering with like-minded friends. Here are some ideas for your Midsummer (Litha) sabbat celebration:

- A bonfire outdoors with plenty of room for dancing and drumming
- A ritual for blessing your garden
- Magickal herb bundles to add to your bonfire or hang above your entry
- Honoring the fae
- A Midsummer feast featuring food grown by local gardeners and farmers
- Greeting the sunrise with mimosas
- A picnic on the beach

JULY

Reveal to me your secret garden and I will tell you what kind of Witch you are.

JULY CORRESPONDENCES

Nature Spirits: Hobgoblins, will-o'-the-wisps

Colors: Green, blue-gray, silver

Herbs and Flowers: Jasmine, lotus, delphinium, hyssop

Scents: Sandalwood, gardenia

Stones: Red tourmaline, ruby, green calcite, white agate

Trees: Oak, acacia, ash

Animals: Turtle, whale, dolphin

Birds: Swallow, ibis

Deities: Cerridwen, Cernunnos, Hel, Khepera

Zodiac: Cancer, Leo

Work spells for success, leadership, dreamwork, strength, passion, and lightwork.

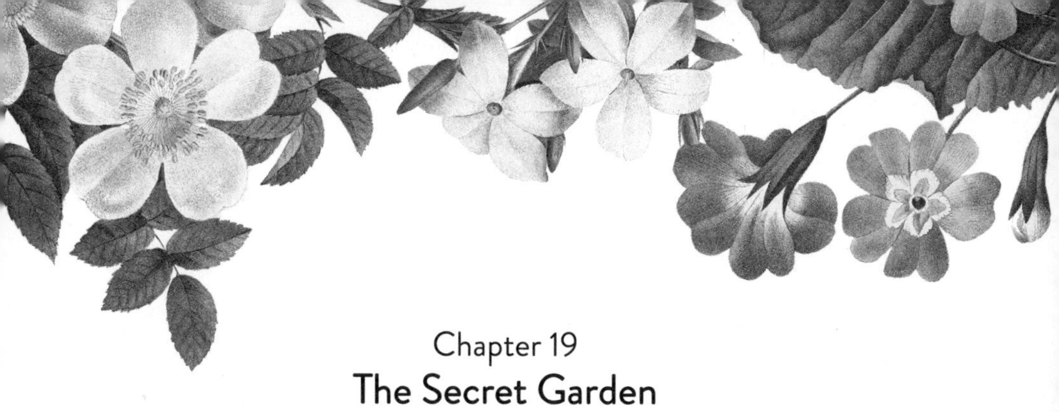

Chapter 19
The Secret Garden

It is in July that the landscape begins to deepen. Gone is the bright, riotous green of early summer when everything is fertile and buzzing with life. July's green is that of summer at its pinnacle—full in its ripeness. It's a deep blue sky vacant of clouds and foothills that glow emerald. It's a warm breeze and the scent of lavender released with the slightest brush of my leg.

Sometimes when driving the winding roads of my narrow valley, I stop to watch how the field grass, dotted with fireweed and oxeye daisy, undulates in the midday heat. Just as I talked about with the taste of strawberries, it is fields like this that begin to draw memories of a life I can't quite place. So distant are the images of myself walking down a path through a tall grassy field that I wonder if it's my overactive imagination playing tricks. But there I am as the trail widens to a dirt drive surrounded by hedges, so thick it's as if I'm walking into a tunnel. That is where the memories stop, but I know that at the end of that drive is a cottage surrounded by the plants that I love so well. One day, I might go under hypnosis just to take a peek at this hidden place that my spirit tells me truly once existed for me. But for now, I know I was happy there and maybe that's all I need to know. Some treasures, I suppose, are meant to stay buried. It gives us something to dream about.

In my present life along the Sauk River, where moss softens and hides those imperfections of our life, I have two tiny gardens that I keep to myself. There is a small garden I made where the rocky slope rises on the south side of our property, a grotto of sorts, where maidenhair fern grows from cracks in the rocks and vine maple branches curve to keep prying eyes at bay. In the summer, I bring pots of shade-loving begonias and coleus and hang a small candle chandelier from a tree. During long summer evenings, I bring a book to this spot and lose myself between the pages.

On the river, a large cedar guards the bank, and near its protective arms I sit with wild bleeding heart, Jacob's ladder, vanilla leaf, and salal, while willow, alder, and elderberry watch from the periphery. Magick feels right here in this liminal setting where I am at home with the spirits of nature. These are my secret gardens: one for magick and one for dreaming. My escape from the mundane when the world becomes overwhelming.

Somewhere, down deep, don't we all long for our own secret garden—our very own private little getaway for meditation, relaxation, and ritual? Come with me down a pebble path and through the trellised entry that leads to the perfect witchy hideaway. It's simpler than you might think.

A Garden Room of Your Own

Imagine a space of your own that evokes a feeling of magick and mystery, a place to solidify your connectedness with nature and embrace your own wild nature. You don't need to own acreage or even have a yard to accomplish this. A balcony, porch, or even a small corner of your home where the light suits the needs of your plantings will do just fine.

To accomplish this, you could most definitely deem your corner of the world as your space, place some plants around you, and call it good. But what if I told you that you could manipulate the vibrations of your garden space to invoke a harmonic energy that lightens your soul and complements your magick? How will we do this? By controlling chaos both energetically and visually. We can do this with color, by employing creative planting techniques, by adding elements that help you establish your secret garden as sacred, and finally, by putting together your garden in a way that is harmonious to you.

The Power of Color

Every color has a vibration, and those color frequencies have a general quality that affects our moods that can be used to enhance our magick or change the energy of our environment. This goes for our gardens too. If the color and plant combination is too uniform, the energy can feel dull, boring—the equivalent of a pair of khaki pants. But if you have too many things going on with your plant and color combinations, the eye has no place to rest, and this can create a nervous energy. Here are a couple of ways to incorporate color and texture that will evoke the mood you're looking for while maintaining interest.

Is your secret garden set up for relaxing and possibly to practice divination? A palette of cool shades of blue, lavender, and deep purple would be nice. Maybe you want a place to raise energy—try plants in shades of orange and red with splashes of yellow. Sticking to a simple analogous color scheme is the easiest way to conjure the vibrations that suit your needs as well as maintain a sense of harmony.

So you want a specific vibe but want to amp up the color a bit. Pull out your color wheel. Complementary colors (a primary color directly across from a secondary color) create a unique energy by adding a "pop" to your space. Try a burst of yellow to your palette of purple flowers. Another way to add vibrancy is by employing "triads," which use three colors equally spaced around the color wheel. Try warm reds and yellows with touches of cool blue.

If you are set on the use of just one color, like lovely pink blooms for peaceful vibes, add texture to your garden with ferns, ivy, or grasses that add interest without taking away from your blooms.

Keeping It Private

The whole idea behind a secret garden is to create a private space where one feels comfortable working magick, meditating, or just hanging out, as well as conjuring an air of mystery for those who pass by. This can be easily done by incorporating vining plants, trellising, or small shrubs or trees into your landscape.

Vining plants can be an inexpensive way to create a privacy screen for your secret garden. Climbers such as clematis, climbing roses, ivy, hops, star jasmine, wisteria, and climbing hydrangea are among the many plants that can be incorporated into your garden design to provide privacy and beauty.

Small trees or shrubs can be a great way to enclose a secret garden. Plants such as emerald greens, privet, laurel, boxwood, bamboo, and fan palm can be used to keep noise levels downs and the neighbors left wondering what you're doing over there.

Incorporating the use of screens is another way to create privacy. But if you want to express a bit of your creativity and go beyond the typical trellis panels, use items one doesn't usually think of when planning a garden. Sheer curtain panels can be hung on wire. They are inexpensive, add the perfect touch of magick and mystery, and come in large array of colors. How about antique or vintage doors repurposed to make screening? Old windows can be painted and hung in trees or off a balcony or side of a porch. The possibilities are endless.

Finishing Touches

No secret garden is complete without those finishing touches that personalize your garden room. Relate your garden accessories to your magick or echo the style of your home. So many details that can be added to a garden have magickal symbolism attached to them. Here are a few to consider:

Altar: Your central point for ritual and ceremony

Animal/Bird Feeder: A symbol of an offering to nature, the element of earth (or air)

Arbor/Bridge/Gate: Thresholds designating the crossing into sacred space

Bells/Chimes: The element of air and the release of prayers, attracting peaceful energies, banishing negative energies

Fire Pit/Fire Table: The element of fire, protection

Fountain: The element of water and the flow of life

Gazebo: May represent a temple, a place for ritual, ceremony, and protection

Labyrinth: Womb of the Mother, purposeful journey, to go inward

Lantern: Guidance

Moon Gate (Circular gate): Transition and the cycles of life

Obelisk: Phallic symbol, masculine power

Prayer Flags: To attract good spirits and send prayers heavenward

Shrine: Focal point associated to a deity, sacred being, or relic; a reflection of life's mysteries and blessings

Spiral/Serpentine Path: Going inward, growth, development, cycle of life

Statuary: Protection

Stones: The element of earth, strength

Sundial: Cycles of life (the seasons)

Vessels: The sacred feminine

Witch Ball: Protection

Incorporating Feng Shui

We've discussed many ways of planning a magickal garden space to suit your needs. But no discussion about creating harmony in the garden is complete without discussing the basic concepts of feng shui. With its roots in early Taoism, the discipline of creating positive qi (energy) is said to bring one's life in balance. Though some of the practices of feng shui are simple placements based on the elements and balance within an environment, to be a true practitioner requires practice, study, and initiation.

In the garden, things to consider that may provide overall harmony include adding a focal point to draw the eye and create a sense of ease or a path that winds through the garden and directs the energy. Balance yin and yang energy by placing hard (yang) and soft (yin) elements together within the garden: a bowl of hard stones nestled in a bed of moss or tall trees with softer ornamental ground covers. Adding features that represent the five elements is another simple way to create balance and harmony within your secret garden:

Wood (Growth and Vitality): Wood bowls or carvings, green trees or shrubs

Fire (Passion and Success): Candles, solar lighting, red flowering plants

Earth (Stability and Nourishment): Well-placed stones, pottery, yellow flowering plants

Metal (Clarity and Ease): Wind chimes, singing bowls, white flowering plants

Water (Flow and Freedom): Water features, black or dark blue flowering plants

The Vine That Binds: Honeysuckle

I have been planning my home since I was a child. I knew I would never live a conventional life—no split-level in the burbs or townhouse in the city. In fact, I knew deep down that my future home was somehow interconnected with our neighbor. You see, she was a collector of architectural salvage. Vintage leaded windows, ornate doors, crown molding, and porch columns were a few of the things that were stacked in her shed and littered her yard.

I remember one morning, just after a heavy summer rain that left the landscape misty and the air scented of the honey locust blooms that grew along our country road, I had heard the neighbor call me over. A shy eleven-year-old, with better ways to spend my day than to help her out, I took a breath and reluctantly walked over.

"Is everything okay?" I asked.

"Hubby's gone, sweetheart. And I sure could use your help getting some things out of the back of the truck and under cover."

"Okay," I said, relieved that I wasn't being asked to babysit or help with her yard work. I hopped into the bed of the truck and pulled back the tattered tarp. What was revealed wasn't the most ornate of her collection, but somehow the objects connected with me. There were four large lead-paned windows and a set of solid wood doors with warbled glass and peeling paint. I was enamored.

"I can tell you like them." She smiled.

I nodded.

"Those will be incorporated into a studio for me." She pointed to the spot in her yard where she planned for the building. "I really love them."

I helped her tuck them up under a lean-to that attached to her garage. When I went home, I told my mother about them and about her plans. She shook her head and said, "Aw, poor thing. She has so many plans, but nothing ever seems to come of them."

"Maybe I can buy them from her someday," I said. "I would put them in my house and grow honeysuckle around them. Just like the honeysuckle here."

My mother patted my head and said, "I bet it'd be lovely."

Years passed, and I went over to the neighbor's occasionally to babysit or help move her treasure, but my mother was right. They never used any of the pieces they acquired. In fact, the windows and the doors I loved so much never moved from underneath their covering. More time went by and the neighbors moved, taking with them almost all of the salvage—including my windows and the doors. I grew up and moved out, but I never forgot about the pieces.

After I was married, my husband and I lived on his cramped fishing boat while we searched for a small home to buy. We purchased a 550-square-foot cottage (before tiny homes were a thing) on the edge of a forest just across the river from our current location and we made it rather charming. But with our family beginning to grow, we knew we had to find something bigger. When the property we are on now came up for sale, we jumped at the opportunity to build something from the ground up. We built our home with salvaged materials found at flea markets, re-stores, the dump, and garage sales.

One garage sale, which was advertised as having vintage and antique items, was at a small home tucked up near an apartment building at the end of a tight gravel road by the airport. We pulled into the drive, and to my surprise I saw something very familiar. My eyes filled with tears, and I clutched my chest.

"What's wrong?" My husband was more confused than concerned.

"Those are my windows." I stammered. "The ones I've talked about for years." I burst from the vehicle and made my way to them. The price tag read five dollars each, which even at the time was inexpensive for four-foot-high antique windows. "Oh my God," I mumbled.

That's when my childhood neighbor walked up to me. We hugged and reminisced before I announced, "I want them all."

She chuckled. "You always did love those windows." Her expression became melancholy. "I loved them too. Still can't decide if I can part with the doors." She pointed to the side of her garage where I saw them leaning.

"If you decide to sell them, I want them. I'll pay anything." I fumbled for my wallet and wished I could take back my last sentence.

She took my twenty dollars and my phone number and promised she'd call me.

I went home more than happy just to have the windows in my life. One month later, she called me. "Still interested in the doors?"

"Of course!" I blurted before remembering I had told her cost wasn't an issue. But I was relieved when she asked if thirty dollars was too much.

We put three of the windows together and the double door at the front of my house, and the remaining window was installed in my bathroom. Around the front grouping of windows grows a honeysuckle plant I had dug as a start from my parents' yard. Growing with our family, it watched over us when in summer, during evening hours, we would open those double doors and take in its fragrance. I'd watch through the windows as my kids would sometimes dance near its creamy blossoms or catch their fascination as they followed the elusive hummingbird moth that was drawn to the magickal flowering vine.

In the winter, the honeysuckle was a perch for birds and didn't seem annoyed as my kids tapped at the windows to say hello to the chickadees that lit on its twisted vines. It was also through the glass of the antique windows that I watched my kids one by one leave to begin lives of their own. The honeysuckle that protected my childhood home is now a part of my family's story, as are the door and the windows that I felt bound to as a child. These are examples of the everyday sort of magick we don't always legitimize—a reminder that objects hold power and the spirit of plants have wisdom to share.

An old-fashioned favorite, honeysuckle (*Lonicera* spp.) is sometimes called woodbine and is a part of a large family of vining and arching shrub plants that can flourish in zones 4 to 9. I know many of us probably have a childhood recollection of sucking the sweet nectar from its trumpet-shaped blossoms or catching their fragrance wafting on a summer breeze.

If I were to recommend any plant for your secret garden, it would be this one, as the scent alone can stimulate psychic awareness. A prolific climber, it can be planted near a trellis to provide quick screening. Honeysuckles can also be planted in a pot with a trellis panel for balconies or decks or even grown in hanging baskets. They do like to have at least six hours of sunlight but can tolerate some shade. Easy to care for, they can grow in almost any soil; just add a balanced fertilizer (10-10-10) a couple of times during the growing season. These are some popular varieties to try:

Common Vine (*Lonicera periclymenum*): This climber is the most recognized variety and is prolific in temperate zones. It boasts pink to white creamy blossoms, turning golden yellow as they mature.

'Gold Flame' (*Lonicera* 'Gold Flame'): Preferring warmer zones 6 to 9, this climber has bright sherbet orange and pink blossoms that bloom throughout the summer.

Winter (*Lonicera fragrantissima*): This shrub variety is an evergreen that can grow without supports in zones 4 to 9. It has lovely white blooms and a pleasant fragrance.

Honeysuckle is a wonderful plant to have in your spell-crafting arsenal. The vines can be used to bind love and the flowers added to sweeten your spellwork. Grown around thresholds, honeysuckle is a protective plant that wards against negative energies and draws in luck. It's said that on Beltane, farmers once hung honeysuckle in their barns to protect the livestock from being bewitched and brought the flowers into the house to promote riches.

Honeysuckle is an important plant for wildlife, as its fragrant blossoms attract night-flying moths such as the elephant hawkmoth and the hummingbird moth to feed on the nectar. Bees love it too, and it is the sole food plant for caterpillars of the white admiral butterfly. The red berries that appear in fall are an important food source for a wide variety of birds and mammals, though mildly toxic to humans. Honeysuckle is associated with Juniper and the element of earth. Use it in spells for love, psychic awareness, luck, money, protection, and dreams.

Honeysuckle Money Spell

- 24-inch piece of honeysuckle vine
- Green candle
- Honeysuckle blooms
- A few coins

On a Thursday during a waxing moon phase, inscribe your candle with symbols for both Jupiter (abundance) and the sun (power) and anoint it with honeysuckle nectar from your blooms. Place the candle in a safe holder and surround it with coins. Surround the coins with your honeysuckle vine. (Remember to be vigilant anytime you are burning a candle near herbs.) As you do this, envision yourself having enough money for your needs. Light the candle and say something like this:

Abundance for my needs
Power within me
I manifest through this flower
Money to fill my bower

Allow candle to burn out. Dispose of the vines in a way you deem appropriate.

Chapter 20
Making Magick: Harvesting and Drying Your Herbs

One really great advantage of growing and foraging for your own herbs is that you know exactly how they were treated throughout the growing and gathering process. This guarantees what you are putting into your body, using to create salves or tinctures, or using in spellwork is organic and has been preserved with loving care. This also provides you with plenty of herbs that will last all year long.

I remember a few years ago, I had run out of rose petals and needed some, so I went to Etsy and purchased a small amount from a dealer who said they had grown them themselves. When the petals arrived, they smelled oddly smoky and had a dull, rusty appearance. Obviously, they were very old and either dried or stored near a woodstove. I learned a valuable lesson about the risks of ordering herbs online—no matter what the dealer says, you never truly know what you're getting, when it was actually harvested, or if it was handled ethically.

Another thing I like to stress to practitioners is that you always have something that grows in your own region that is comparable to many of the exotic or endangered herbs, woods, or resins that are being peddled in the New Age community today. White sage can be easily replaced by garden sage. Frankincense can be replaced by pine, and palo santo can be replaced with cedar or pine bark or fallen branches. Not only does this enhance the connection to the spirits of your region, but it helps the environment.

Harvesting and Drying Herbs

Harvesting and drying herbs is a simple process and can be done all through your growing season, but a few rules of thumb still apply:

Harvesting

Harvest early in the day after plants dry off and before it gets hot, and always use a sharp knife or pruners for clean cuts.

Harvest plants when they have enough foliage to maintain growth. When dealing with perennials, you can cut back approximately one-third of the growth. Annuals can be cut back by half. When wildcrafting, only take what you need, and never take more than one-third of any grouping.

If you are harvesting for leaves, plants are best harvested before flower production begins. Remove flowers as they appear for continued production of new leaves suitable for harvest.

Do not harvest from roadsides, as the herbs run the risk of being contaminated by fumes, runoff, and possibly pesticides.

Drying

Using paper bags to put bunches of herbs in with ends sticking out is the simplest way to dry your herbs. The bags help protect the herbs from contamination while drying and helps maintain their color. Hang your herb bunches in a dark, dry, well-ventilated area such as a garage or shed. This is also the slowest process, with herbs taking approximately a month to dry.

Food dehydrators are an efficient way to dry herbs, but if you don't have one, using an oven set at its lowest temperature and propping the door slightly open can give similar results. Typically, herbs will dry within three to four hours. Monitor closely.

You can also use a screen to dry flower petals or individual leaves. Arrange the herbs in a single layer on a framed screen and set it out of the sun in a warm, dry, well-ventilated area. This can take anywhere from a few days to a week, depending on conditions.

Storing Dried Herbs

I love images of darkened shelves with antique jars filled with herbs alongside bewitching curiosities—a cauldron, bones and feathers, framed pages from old grimoires, black candles, stones, and a collection of mortar and pestles. That's exactly how I envisioned my witchy pantry would look—but alas, my dried herbs are tucked behind the jars of canned pickles and beets above the chest freezer and across from the washer and dryer. No matter what our aesthetic, the important thing is that our herbs are stored properly. I leave the herbs I use most often in their paper bags hanging in an attic space upstairs where I put together my incense blends. Others I have vacuumed sealed or tucked into canning jars. The key to keeping them viable is that they are kept in a warm, dark space. Try not to crumble your herbs when storing, as this breaks down their potency quickly. Crumble just before use. Always mark and date your stored herbs.

Here are a few storage options:

- Vacuum sealing is going to preserve your herbs best. In fact, they will be fine to use in tinctures and salves for over a year, as there is no exposure to air. This is a great option for herbs that won't be used right away.
- Canning jars work great. Just remember to store them in a cupboard, drawer, or darkened pantry.
- If you don't have a pantry or room in a cupboard, use amber-tinted or painted jars or stainless-steel tins for herbs to avoid exposure to light.

Freshness Test

Herbs don't last forever, and depending on your storage techniques and the type of herbs you're storing, their viability can quickly wane. I always suggest keeping your herbs for a year from the date they were stored. But if you think they might be okay, here are some questions to consider:

Color: Is it still green, or do you have something that is the equivalent of brown dust?

Scent: Can you still identify it by scent, or is it faint to nonexistent?

Webby or Chewed: Is there evidence that bugs have gotten into your herbs?

Just like in cooking and medicine, herbs are not going to be effective in your magick if they are too far past their prime. That's why I tell people, if you cannot dry your own, to avoid buying herbs through large online marketplaces. Try to find a local grower whom you trust.

In the Cauldron Goes …

Fragrant smoke from herbs can be used in magickal workings to purify or cleanse your sacred space from negative vibrations and aid in raising energy to suit your intentions. Now that you have a collection of dried herbs, I encourage you to start creating incense. This will not only help you get to know the energies of each of your plants but also infuse your own personal energy into the incense.

If you're new to making your own incense, start with easy noncombustible varieties by picking three herbs and using this simple formula: 4 parts for your main component, followed by 2 parts for your second component, and 1 part for your final component. Grind your herbs, barks, berries, or resins with a mortar and pestle or an electric grinder. They can be stored as you would your individual dried herbs for later use. After you get the hang of it, start adding more components to your mixes; be creative and let your intuition be your guide.

I've added few blends to get you started.

All-Purpose Blend

Bay, basil, cedar, lavender, pine, rose, sage, thyme, and yarrow are great all-purpose herbs for incense making.

- 4 parts sage
- 2 parts thyme
- 1 part pine

Energetic Blend

Cypress, goldenrod, lemon peel, lemon balm, mint, and orange peel all work well for clearing stagnant energy.

- 4 parts cypress
- 2 parts orange peel
- 1 part mint

Divination Blend

Try creating blends with bay, borage, chamomile, elecampane, mugwort, or yarrow when working divination.

- 4 parts mugwort
- 2 parts chamomile
- 1 part yarrow

Dreamwork Blend

Honeysuckle, mugwort, lavender, marigold, rose, and valerian are wonderful for dreamwork.

- 4 parts valerian
- 2 parts rose
- 1 part lavender

Healing Blend

Use lavender, nettle, poplar, rosemary, rose, rowan, or violet in incense blends for healing.

- 4 parts poplar buds
- 2 parts nettle
- 1 part rosemary

Loving Vibes Blend

Try herbs such as apple, betony, catnip, chamomile, elm, gardenia, rose, jasmine, lemon balm, maple, pansy, and vanilla in mixes for love.

- 4 parts chamomile
- 2 parts jasmine
- 1 part rose

Meditation Blend

Meditative herbs include chamomile, hibiscus, juniper, lavender, lemongrass, meadowsweet, mint, sage, and vervain.

- 1 part chamomile
- 1 part hibiscus

Blend of Plenty

Prosperity blends may include calendula, cinnamon, basil, dandelion, dill, ginseng, lovage, and maple.

- 4 parts calendula
- 2 parts ginseng
- 1 part cinnamon

Protection Blend

Try angelica, anise, aspen, basil, bay, birch, broom, cedar, elderberry, eucalyptus, dill, fennel, fern, ginseng, mint, mullein, oak, rosemary, and sage in blends for protection.

- 4 parts birch bark
- 2 parts bay
- 1 part cedar

Psychic Blend

Herbs known for sharpening psychic skills include anise, borage, honeysuckle, ginger, jasmine, mugwort, wood betony, and yarrow.

- 4 parts honeysuckle
- 2 parts jasmine
- 1 part mugwort

Purification Blend

Use angelica, bay, cedar, lavender, pine, sage, and thyme for purifying sacred space.

- 4 parts cedar
- 2 parts bay
- 1 part lavender

Bring It On Blend

Bay, basil, cinnamon, fennel, mullein, oak, and orange peel are excellent herbs for strength.

- 4 parts basil
- 2 parts bay
- 1 part cinnamon

Chapter 21
Herbs of July

July evenings seem created for strolls through a garden. What wisdom can we gain from our plant allies? Healing, protection, and courage are a few of the attributes offered from the plants I chose for this month, when summer is at its sweetest.

Blackthorn (*Prunus spinosa*)

Planet: Saturn

Element: Fire

Energy: Masculine

Deity: The Morrigan

This plant of the hedgerows has a bad reputation. A shrubby tree in the rose family associated with curses and bad luck, it was said to grow from the body of heathens. The most likely cause was the tree's long spines that, when pierced into skin, were known to cause severe bleeding or infection.

Native to Europe and western Asia, it is not an easy tree to find in your local nursery in the United States. But if you choose to order it online or seek it out through a specialty nursery, you'll be pleasantly surprised. Perfect as a hedge plant in zones 4 to 8, it boasts lovely white blooms in the spring that develop into fruit known as sloes. Sloes are used in the making of sloe gin and can be used in jams or jellies if the fruit is harvested after frost has set, as this takes away any bitterness. Use blackthorn in spells for protection, setting boundaries, purification, and hexing.

Blackthorn Protection Salt

With its sharp thorns, not many would dare to cross through a hedgerow of blackthorn. It makes sense to add the thorns to a protective salt. Use this salt in cleansing rituals, to mark protective borders, or in Witch's bottles.

You will need:

- 1 bay leaf
- 1 star anise pod
- ¼ cup sea salt
- 3 blackthorn thorns (available online)

Crush your bay leaf and remove the seeds from the points of the star anise pod. Add both the crushed bay and the seeds to your salt. As always, do this with intention, mixing your ingredients in a deosil (clockwise) motion. As you add your thorns, say,

> By the power of three and the blackthorn tree
> I invoke your protective power
> By the power of the Maiden, of the Mother, and Crone
> May all negative forces in my presence cower

Borage (*Borago officinalis*)

Planet: Jupiter

Element: Air

Energy: Masculine

Deities: Mars, Euphrosyne

Also known as starflower or bee bush, borage is a quick-growing annual that easily self-sows. I love it in my own garden but never know where it will be popping up from year to year. It grows up to 2 feet in height with bright blue starlike flowers that are a must for anyone who wants to attract pollinators into the garden. It also is known to repel tomato hornworm and cabbage worms. All but the root of the plant is edible. The large fuzzy, oval leaves are favored for their cucumber-like flavor, and the flowers are lovely as a garnish or in salads. Medicinally, it has been used as a sedative, to aid in depression, and as a fever reducer and cough suppressant.

In ancient Rome, borage was thought to aid in bravery and courage during times of war. Wine was steeped with the herb and weapons were consecrated with it. It was also said that women who wanted to encourage their suitors to ask their hand in marriage would sometimes slip a sprig of borage into their drink. In magick, use borage for courage, happiness, and psychic powers.

Courage Wherever You Go

A simple way to take the magick of borage with you is by placing pressed borage flowers in a simple cabochon pendant.

You will need:

- 32-millimeter glass cabochon pendant from a craft store
- Borage blooms
- Scrapbook paper (your choice of color)
- Spray adhesive
- Paint brush
- Mod Podge

Your pendant will come in two pieces—the clear cabochon and the bezel it is set in. Pick fresh borage flowers and press them in the pages of a heavy book for approximately a week before starting this project. Make sure they are completely dry before use. When you're ready, take your scrapbook paper and trace the shape of the clear cabochon on it. Cut out the shape. This will show slightly from behind your flowers. On the back, draw the planetary symbol for Mars or a sigil of your own choosing.

Mars symbol

Take your spray adhesive and lightly spray the flat side of your cabochon. Carefully lay your borage flower(s) on it face down and smooth it the best you can. When dry, take the paint brush and paint Mod Podge over the back of the cabochon (including the flower). Press your scrapbook paper shape on top and let dry. Finally, use the Mod Podge to paint the setting of the bezel, press the prepared cabochon in the bezel, and let it set. Use a pretty ribbon or chain to hang it from your neck or carry it with you.

Ivy (*Hedera helix*)

Planet: Saturn

Element: Water

Energy: Feminine

Deities: Bacchus, Osiris, Artemis, Ariadne

This voracious evergreen climber, sometimes called bindwood, is native to northern Europe and some areas of southern Asia. It was introduced to both North America and Australia by English colonists. It is beautiful as a ground cover in a woodland garden or when used to climb unsightly walls or fences. But be careful when adding this plant to your garden, as it can be very invasive if not kept trimmed back.

Common ivy was associated with Bacchus, and to wear a wreath of ivy was said to prevent drunkenness. It was believed that if ivy, a common sight in graveyards, refused to grow on a grave, it meant that the deceased was unhappy in the Otherworld. And if ivy grew profusely upon a young girl's grave, it signified that she died of unrequited love. It was also believed that where ivy grows, no negativity may harm those who dwell nearby. Use it in magick for protection, growth, fidelity, love, and healing.

Dreams Becoming Reality

On a piece of paper, write down one dream that you will be focusing on over the coming year. Draw the ogham for *gort* (ivy) onto your paper and fold it three times.

Gort ogham

With a piece of ivy, wrap your folded paper three times. As you do this, envision your dream becoming reality while saying something like:

Knowledge and acceptance
That dreams come true
I attach my power three times to you
By the power of the root
Of the leaf and vine
With the power of (deity of choice)
The reality is mine

Larkspur (*Delphinium* spp.)

Planet: Jupiter

Element: Air

Energy: Masculine

Deities: Mother Mary, Ajax

Beautiful bloom of reclamation, you guide us on our path of self-discovery. Larkspur is in the buttercup family and is just as baneful as its aconite cousin. As a cottage garden favorite, its spire-like stems bear blue, purple, lavender, or white flowers. Larkspur is an annual that may be grown in zones 2 to 11. And though they are drought tolerant and easily reseed, they prefer a cooler climate. Because of their toxic nature, animals such as deer and rabbits stay away from this lovely plant, but their blooms draw pollinators to the garden and are an excellent addition to a butterfly garden.

Medicinally, larkspur seeds were once tinctured and used to treat internal parasites. The plant was also used to treat hemorrhoids, colic, and lice. The flowers were once used to make a blue dye and also ink.

Associated with Ajax and the Trojan War, larkspur can be used in spells for healing or for battle. And as a plant that can thrive in a barren landscape, it can be used in reclaiming spells and rituals. It is also a protective plant that can be planted near your home to keep ghosts or negative spirits at bay.

Natural Flower Ink

Creating ink from dried blooms to use in your spell crafting can add a real punch to your spellwork. And since larkspur is connected to protection against ghosts and evil spirits, you can use the ink to draw protective symbols on paper and tuck them around your home or workspace.

You will need:

- Mortar and pestle
- Dried larkspur petals (or flower petals of your choice)
- Water
- Coffee filter
- Funnel
- Bottle for storing

Use your mortar and pestle to grind dried flower petals until they form a powder. Bring a small amount of water to a boil and add enough water to your powder to cover it. Place your mortar in a sunny window for 24 hours. Using a coffee filter placed in a funnel, strain the powder from the liquid into a bottle. Use a small paint brush or a quill to create powerful symbols.

Lavender (*Lavandula* spp.)

Planet: Mercury

Element: Air

Energy: Masculine

Deities: Aphrodite, Venus, Circe, Brighid, Cernunnos

The scent released as I brush past this plant on drowsy summer afternoons is enough to lull me into a blissful state. Lavender is a must-have in my Witch's garden. A native to the Mediterranean, this shrubby perennial that is a member of the mint family requires good drainage and lots of sun to maintain healthy plants. It's perfect to grow along walkways and near seating areas where its scent can be appreciated most.

Medicinally, lavender has been used to treat skin ailments and for joint and muscle pain. As an aromatherapy agent, it helps ease anxiety and fatigue.

Lavender is one of those herbs that I am never without. The flower has a long history of being used in love spells but can also be used to add peaceful vibes to your spellwork, especially when working spells for self-love or care. It was once thought that carrying a sprig of lavender would help one to see ghosts, and the scent alone could add years to your life.

Add lavender to your dream pillow mixes, add it to purification bundles, or use it in spells to ward against the evil eye. Lavender, for me, is truly an all-purpose Witch's herb. Use it in spells for faery magick, purification, sleep, love, self-care, happiness, peace, and protection.

Lavender Faery Wand

These whimsical wands are perfect for working with the fae or as a craft to share with your Witchlings.

You will need:

- 21 to 25 freshly cut long lavender stems
- Approximately 60 inches of ⅜-inch ribbon in color of your choice

Trim all the leaves and side blooms from the lavender. Tie the end of your ribbon with a knot around the base of the flower heads. Carefully bend the stems up over the top of the flower heads to encase them within the stems. Weave your ribbon under 2 stems and over the next 2, continuing this pattern all the way around and repeating until just past the bottom of the flower heads. Tie off or trim your ribbon in a way you find pleasing.

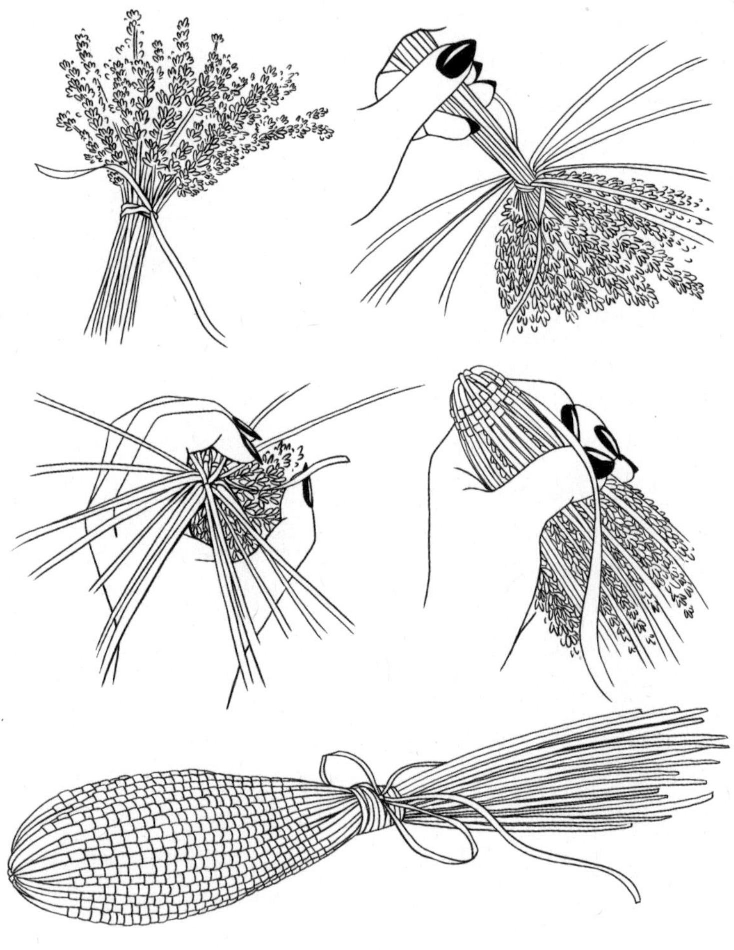

Around the Garden
To-Do List for July

If you plan on planting a fall garden, this is the time to start seeds. Check to see what plants grow best for a fall harvest in your zone. Because July's heat can be hard on your plants, remember to water deeply at the base of the plant during the early morning or at dusk to prevent sun damage to your plants.

Stake tall plants to keep stems from breaking. Fallen plants are also more susceptible to disease. Remove dead or diseased plants, and harvest regularly to ensure your garden stays productive.

Practice succession planting. This is done by continuously sowing herb and vegetable seeds such as spinach, radishes, parsley, and cilantro every two weeks for a constant supply.

Grow Your Magickal Knowledge

Harvest your magickal herbs in the morning just after the dew evaporates or at dusk. Some practitioners use a ritual knife called a boline to gather herbs. A boline (or bolline) is traditionally a white-handled knife with either a straight or crescent-shaped blade used for cutting herbs or inscribing candles. You can designate any blade or shears for the job.

Make gathering herbs a ritual. Harvest your magickal herbs with intention and gratitude. As you gather, you may say something like this:

Flower and root and herb and vine
Much gratitude for your wisdom divine
Vine and herb and root and flower
Much gratitude for your healing power

To avoid clutter and waste, instead of packing your Witch's pantry with dozens of exotic herbs you may or may not use within a year, come up with a short list of herbs you know and trust. Start with herbs that you have foraged or grown yourself or, at the very least, herbs that can be grown in your region.

Here's a Witch's dozen of practical herbs you may want to consider: basil, yarrow, rosemary, lavender, rose petals, garden sage, mugwort, comfrey, lemon balm, sweet woodruff, hyssop, and horehound.

AUGUST

I have seen the signs—old stories rustle in the leaves of the trees and stir my soul.

AUGUST CORRESPONDENCES

Nature Spirits: Phoenix, dryad, dragon

Colors: Dark green, yellow, gold

Herbs and Flowers: Poppy, chamomile, fennel, bay, all grains

Scents: Frankincense, rosemary

Stones: Green sapphire, peridot, onyx

Trees: Hazel, cedar, cypress

Animals: Rooster, calf, stag

Birds: Crane, falcon

Deities: Lugh, Demeter, Hathor, Diana, Thoth

Zodiac: Leo, Virgo

Work spells for harvest, gratitude, vitality, appreciation, clarity, and reemergence.

Chapter 22
What's Your Sign?

As a Witch who weaves her magick in tune with nature, I am acutely aware of my surroundings. I know every point the moon rises month by month as it inches its way along the length of the bluff that guards the river, from December, when it crowns the high rocky peak and spills silver light through my windows, to June, when it presents an ethereal halo in the curve of the hill below the tree line. I delight as the sun rises higher and higher throughout the light half of the year, bathing my garden with golden loveliness. But as August approaches, I must accept the sun's steady decline. Shadows begin to grow noticeably longer, and the dew seems heavier. Birds begin their journey to their winter homes, and the air is tinged with the sweet scent of fruit that hangs from both bramble and bush. This is a busy time in the garden, for everything is ripening all at once and I feel the hard work of preserving the fruits of my labor will never end.

We all see the signs of nature shifting from one season to the next with different eyes. And I encourage anyone to slow down and be mindful of the rhythms of your region. Watch the skyline—where do the sun and moon rise and set throughout the year? If you have a garden, what are you growing? What is your soil type? What are vendors at your local farmer's market offering? Are there festivals happening in your community? Where is the nearest body of water? Is it fresh or salt water? What is the oldest tree in your community? Is it coniferous, deciduous, or evergreen? What native plants are producing fruit, nuts, or flowers around you? Can you name a plant that best represents each of your seasons? Do you see wildlife in your surrounding neighborhood? What do you see? Answering these questions may help you make a better connection to the rhythms of your community and the surrounding landscape. Local festivals and the foods produced near you give an insight to your community's history and folklife. Being familiar with your local flora and fauna and the subtle changes as the Wheel of the Year turns allows you to be sensitive to the spirits of your land. Because every good Witch knows we should not work with energies with which we are not well acquainted.

I find it wondrous that no matter where we are in this world, we all dream under the same moon as it waxes and wanes, marking out the passage of months. And the sun has been a loyal companion to us all, trusted to draw us from sleep to greet the eastern dawn and lull us to rest as it too settles down into the western landscape. Patterns in the sky guided ancient peoples as they tried to predict and measure the movement through the passing seasons. The moon's phases and the movement of the stars as well as the sun's steady seasonal cycle all played a part in planning when to plant, when to forage, when to hunt, and when their animals would give birth. It also indicated times of celebration, to give thanks to their deities or bless their cattle and crops.

To encourage you to become more attuned to the rhythms of your natural surroundings, I would like to challenge you to create a calendar from observations of your region, community, or even backyard. You could create a calendar (or monthly associations) named for the full moons or constellations as you experience them or the flora, fauna, or spirits that occupy your area. Add magickal correspondences, symbols to represent them, and keywords for divination practices. These can be added to your garden BOS, can be used to give your magick a personal touch, and, more importantly, can connect it specifically to the spirits of your land.

I have included thirteen rituals based on the Celtic tree calendar, a modern interpretation of the ogham alphabet. Use them as they are to celebrate the changing seasons, or modify them in a way that suits your own magickal practice. Better yet, use them as a source of inspiration to create your own ritual calendar.

Following the Modern Celtic Lunar Cycle

It should be noted that the Celts did calculate their time based on a lunisolar calendar system. Evidence of this was found near Coligny in France in 1897. Seventy-three bronze plates, dating to around the first century BCE, were discovered that contained both Roman numerals and Gaulish names. This calendar has 12 months based on a 354-day year, with an added extra month every 2.5 years. That being said, the modern thirteen-month Celtic tree calendar has become near and dear to many practitioners, enhancing our magickal practice and nurturing the souls of those who seek a connection to the trees that were undoubtedly sacred to an ancient people.

Birch Moon (Beth): December 24 to January 20

The Birch Full Moon finds us in a time of incubation. We busied ourselves throughout the festivities of the wintertide celebrations, and now we are biding our time until the earth unfurls itself and allows us to grow—a time between time, of sorts. On the night of the Birch Full Moon, let us call upon the Lady of the Woods, the faery being who is connected to the birch, that papery white tree of new beginnings and of clearness of mind, to sweep away those wintery cobwebs and open us up to change.

You will need:

- Birch besom (see page 26), but any besom or broom will do

Stand under the glow of January's full moon with your besom high above your head. Call out,

> Lady, faery queen of the woods
> Lend me your light and guide my way
> Through wintertide's long nights and darkened days
> Clear my path so I may see
> My own light burn bright within me

Now take your broom and ritually sweep deosil (clockwise) in a sweeping circle around you. Focus as you figuratively sweep the cobwebs from your mind, clearing your focus and allowing your own inner fire to kindle. What goals will you set as the light of spring slowly returns?

When you have completed the circle, thank the Lady of the Woods in your own way. Remember to write down ideas, goals, or changes you would like to make in the coming months as the light slowly gains strength.

Rowan Moon (Luis): January 21 to February 17

As the Rowan Moon makes its way above the tree line, take a deep breath and know we have made it through the darkest part of winter, and soon the lemony light of spring will brighten our days. Winter can be a struggle for many of us—financially, physically, and emotionally—leaving us feeling vulnerable. Rowan is a tree of protection and clarity, so we will call upon the Fiery Arrow, Brighid, to rekindle our spirit and surround us with her protective flame by creating a rowan wood solar cross.

Rowan Protection Ritual

- 2 small (4-to-6-inch) rowan wood twigs (either collected ethically or purchased from a trusted supplier)
- 12 to 14 inches red string, twine, or yarn

Under the full moon, call upon Brighid in your own way. Hold the rowan branches crossing one another in the shape of a solar cross and wrap the red string 3 times, saying,

> Rowan, tree of light, tree of protection, tree of power.

Wrap the red string another 3 times while saying,

> Unfurl your magick as the moon rises high above me.

Wrap the red string 3 more times, saying,

> Sparking the green fire within me—my spirit empowered.

Hold the solar cross above your head directly in the moonlight. Close your eyes and imagine the green fire of Brighid growing around you. Feel the power of rowan making you stronger and rejuvenating your spirit.

When you feel ready, thank Brighid in your own way. Hang your rowan solar cross in your home where you can see it as a daily reminder that you are stronger than you know and have the fire of Brighid burning within you.

Ash Moon (Nion): February 18 to March 17

In our productivity-orientated world we tend to think of time as linear, but if we look to nature, we find it is a never-ending cycle—the moon waxes and wanes across the sky in continuous motion month after month; seeds grow, bear fruit, then die, only to be resurrected in the spring. And as we follow the Wheel of the Year, we too feel the exuberance of life as the sun gains his strength, only to settle inward as the moon bears her crown during wintertide.

It is the European ash tree (*Fraxinus excelsior*) who rules this moon. Native to Britain, the ash can grow up to 150 feet tall with an ashen, irregularly ridged trunk. Leaves are compound with between four and eleven leaflets. The ash tree plays heavily in mythology and folklore but most notably in Norse lore. Odin hung from Yggdrasil, an ash tree that stood in the middle of Asgard, for nine days and nights so that he might be granted wisdom.

In northern England, it was believed that if a young lady placed an ash leaf under her pillow, she would dream of her future lover. Magickal staffs made of ash are thought to connect the user to the realms of earth and sky. Cradles carved of ash were thought to protect the child from being taken away as a changeling by mischievous faeries. Other folklore indicated that carrying the leaves of the ash would attract wealth and advised giving the sap of the tree to a child before leaving their mother's bed to prevent disease. It's no wonder the ash is used in magick, not only for protection but also for wisdom, divination, healing, wealth, love, and transitions between the worlds.

March is a transitionary month: the Crone silently gives up her reign, allowing the sleeping Maiden to rise from the earth. Let's take this time, under the Full Ash Moon, to meditate on our interconnectedness with the earth and the spirits of the land. Gather a blanket, notebook, candles, and a favorite incense, and brew yourself a cup of magickal awakening tea (recipe follows). Go outside or near an open window, sit under her reflective light, and contemplate the lessons the Crone has left with you as winter exits. What does the light half of the year hold for you? How will your garden play a role in your spirituality? Listen past the sounds of the mundane world and take in the messages being whispered by the spirits of your land. Take time to write down whatever wisdom comes to you to reflect upon later.

Magickal Awakening Tea Blend

- 4 parts ginger (power)
- 2 parts calendula (prophetic dreams)
- 2 parts yarrow (courage)
- 1 part thyme (healing, health)

This is the perfect combination of herbs to take us from a place of healing and dreams into the light with a magickal punch.

Alder Moon (Fearn): March 18 to April 14

The ghostly appearance of the alder tree (*Alnus* spp.), whose leaves shiver under nature's breath, can make the forested areas they prefer feel haunted. Because they can be found growing along streams, rivers, and swamps, alder has always been a tree of mystery and secrets.

The wood of alder is quite light, but it turns a deep reddish orange color when it is cut. This gives the impression of bleeding and has linked it with war and the supernatural. Because alder thrives in primarily swampy areas or by riversides, the alder's wood does not rot in wet conditions and becomes as hard as stone when left immersed in water. Out of water and out of doors, however, the timber rots easily. Alder is very well known by fiber artists, as the leaves, bark, cones, and twigs can be used to make dyes.

Setting Boundaries with Alder

Alder magick eases doubt, gives courage, provides protection from negative vibes, encourages balance, and guides us in communication with the Otherworld.

Under alder's full moon, we will focus on balance and setting boundaries as we burn alder wood in a fireproof container.

You will need:

- Alder wood chunks (can be purchased in the grilling or barbecue section of any grocery store) or dry alder that has been ethically gathered and cut into kindling
- Clean, firesafe container (large cauldron, grill, firepit, etc.)
- Sea salt

On this full moon, we will light a fire using only alder. As the fire burns, slowly add more alder. With every piece added, focus on setting healthy boundaries—with work, family, friends, and so on—and envision how those boundaries will allow you to become the well-balanced person you know you can be. When you are finished, you will be left with alder ash. Let the ash cool for 24 hours, and then mix the ash with an equal amount of sea salt. Use the mix in spells for setting boundaries, spells of protection, or banishing.

Willow Moon (Saille): April 15 to May 12

There is a rhythm to spring. I hear it in the drum of a hummingbird's wing, the buzz of bees that dart eagerly between blooms, and the frogs whose mating calls serenade me well past dark. I sense it in the musky scent of earth that rises from my garden beds and the riotous shock of green that draws me to the forest—down a path that winds among the deciduous trees to the river's edge. This is my liminal space where the willow dips her branches gently in the water. Twilight is when I can be found there sitting beneath that graceful tree, who is associated with female rites, drinking in the moonlight, and communing with the spirits of nature. When I feel it is time, I stand and cry out as loud as I can. I dance, I chant, and I celebrate the wild woman that I am.

One with Nature Ritual

For this full moon ritual, we will give in to that rhythm that draws us into the wild. For it is in May that we are reminded to be passionate, to sing, to chant, to dance, to drum.

Go to that place where you feel most alive on the night of the full moon, either alone or with a group. Bring along a drum or your favorite drum track that you can play. Start out slow, build a fire, meditate in a favorite spot—make that connection with the spirits of nature. When you feel ready, jump up and cry out. Bang your drum (or turn on your drum track), sing or chant, dance—do whatever makes you feel alive.

Here is one of my favorite chants:

I am one with water
Water is my blood
I am one with air
Air is my breath
I am one with earth
Earth is my body
I am one with fire
Fire burns in my soul
I am one with the Goddess
Magick dwells in me

Hawthorn Moon (Huath): May 13 to June 9

In the Pacific Northwest, if our spring temperatures are cooler than normal, it's not unusual to find hawthorn blooming in June rather than the end of April or early May. It brightens the hedges that line some of our country roads, releasing a scent reminiscent of how rain smells on a spring day. It's a scent that eases the heart and quiets a restless spirit. Maybe it's because it is intrinsically connected to the spirit world that I find myself drawn to it. I have been known to tuck myself near its thorny branches just to take in the energy that radiates from its blossoms. And for this full moon, it is this tree of the fae we will go to for healing of the heart.

Releasing Burdens with Hawthorn

- White candle
- 3 hawthorn thorns
- Dried hawthorn blossoms (optional)

If you have hawthorn growing on or near your property, prepare a comfortable place near the tree facing the moon. If not, a pretty bowl of dried hawthorn blooms will do perfectly well to symbolize this tree. Ground and center. Call your quarters or prepare yourself in any way that feels appropriate for this ritual. Light your candle to symbolize the spirit of the tree. Pick your thorns up one at a time. Whisper to each thorn something that lies heavy on your heart, then set them around the lighted candle. When you are done, say aloud,

> Spirit of the hawthorn, I ask of thee
> To take my burdens one, two, three
> And as I release them to your hallowed ground
> May my heart open and peace be found

If you are sitting beneath a hawthorn, bury the thorns in the soil beneath it. If not, bury the thorns in the dish of dried hawthorn blooms, which can be buried in your compost pile or be disposed of as you feel appropriate.

Oak Moon (Duir): June 10 to July 7

As one who grew up in a region suited for dark fairy tales, with jagged peaks and trees so tall they seem to scratch at the clouds that hang for months on end, the trees have become a security blanket of sorts for me. They obscure the sky, which can feel far too big at times. You see, when presented with a wide-open landscape with an endless sky, I have literally had panic attacks and rushed for cover under the nearest tree to press my anxious body against its trunk. I know it seems strange, as there are so many who say they feel claustrophobic in my landscape. But it is my truth; I cannot be without the sentinel giants who protect me.

As the largest plants, trees offer protection and strength to those who seek their comfort. For modern Witches, the oak may be the most synonymous with strength, and as one of the tallest and strongest trees of Europe, it was venerated and worshipped by ancient peoples for thousands of years.

Finding Strength with Oak

For this full moon ritual, if you are privileged enough to have an oak tree in your yard, in a nearby park, or even at a friend or family member's property, plant yourself underneath its canopy as the moon rises. If there are no oaks in your area, any tree is strong enough to take you on. With the moon high above you, feel free to lean into the tree's trunk. As you do this, release your anxiety into it. Feel its comforting energy. Feel free to cry or scream. The tree can handle it. Just like the tree takes in carbon dioxide and turns it into oxygen, it can also absorb our negative energy and turn it into positive energy. When you have given the tree all you can, take a deep, cleansing breath and rise slowly, as you may feel a bit weak. Remember to thank the tree in your own way.

Holly Moon (Tinne): July 8 to August 4

The Oak King reigns over the light half of the year, relinquishing his crown at the summer solstice to the Holly King, who reminds us of the darker days ahead. The days leading up to August are some of our warmest, but there are subtle signs that the Holly King has been at work. We see it as the sun inches its way lower and lower across the horizon. Shadows reach longer across the garden and the plants grow weary in their beds. Holly (*Ilex* spp.) is a protective Mars plant that is hardy in zones 5 to 9. It reaches a height of approximately 30 feet with spiny green leaves and red berries that appear on successfully pollinated female flowers in the autumn months. This plant, which most of us associate with Yule, can be used for protection anytime we feel the need to use its masculine energy.

House Cleansing with Holly

On the night of the Holly Moon, have with you a bowl of fresh, clean water (or moon water) and a sprig of holly. Start at the main entry of your home (this can be done inside or outside of your home). Work your way deosil as you dip the holly into the water and use it as an aspergillum to sprinkle the water around your home. As you do this, say,

> Summer wanes and darkness creeps into the corners and the cobwebs
> I invoke the moon and the tree of holly as the protective thread
> Negative vibes and energies that have made themselves at home
> I demand your exit as summer descends—go, leave me/us alone

Hazel Moon (Coll): August 5 to September 1

Late summer offers a soft light that gently sparks our creativity. There is something about the sun's slanted gaze through the trees that takes on an Otherworldly glow and allows us to dream of the possibilities that await us in the spring. Its wisdom is softly spoken and may come to you when you least expect it. For illumination finds us in the most unlikely places—the gentle falling of the first leaves or the chill of autumn's first breath.

Finding Inspiration with Hazel

Under hazel's full moon, we will peek into the cauldron of inspiration reflected by moonlight to discover what illuminates our soul.

You will need:

- Hazel stick
- Cauldron or dark bowl filled with water

Hazel is a tree of wisdom and inspiration and is a wonderful ally to work with to heighten our senses as we begin our journey into the dark half of the year. On your hazel branch, draw or carve the runic symbol for Kenaz, the rune of inner knowledge, guidance, and light.

Kenaz rune

Under the moon's golden light, sit with your cauldron in way that the moon reflects off the water. Take a few cleansing breaths, then use the hazel branch to stir the water in your cauldron in a deosil (clockwise) pattern. Stir the magick well, dear Witch. Open your third eye and divine what your soul seeks. Use your journal to write down patterns or images you see. When you are finished, close your eyes, and take in the moon's gentle energy.

Vine Moon (Muin): September 2 to September 29

September marks a time of equal darkness and light. It is a time of bounty and celebration for a harvest well done. Grapevines are heavy with fruit under the glow of September's mellow sun. Their offerings provide us with the fruit whose juice, when fermented, gives us wine.

The vine was sacred to the lusty Greek god Dionysus (called Bacchus by the Romans) and may have been one of the earliest cultivated fruits. Associated with fertility, merriment, money, and abundance, a full moon ritual under the Vine Moon can be one of pure joy. Let it be a celebration of abundance and of wild elation.

Celebrate Joy

On the night of the Vine Moon, light a bonfire outdoors somewhere where you have plenty of room to dance and be as raucous as you like. Invite like-minded friends and make sure to have plenty of wine. Eat luscious foods, dance to the beat of drums (provided by a drum track if no one plays), and make merry by keeping the wine flowing.

When ready, raise your glasses to the moon and say something like this:

Hail to thee, Vine Moon!
Harbinger of joy and prosperity
May our days be filled with abundance
And our nights filled with wild abandon under your merry glow

Have everyone pour a few drops of wine onto the ground, then say together:

Blessed be!

Ivy Moon (Gort): September 30 to October 27

The season of the Ivy Moon reflects both endings and new beginnings. For as the darkness and cold begin to set in, marking the end of the growing season, it becomes a time of dreaming and planning for what lies ahead. So on this full moon of both shadow and light, we look to ivy as our ally. Ivy is a potent symbol whose protective powers remind us that even as darkness approaches, life persists. An evergreen that thrives in shady spaces where little else can survive, it clings to walls and winds its way up trees to find the light. Even when cut back, it finds a way to continue to grow.

Ivy Cord-Cutting Ritual

Let us use the golden light of October's full moon to reflect on those things that have served us well and to sever those connections or experiences that we know are unhealthy for our well-being.

You will need:

- 4 feet of ivy vine
- 2 candle tapers (1 white, 1 black) and holders
- Natural twine
- Scissors

Form a circle with your length of ivy and place your 2 candles within it. Loosely tie your twine around the candles, connecting them. This represents your tie to the unhealthy person or experience you need to sever. As you light the candles, focus on your intent. Imagine your life without the person or experience in it. Imagine cutting away that part of your life that is stunting your growth. And like the ivy, imagine yourself growing back stronger.

As you cut the twine, say something like this:

I release the ties that bind
(Name or emotion) no longer holds power over me
By the power of root, leaf, and vine, so mote it be

Snuff out the black candle as a symbol of your release. Allow the white candle to burn as a symbol of your freedom and growth. Dispose of the black candle and twine in a way that feels appropriate to you.

Reed Moon (Ngetal): October 28 to November 23

November takes us to the threshold. Death and renewal are on full display in the garden, and we have watched it play out since spring when we planted those first seeds. We nurtured and observed in awe as our gardens matured and bore fruit. We danced circles in the rain and praised the Earth Mother for her bounty. We harvested and celebrated our yield even as we bid the God farewell. Now it is November, and in many regions the dark days of winter have already begun, but just under the soil new seeds lie waiting for spring's return.

Reed is a common name for several varieties of grasses with hollow stems and broad leaves that grow in wetlands. They have been used to create roofing, arrow shafts, and flutes; weaved into baskets; and utilized for both food and medicine. A plant of gateways, it settles between the elements of earth and water. Magick in liminal spaces takes on a deeper connotation. It is there we touch the hand of spirit.

Honoring Gateways

On the night of November's full moon, we will settle into a space that is betwixt and between—just as the clock strikes 12 a.m., the time between "what was" and "what has yet to be." In this liminal space, we will honor each of the different aspects of ourselves: The self we are. The self we strive to be. The self we want to change.

You will need three candles in your choice of colors that best represent the three aspects of you. As you light the first candle, say,

> I honor the journey that has brought me to this place in my life. I am (fill in the blank).

Light the second candle and say,

> I honor the light that leads me through the darkness. With courage, strength, and power, I will (fill in the blank).

Light the third candle and say,

> I honor the threshold of new possibilities and release those things that no longer serve me. As I continue my journey, (fill in the blank) will no longer burden me.

Allow the candles to burn out on their own.

Elder Moon (Ruis): November 24 to December 23

The elder grows in those forgotten places that border the liminal—the edge of a forest or near streams and along riverbanks. Neither grand as the oak nor stately as the cedar, the elder embodies the energy of the diminishing light of December. And though the elder may not catch your eye right away, you will definitely feel the presence of the Elder Mother, whose spirit occupies the tree.

Release with the Elder Mother

For December's full moon ritual, we will call upon the Elder Mother for resolution to matters that might restrict future growth. For December is a time of renewal, a time to heal and release the wasted energy that may restrict future growth.

You will need:

- Candle
- Elderberry tea
- Incense of your choice
- Piece of paper
- Pen
- Cauldron or firesafe container
- Elderberry twigs gathered from underneath the tree (optional)

Light a candle and sip your tea. Burn some incense that resonates with you. Light a charcoal tab and place it in a cauldron or other firesafe container. On this night, you will take out the paper and pen and write down every failure or bad memory you can recall from the past year. As you do this, remember it's okay to express strong emotions. Be sad, mad, or disappointed. Let it out. When you're done, take a deep, cleansing breath. If you have some elder twigs, add them to your fire. Fold the paper in half, hold it over your cauldron, and begin to rip it into strips. As you drop each strip of paper into the fire, say,

Pain into healing
Smoke on the rise
Spirit of the elder
Spirit who is wise
Healing into renewal
Smoke on the rise
Spirit of the elder
Spirit who is wise

With the last strip, say,

Into the flames I release the past
As I journey into the light, may I never look back
Blessed be

Chapter 23
Signs of Summer's End

Cascadian Farm was established in 1972, not too far from where I lived, by a young grad student who had a desire to farm in a manner that would not only produce healthful fruits and vegetables but also make a positive impact on the earth. The farm was quickly a success, and for many of us in eastern Skagit Valley, their story became part of our own families' stories. Three generations of my family have worked for Cascadian Farm in some capacity. My parents were field bosses, supervising field workers and enforcing quality control. I, my sisters, and many of our friends spent the summers harvesting fruit and vegetables for the company alongside the founders. Years later, the company outgrew the small farm site and was eventually sold to General Mills. The corporation continued to use the land tucked in the Skagit Valley, and two of my three children have been employed there.

As a teen, berry season at Cascadian Farm marked out the passage of summer. June, with an energy that was as bright and raucous as the surrounding landscape, was strawberry season. Still bleary-eyed, we'd begin picking just as the sun reached its shining fingers above the mountain. My sister, goal-oriented and hard-working, would have a flat almost filled before the sun had fully risen. I, on the other hand, needed time to test the sweetness of the plump, dew-kissed berries. I had to interpret the messages found in the flight patterns of birds. And take a moment to talk of faeries to the girl who, during the school year, was too cool to give me the time of day. But at the farm she wasn't a cheerleader or homecoming queen. She was just another field worker who thought I was funny and liked my crazy hair.

July was always sun drenched and dreamy, the time when raspberries reigned. I worked alongside the girl from my high school in raspberry rows that seemed to go on forever, where we wasted most of our time throwing the sweet-tart berries over the raspberry hedges at my sister, who always threatened to turn us in to the field boss (a.k.a. Mom). Sometimes a breeze would pick up the scent of earth and sweetness, and I would shake my head and tell the girl we'd been faery blasted just to watch her nervous expression…which always turned to fits of laughter.

August brought sunflowers and fields of tall grass that rustled and waved near the blueberry bushes that hung heavy with fruit in late summer. Blueberries were by far the easiest to harvest, and I could fill my flats without having to take my eyes off the family of deer who nibbled around the periphery. The girl, who I knew would only be my friend for a few more short weeks, talked of the school year ahead—games and dances and parties that she thought I should attend. I nodded my head in agreement, knowing I would never go. For I had too many books to read and forests to explore, too many stories to write about the faeries who dwelled around me.

By the time the blackberries that grew along the country roads were ripe, school had started again. My sister had made quadruple the amount of money I had, and the girl who picked alongside me all summer long walked past me in the hall, decked out in her cheerleading uniform and giggling with friends, as if I were a ghost.

I remember one day I walked quietly after school down a lonely road in the mellow light of a dying sun and snacked on the blackberries that to me tasted best of all. The girl pulled up alongside me in her mother's car. She rolled down her window and smiled.

I politely said hello, and she responded with, "I hope you're not mad about me not hanging out with you at school. I try to only hang with the athletes there." She nervously smiled, then added, "You know how it is."

I just smiled back and said, "I guess it's your loss." I popped a blackberry in my mouth and walked away from her and toward the forest, free of any silly human need to fit in. I understood, even then, that it was the kids like her who were still finding where they fit into this world. You see, the ones like me—the dreamers, artists, gamers, nerds—we were content with who we were and didn't give a damn about what anyone thought about us. It was that transitional moment in my life that cemented the importance of self-worth into my psyche. And being among the blackberries made it even more powerful.

Blackberry and Transition

For me, blackberry (or bramble) will always be a plant of transition. For it is a plant that is connected to the fae and the transition from one season to the next. In many regions, blackberries are the last of the summer fruits. In the Pacific Northwest, we typically begin picking in late August and our harvest continues well into the autumn months.

Some superstition dictates that the first berries to ripen should be left for the fae. If one does not heed this warning, continuing harvest will be full of nasty grubs and rot. And, depending on the folklore, it is thought that harvesting must end by either Michaelmas (September 29), after which the devil will have stomped or spit upon them, or Samhain (October 31), when they may be befouled by the fae.

Arched bramble canes were crossed through to cure all manner of illnesses, including boils, hernias, whooping cough, and blackheads. This too is a form of transition, as you are crossing through a portal (of sorts) from sickness into wellness.

A wonderfully cooling herb, blackberry leaves have been used to ease burns and conditions such as eczema and hemorrhoids. Rinses made from the leaves are excellent for relieving a sore throat. An incredibly nutritious fruit, the blackberry is high in fiber and contains many vitamins and minerals, including vitamin C and manganese, so it makes an excellent berry syrup to help relieve the effects of winter colds.

Magickally, blackberries are considered a protective plant. Connected to Venus and the element of water, their canes can be made into wreaths and hung over the entrance of a house to keep out negative spirits. Their leaves can be used in charm bags or spells for wealth, regeneration, protection, or fertility. And the fruit can be used to whip up magick for abundance. Blackberry pie is a wonderful addition to a harvest festival feast.

Blackberries grow wild in many parts of growing zones 5 to 8, and with their distinctive oval compound leaves (grouped in three), thorny bramble, and classic black aggregate fruit, they are very easy to identify. Growing blackberries in your home garden is super easy and provides convenient harvesting for those too busy to drive into the country to find them. And best of all, you can find cultivars that are suited for zones 3 to 9. Blackberries like loamy soil and six to eight hours of sunlight per day. Give these blackberry varieties a try:

Lawton Blackberry (*Rubus ursinus*): This cold-hardy variety boasts large black aggregate fruit and few thorns. Zones 3 to 8.

'Apache' Thornless Blackberry (*Rubus fruticosus* 'Apache'): This popular thornless variety can be ready for harvest as early as late June. Zones 5 to 9.

'Kiowa' Blackberry (*Rubus fruticosus* 'Kiowa'): A thorny variety that produces fruit up to 3 inches long. An early producer, it is great for baking and winemaking. Zones 5 to 8.

'Triple Crown' Blackberry (*Rubus fruticosus* 'Triple Crown'): A fast-growing, thornless cultivar with semi-erect canes that bear sweet-tart fruit perfect for baking. Zones 5 to 9.

Consider these other berries for your late summer garden:

Blueberry (*Vaccinium spp.*)

The blueberry is a member of the rhododendron family that offers tasty berries in the summer and bright red foliage in the fall. It's known for its protective powers against psychic attack, and eating blueberry-infused foods or sipping blueberry tea is a good way to protect yourself from intense energy. Dot dried blueberries around your protective circle during ritual. Ruled by the moon and the element of water, blueberry is also connected to peace, rebirth, and motherhood.

Try these cultivars:

'Bluecrop' (*Vaccinium corymbosum* 'Bluecrop'): There's a reason this is the most popular variety to grow. It's cold hardy and produces clusters of beautiful berries perfect for baking. Zones 4 to 7.

'Northsky' (*Vaccinium corymbosum* × *Vaccinium angustifolium* 'Northsky'): This cultivar is cold hardy and perfect for container gardening. It provides small, sweet berries reminiscent of wild blueberries. Zones 3 to 7.

'Biloxi' (*Vaccinium corymbosum* 'Biloxi'): For those of you who live in zones 8 to 10, this blueberry bush provides excellent yields and will remain evergreen in a warmer climate.

Gooseberry (Ribes *spp.)*

Gooseberry is a plant of empathy and nurturing that is connected to Venus and the element of earth. Use gooseberry in spells and rituals for assurance, healing, and loving protection.

Try these cultivars:

'Poorman' (*Ribes hirtellum* 'Poorman'): A highly flavored, sweet table variety that can be eaten fresh or used in recipes. Zones 3 to 8.

'Hinnonmaki Yellow' (*Ribes uva-crispa* 'Hinnonmaki Yellow'): With yellow gooseberries with a flavor reminiscent of apricots, this variety offers tasty fruit and lovely fall foliage. Zones 3 to 8.

'Orus 8' (*Ribes ×nidigrolaria* 'Orus 8'): A cross between a currant and a gooseberry (known as a jostaberry), this cultivar has shiny black flesh and can be eaten fresh or used in recipes or in winemaking. Zones 3 to 8.

Huckleberry (Vaccinium *spp.)*

A lovely Venus plant that is connected to the element of water, huckleberries can be used in spells for luck and protection and in dream magick. Add huckleberry leaves to your favorite dream pillow mix to make your dreams come true. Huckleberries are related to blueberries, and both deciduous and evergreen varieties are available.

Try these cultivars:

Evergreen Huckleberry (*Vaccinium ovatum*): Shade-loving, this variety makes an excellent hedge plant and provides tart, flavorful fruit in mid to late summer. Zones 7 to 9.

Red Huckleberry (*Vaccinium parvifolium*): A deciduous variety with small, tart berries that are wonderful mixed with sweeter berries in pies or in savory dishes. This plant refers partial shade and is a great addition to your woodland garden. Zones 5 to 8.

Celebrating the First Fruits

The signs of harvest are all around us. In my garden, the summer heat has taken its toll, and for many of my perennials, it's time to be cut back. The early summer fare is gone, and I focus on the preservation of the late summer harvest. In the farming communities to the east of my mountainous region, wheat and other grains undulate in golden waves across the fields. The scent of ripened fruit rises with the afternoon heat, and sunflowers follow a noticeably declining sun. These are the days that mark our descent into autumn, when communities would gather to harvest and to celebrate the fruits of their labor.

The importance of the corn (grain) is seen in the many folk customs and ballads that are connected to the harvest season. The first sheafs were typically made into bread or brewed into beer. The last of the harvested sheafs were made into a grain idol, sometimes called a "corn dolly," that represented the spirit of the vegetation. Corn dollies would be ritually placed above an entrance or the hearth as a symbol of abundance and protection, then plowed back into the earth with the first harrowing of spring.

Lughnasadh is a Celtic cross-quarter festival in celebration of the first fruits. It is typically celebrated on or around August 1 and marks the beginning of the harvest season. During this time, the God departs from the Earth Mother's side, and his power is present in the fields. We reap from him the nurturing spirit that is present in the grain. And we thank the Earth Mother, from whom all life springs, for the continuous cycle of life, death, and rebirth.

This time of celebration as harvest is in full swing is a great time to take part in community events such as county fairs or festivals that celebrate the predominant produce of your local region. Visit local breweries or plan a trip to a U-pick farm. If you haven't made bread, this is the time give it a try, be it a simple quick bread such as zucchini or banana bread or complicated braided yeast breads flavored with the herbs of the season.

As a Witch who spends so much of her time in the garden, this is an important sabbat for me, as it is a time to celebrate the gifts of the soil and the hard work that is put into creating a garden. It is also a time to acknowledge our symbiotic relationship with the earth and a time to validate our connection to the spirits of our region.

Triple Wild Berry Pie

I have always served (almost exclusively) food that I have grown, foraged, or purchased from local growers for the meals of the three harvest festivals that make up the Witch's Wheel of the Year. I even stumbled upon a local flour mill for bread and pie crusts a few years back. The recipe for triple wild berry pie below is a wonderful addition to your Lughnasadh celebration. You can replace the berries in my recipe for berries that are in season in your region. For ease, I did not add a pie crust recipe but offered the option of buying a pie crust.

- 2 cups blackberries (for seasonal transition)
- 2 cups blueberries (for protection during the dark days to come)
- 2 cups red huckleberries (for the dream of spring's return)
- 1 cup sugar, plus 1 tablespoon for sprinkling
- 6 tablespoons cornstarch
- 1 teaspoon lemon juice

- 2 premade pie crusts for a 9-inch pie pan (or use your favorite pie crust recipe)
- 1 beaten egg white

Preheat your oven to 400 degrees Fahrenheit. Mix together the berries, 1 cup sugar, cornstarch, and lemon juice. Line the pie pan with a crust and place the mixture inside. Place the second crust over the berries with holes for ventilation. Crimp the edges. Brush a thin layer of beaten egg white on the crust and sprinkle lightly with sugar. Bake for 40 to 45 minutes. Check after 25 minutes; if it's browning too quickly, cover with aluminum foil. Cool for several hours before serving.

Chapter 24
Herbs of August

Success, revelations, and wisdom are some of the attributes of our herbs for August. The signs of transition are at hand as we pay homage to the Earth Mother—the harvest season has begun.

Bee Balm (*Monarda* spp.)

Planet: Mercury

Element: Air

Energy: Masculine

Deities: Osiris, Sobek, Nephthys

There is something absolutely enchanting about the scent of this perennial that keeps me under its spell every gardening season. Native to North America, it is a favorite to pollinators such as butterflies, bees, and hummingbirds. It prefers full sun but will grow in partial shade and loves rich, well-draining soil. It grows well in zones 3 to 9, and because it is a member of the mint family, it may spread rapidly.

Medicinally, bee balm can be used in teas to aid in digestion and applied topically as a natural antiseptic for minor abrasions. Use leaves to flavor cooking or to add a slight citrus flavor to drinks or salads.

With its bright scent and connection to the element of air, use bee balm when seeking clarity in your life. It is wonderful added to ritual baths and used in spells for success, prosperity, contentment, and peace.

Spell for Clarity

Create an incense blend with 2 parts dried bee balm leaves and 1 part dried garden sage.

Position yourself comfortably outside and sprinkle your incense over a lit charcoal tab in a small cauldron or firesafe dish.

Invoke the element of air by saying something like this:

I call upon the power of air
To ease away clutter and chaos from my mind
And allow the flow of wisdom and clarity divine
May contentment soothe me
May wisdom move me
May clarity fill me
Blessed be

Beech (*Fagus* spp.)

Planet: Saturn

Element: Air

Energy: Feminine

Deity: Cerridwen

A popular shade tree that can live up to 300 years old, the beech thrives in zones 3 to 9 and grows to an average of 60 feet in height. Of the thirteen species of beech, *Fagus grandifolia* (American beech) is the only one native to North America. Before the last ice age, it flourished throughout the continent, but it is now confined to the eastern region of North America. Other popular cultivars for the garden include European beech (*Fagus sylvatica*) and Japanese beech (*Fagus crenata*).

Beechnuts are distinguished by their triangular shape and spikey husks and are edible, as are the inner bark and young leaves. High in tannins, beech has been used medicinally for external wounds and internally to ease sore throats and inflamed tonsils.

Beech is a tree of wisdom, knowledge, and revelation. Some of this may have come from the thought that early Germanic peoples used strips of beechwood to write on. Carrying a piece of beechwood is said to bring you luck and increase your creative power. Burying a piece of beech with your wishes written on it will help manifest your desire. Use beech in spells for communication, wisdom, revelation, wishes, luck, and creative power.

Manifest Your Power Through Writing

Writing allows you to tap into your inner self and manifest a power you may not be aware you had in you. Handwritten spells, words of power, sigils, symbols, and magickal observations are important aspects of your spell crafting, as they allow you to physically clarify your goals. That's why I suggest you fill your BOS with as many handwritten entries as you can. Use your pen as your wand and manifest your desires.

To remind yourself of the power of the pen, use a gold pen to write on a beech tree leaf "My words hold power." To preserve your leaf, generously coat one side of the beech leaf with Mod Podge and allow it to dry. Repeat on the opposite side. When completely dry, tack your leaf up in your home office or wherever you do your writing.

Poppies (*Papaver* spp.)

Planet: Moon

Element: Water

Energy: Feminine

Deities: Demeter, Kore, Hypnos, Ceres, Aphrodite, Hecate

There's a reason this flower has been an inspiration for so many artists, for it is a bewitching sight indeed when planted in masses or allowed to spread in a field, and there are varieties that grow in zones 2 to 10. With both perennial and annual varieties and colors ranging from the classic red, yellow, and white to soft pink and plum, it's a perfect fuss-free flower for any gardener.

Medicinally, poppies have a history of use as a painkiller and a mild sedative. Their seeds are popularly used in baked foods such as bagels, muffins, and cakes.

Since Greek and Roman times, poppies have been connected to remembrance and the dead, and their images have been used on gravestones to represent eternal sleep. After World War I, poppies spread in Europe due to large amounts of lime left from the rubble, and now paper poppies can be seen worn on Remembrance Day, or Memorial Day in the US, as a symbol of remembrance of fallen soldiers.

In magick, poppies have been used in love spells—try an almond poppyseed cake to evoke loving vibes. Seeds may be carried on you to draw wealth or used in dream magick. Use poppy in spells or rituals for remembrance, release, death, luck, wealth, love, dream magick, sleep, or invisibility.

Dream Magick with Poppies

Fill a drawstring bag with one part each mugwort, poppyseed, and lavender. On a piece of paper, write a question you would like the answer to and add it to the mix. Place the bag under your pillow before bedtime. Keep a journal with you and write down any symbols from your dreams that may help you answer your question.

Sunflower (*Helianthus annuus*)

Planet: Sun

Element: Fire

Energy: Masculine

Deities: Baba Yaga, Ra, Apollo, Helios

Is there anything more delightful than sunflowers in full bloom? A true joy of late summer, these heliotropic plants turn their flowers to follow the sun as it makes its way across the sky. The largest varieties can grow over 16 feet tall and are an impressive addition to your garden. The smallest varieties reach around 24 inches and can add a touch of enchantment to borders and containers.

Native to North and South America, the over seventy varieties of the annual sunflower range from the classic bright yellow to deep maroon and chocolate hues. They are a wonderful plant for beginning gardeners or for children, as they are easy to sow in zones 4 to 9 and fast growing. Their seed heads can be dried and the seeds enjoyed all winter long (try *Helianthus annuus* 'Mammoth Grey Stripe' or *H. giganteus*), or they can be left on the stalk for local wildlife to enjoy in the autumn. Sunflowers contain high levels of vitamins and minerals that promote healthy bones and joints. The leaves of the plant have been used as fodder for livestock, and the petals yield a yellow dye.

The plant is connected with fertility, and it was thought if a woman consumed sunflower seeds, it would help her conceive. Other folklore dictates placing the petals of the flowers under your pillow at night for truth (revealing dreams) and adding a few drops of sunflower oil to a person's food to gain their loyalty. Use sunflowers in magick for joy, fertility, loyalty, wishes, wisdom, and health.

Joyful Salutations with Sunflower

Greet the sun as it rises with a woven crown of sunflowers (smaller varieties such as 'Junior' or 'Firecracker' work best). Raise your arms and say something like this:

> May the joy I feel this moment continue with me throughout the day, the week, the month, the year. Joy fills me up. May the joy I feel at this moment spread to everyone I meet throughout this day, this week this month, this year. Let joy be my gift to all I encounter. Blessed be.

Wood Betony (*Stachys officinalis*)

Planet: Jupiter

Element: Fire

Energy: Masculine

Deity: Juno

With its unusual flowering pattern, betony makes an eye-catching addition to your woodland or shade garden in zones 4 to 8. A hardy perennial of the mint family, it is native to Europe and Asia and prefers a damp, acidic soil that easily drains. It grows to about 12 inches in height with light purple blooms.

"He has as many virtues as betony" is an old saying that relays the reverence once held by this simple plant, as it was well esteemed for its mild bitter and astringent qualities. Today it is primarily used in calming herbal tea mixes.

Wood betony has always been a plant of protection and purification since ancient times and was once worn as a protective amulet to ward off evil spirits. Grow it near the borders of your property or sprinkle the herb around the corners of your home or threshold to protect all who dwell within. Use it in incense blends for purification. Use it in spells for protection, purification, and passion.

Purification Smoke-Cleansing Bundle

- 4 to 10 fresh sprigs of herbs, 6 to 8 inches long (use a combination of wood betony, rosemary, and lavender)
- Natural twine (such as hemp or cotton)

Lay out your sprigs in a uniform manner with stems together. Wrap twine several times around the stems and tie off. Working at an angle, wind the twine upward around your bundle. Wrap around the top of the bundle and continue wrapping back down the stem. Wrap around twice and tie off. Dry it in a dark place or in a paper bag for at least 2 weeks before use.

Around the Garden
To-Do List for August

In many regions, there is still time to sow another round of quick-growing vegetables for an autumn harvest. Try 'French Breakfast' or 'Pink Beauty' radishes; loose leaf lettuce varieties such as 'Black-Seeded Simpson' and 'Mascara'; 'Verdil' or 'Butterflay' spinach; and Asian mustard green varieties such as 'Garnet Giant' or 'Mizuna'. Don't forget other greens, such as 'Astro' arugula, frisée endive, and 'Red Russian' kale. All of these are ready for harvest in just around thirty days.

As vegetables stop producing and begin to die, pull them up and add them to the compost heap. Berry canes that have stopped producing fruit need to be clipped back. Direct sow flower seeds such as poppies, calendula, and cornflowers for beautiful blooms next season. Continue to deadhead flowering plants to prolong their lifespan. And add mulch or plant cover crops in vegetable beds that are done for the season to protect the soil and add nutrients.

What Are Cover Crops?

Cover crops, which include clover, rye, alfalfa, vetch, winter peas, and more, are planted to protect and nurture the soil rather than to be harvested at the end of the growing season. They are an easy way to return much-needed nutrients back to the soil, suppress weeds, and control disease. They can be dug or tilled back into the soil in the spring.

Grow Your Magickal Knowledge

We stand at the edge of summer with autumn firmly in our sight. What have you learned so far from working so closely with the earth? You may have discovered new energies that you were never familiar with before. As you become more attuned to nature, you will learn the language in which the spirits of your land speak with you, be it through animals that cross your path, the way the wind brushes your face, or that whisper woven into the movement of trees. Pay close attention to the signs.

Don't forget to involve yourself or your family in community harvest celebrations as another way to get to know what makes your region unique. Host a Lughnasadh (or Lammas) celebration for your circle or coven or just a close group of like-minded friends and family. Share homemade dishes made from homegrown or local produce.

SEPTEMBER

The shadows of autumn stretch darkening fingers over the land … Change is coming.

SEPTEMBER CORRESPONDENCES

Nature Spirits: Cwn Annwn, trooping faeries

Colors: Golden yellow, brown, yellow green

Herbs and Flowers: Goldenrod, thyme, rye, skullcap, wheat, valerian

Scents: Bergamot, apple, myrrh

Stones: Carnelian, lapis lazuli, peridot, sapphire

Trees: Bay, larch, hazel

Animals: Snake, boar, jackal

Birds: Sparrow, ibis

Deities: Demeter, Ch'ang-O, Ceres, Attis, Pomona

Zodiac: Virgo, Libra

Work spells for harvest, hearth and home, balance, purification, transformation, and focus.

Chapter 25
Bittersweet Are the Shadows of Autumn

Even though I long for cool, crisp nights that allow me the comfort of old woolen sweaters and coffee by the fire, it's sometimes hard for me to release my grasp on summer. For I know once the Cailleach brings down her staff, darkness will encroach, and I will be pulled into the shadows, where I am faced to take a hard look at myself. Do I like what I see? The Dark Goddess will howl, the sky will turn to charcoal, and I know the sun will once again be a fleeting object talked about in the past tense, as if it were a long-lost friend. Do I have a sturdy-enough constitution to face another winter?

But even as I ponder the upcoming winter and all that it brings, there is something about the slanted light that bewitches me. Picking and processing apples and plums completes the enchantment, as my home is filled with the scent of the fruit and spices that ease my spirit and draw me under autumn's spell. September brings us equal day and night and coaxes us to slowly surrender ourselves to the stillness to come. But for now, there is still so much work to be done as we begin to prepare the garden for dormancy.

Divide and Conquer

We look over our September landscape and smile. We have treated the land well, and in return we are gifted with flowering herbs and edible gems that will keep us fulfilled throughout wintertide. But we're not quite finished yet. Just as we have our own rituals before we tuck ourselves into our beds to sleep, there are things we can do to ensure our plants will awaken from their dormancy healthy and vibrant, their beds free of weeds and disease.

Weeding

Did you realize that autumn is probably the most important time for weed management? Think about it: this is the time that weeds are setting seed, and if the weeds are not removed, those seeds will drop into your beds. Some weed seeds can stay viable for decades, so instead of fighting weeds in the spring, it's best to take care of them now.

Dividing Perennials

By splitting large or overcrowded perennials into smaller sections, you are reducing competition for nutrients, stimulating growth, and increasing bloom development. It's an inexpensive way to increase the number of plants in your garden and a nice way to share your plants with other gardeners. This is a perfect autumn garden chore for perennials that are spring- or summer-blooming and should be done four to six weeks before the first frost. Divide autumn- or winter-blooming plants in the spring just as new growth emerges.

- Water plants 24 hours before dividing. Cool or overcast days are best.
- Use a spade or fork to gently raise the plant from the soil.
- Separate the plant by gently pulling it apart or by cutting with a knife or spade.
- Plant splits in appropriate containers or move them to a new bed. Water thoroughly.

Care for Tender Bulbs

I am using the term *bulb* to refer to plants whose storage systems are held in bulbs, tuberous roots, corms, rhizomes, and tubers. Tender bulbs are those that are typically planted in the spring for summer blooms. Included are plants such as amaryllis, gladiolus, canna lily, tuberous begonia, dahlia, colocasia, caladium, and taro. In contrast, hardy bulbs are planted in the fall and require vernalization for spring blooms to occur. Included are tulips, crocus, stargazer lily, daffodil, allium, hyacinth, and fritillaria.

Most tender bulbs must be dug up and stored for the winter if you live in regions colder than zone 7 or 8 (depending on the type of bulb and area planted). Once the blooms have dropped and foliage has turned yellow, dig around your plant with a spade or fork and gently remove the plant from the soil. Gently shake and rinse off your bulbs with a hose. Gladiolus should not be rinsed but allowed to dry and soil gently removed.

Allow bulbs to "cure" (or dry out) at 60 to 70 degrees Fahrenheit, out of direct sunlight. Most bulbs only require one to three days. Gladiolus should be left to cure for three weeks.

Remove any remaining stems or foliage and label bulbs for easy identification next season. Fill ventilated storage containers with peat, shredded paper, or shavings. Layer the bulbs and try to avoid them touching each other. Store in a cool, dry place (45 to 50 degrees Fahrenheit). Check several times over the winter and remove any bulbs that have shriveled or rotted.

Adding Mulch

Adding an insulating layer of organic matter to your beds in the fall helps prevent weeds, protects roots, and adds nourishment to the soil. Here are a few common mulch varieties:

Compost: Decomposes quickly and adds nutrients to your garden. Use in vegetable and flower beds.

Pine Straw: Decomposes easily and great for filtering water and protecting soil from erosion.

Shredded Bark: Inexpensive and great for landscaping around trees and shrubs.

Shredded Leaf Mulch: Breaks down easily and adds nutrients to perennial and vegetable beds.

Straw: Inexpensive and decomposes easily—great for vegetable and raised beds.

Wood Chips: Slow decomposer—best for landscaping in undisturbed areas.

Wood Shavings: Holds moisture well and is a great deterrent for slugs and snails. Great for walkways between beds.

Dahlia for Grace: Magick for Facing the Darkness in Our Lives

Dahlia stands in the garden with a graceful nod to the dying sun. It is the beautiful showstopper that charms the garden long after other summer favorites begin to fade. It has been said that no other plant gives so much reward with so little effort, and it might just be true. Native to Mexico and Central America, dahlias are popular tuberous, herbaceous perennials in zones 9 to 10 and tender perennials in colder zones. They are typically grown for cut flowers and come in a rich and varied array of colors, shapes, and sizes. From the small single 'Mignon' dahlias, perfect for a boutonniere, to the large dinner plate dahlias, which are pillowy and fantastical, the dahlia is definitely one to add to your magickal garden. And with thirty-six species and thousands of cultivars, every gardener is bound to find a favorite.

The dahlia (or *dalia* in Spanish) grows wild in the mountainous regions of Mexico and Central America and was an important plant to the Aztecs. They used them in food and medicine, and the stems of imperial dahlias, known as *acocoxochitl*, were used to transport water. The dahlia was also an important part of ritual and was associated with Xochipilli, the Aztec god who presided over flowers, pleasure, and the arts, as well as their god of war, Huitzilopochtli.

The first dahlia specimens arrived in Europe in 1791, and the flower was renamed in honor of Swedish botanist Anders Dahl. Dahlias graced the garden of Empress Josephine, who was very protective of the flowers she loved so much. The flower has since become one of the most popular garden flowers in the world, with societies dedicated to enthusiasts.

Dahlias grow best in rich, loamy soil. Plant tubers in late spring directly into your garden bed after the soil has reached approximately 60 degrees or in containers to grace your porch or balcony.

After the exuberance of summer, we begin to draw our energy inward, knowing that that dark half of the year is closing in. As a flower of grace and resiliency, dahlia helps us face the melancholy that can occur as we confront the realization that a chapter in our life is drawing to a close. It is a flower to go to for reconciliation when we feel as if things have not gone our way, for it blooms the most stately at season's end. As a Mars plant, connected to fire, dahlia can be used in magick for resiliency, acceptance, protection, self-love, grace, reconciliation, elegance, and dignity.

Ritual Bath for Resiliency

The dark half of the year can be stressful for many of us. And though many of us love a good pumpkin spice latte and a romp through a corn maze, the darkness and cold only intensify once spooky season has passed and the Samhain fire is extinguished. Our spirit loses its light as we wish the darkness away. But the reality is that it's not going away. This is true for anything in our lives that may feel adverse or traumatic. Resilience will not take those problems away, but it is what allows us to take on difficult situations with strength and grace. It gives us the courage to seek help when we need it and allows us to develop the skills for dealing with our emotions in a healthy manner.

So whether you're dealing with the effects of seasonal change, a change in your personal life, or other difficult challenges, a little reminder of your own resilience is sometimes needed.

You will need:

- As many candles as you would like
- Dahlia flower essence
- Dahlia petals (dried or fresh)
- Incense blend of 2 parts dragon's blood, 1 part ginger, and 1 part basil

Fill your bathroom with as many candles as you would like to set a comforting mood. Play music that resonates with you. In a firesafe dish or cauldron, sprinkle your incense blend over a heated charcoal tab and set the dish in a safe location. Fill your tub, add a few drops of dahlia flower essence, and sprinkle your bath with petals.

As you soak, allow yourself to express whatever emotions you may be feeling about your challenge. Your feelings are valid; let them out. When you feel ready, take a deep breath and exhale slowly. Allow dahlia's flower essence to reconnect you with happiness from a place of resiliency. Remind yourself, in whatever way feels right to you, that you have a warrior's spirit and that you can take on the darkness in your life with courage and grace.

The Gathering

The last of summer's fire dances across the landscape, reflecting sparks of golden light through growing shadows. This is the time of year when I reflect on the bounty of the season and am thankful for all that the Earth Mother has blessed us with. As I prep tomatoes, harvest pumpkins and winter squash, or even cut a few dahlias for the table, I also think about my ancestors who passed down the seeds and plants that have been in our family for generations. In fact, if you take a look, my entire garden tells a story of family. The roses and the rhubarb, the honesty plant, flag iris, columbine, tomatoes, pumpkins, beans, chives, some of my raspberry varieties, my hawthorn tree, the snowball bush, and my beloved honeysuckle all hold within them the wisdom of those who worked the soil before me.

As I harvest, I manifest their ancestral knowledge and sometimes hear myself answer aloud to their murmurs that fill my head. "Yes, Grandfather. I remember," I mutter as I shell heirloom beans. "Thank you, Great-Grandmother," I whisper as I carefully process tomato seeds.

Seed saving for me is not only a way I connect to my ancestors but also a way of passing on family tradition and keeping alive a way of life that has all but diminished. Saving the seeds from your food and flowering plants is a wonderful way of preserving your own family history, but it is also an inexpensive way to preserve the genetic diversity of heirloom and open-pollinated plants.

You see, many of the seeds that line the shelves every spring are not intended to be passed down from generation to generation, but were bred instead for longer storage, uniformity, and improved shipping quality. These types of seeds are called hybrid or F1 hybrid seeds, and though they produce vigorous, high-producing plants, they do not always breed true to type. The heirloom seeds that your ancestors lovingly saved from their largest and most vigorous plants created cultivars that were well adapted to their region's growing conditions which made them naturally more disease and pest resistant. And though not always uniform, these plants have amazing flavor and always breed true to type.

So, let's take a closer look at the markings on your seed packets to give you a better understanding of which seeds to save from your garden.

Hybrid (F1 Hybrid)

Bred to produce large yields, more vigorous plant growth, and a more uniform fruit, F1 hybrid plant varieties are a result of pollination between genetically distinct plants to create a desired trait. Hybrid seeds are a great choice for "one-season" planting and for gardeners with a short gardening season. But because they are designed for only one growing season, second-generation plants typically have less or no fruit, and physical characteristics vary greatly from first-generation plants. They also have a lower adaptability to stresses such as pests and disease. These are the reasons we want to avoid saving seeds from F1 hybrids.

Open-Pollinated (OP)

These genetically diverse seeds are a result of pollination between similar parents, which means the seeds will breed true to type and plant populations can slowly adapt to local growing conditions. Though the fruits may not be uniform, they will have great flavor. As open-pollinated plants may cross-pollinate, it is important to keep similar varieties separated. These are perfect for saving seed. Great open-pollinated seeds to begin with include peas, leaf lettuce, beans, and tomatoes.

Heirloom

Heirlooms are open-pollinated plants. Most sources agree they must be over fifty years old to be considered heirlooms. Handed down from generation to generation, these plants are perfectly adapted to their growing region. Great heirlooms to start with include beans, tomatoes, beets, and cucumbers.

Seed Saving

Saving your own seed is relatively easy and can save you a lot of money in the spring. Before you get started, consider that many common vegetables are biennials, meaning you will have to wait until their second season to collect seeds. This includes cabbage, brussels sprouts, root vegetables, and herbs and flowers such as parsley, hollyhock, foxglove, honesty plant, and alliums, to name a few. You also must consider cross-fertilization, which can take place when pollen is exchanged between flowers on different plants of the same genus. This can be remedied by planting only one variety of a plant at a time.

Dry Seeds

Dry seeds develop in pods, husks, or ears and dry on the plant rather than inside a fruit. You can leave a few pods on the plants until they are "rattle dry" for capsulated seeds or pick seedheads when they are brown and dry looking. After picking the pods or seedheads, allow them to dry completely, either by open air on a lined screen (use baking parchment or coffee filters) in a single layer on a tray in a dry, dark area or by clipping them into a paper bag. In the case of legumes such as bean or peas, you may consider pulling the entire plant after they have died back and hang them upside down in a shed or garage.

Wet Seeds

Any plant that houses its seeds inside the fruit, such as pumpkins, squash, watermelons, and tomatoes, produces wet seeds. When the fruit is fully ripe, cut open and scrape out the seeds into a bowl. Remove their slimy coating by rubbing them gently along the inside of a sieve while washing them. Drain and lay them in a single layer to dry. They are ready for storage when they break and no longer bend.

For cucumbers and eggplants, leave the fruit on the vine until they turn yellow, then continue the process above. For peppers, open mature fruit and scrape the seeds onto a plate. Allow them to dry in a single layer until the seeds break rather than bend.

Storing Your Seeds

Humidity and warmth are the enemies of any stored seeds. I like to place my seeds in envelopes labeled with their common and botanical name as well as the date. Tuck the sealed envelope into a clear mason jar and place them somewhere cool and dry. Mine are kept in the pantry alongside my herbs and behind the canned goods. Your refrigerator is another great place to store your seeds. Stored seeds, if kept properly, can last an average of two years. Though I have successfully planted seeds that were much older, I don't recommend it.

Chapter 26
Mabon Blessings

Autumn's first kiss is dreamy and chill. The mellow light and change of color that happen as September wanes seduce us into releasing summer's hold and immersing ourselves in the delights of the season. The autumn equinox, or Mabon, falls between September 21 and 23 and gives us equal hours of day and night. For my agricultural ancestors, the end of the harvest brought a close to the farming year and the completion of a successful yield.

Many agrarian societies took an animistic approach to farming, as seeds held the very essence of life within their casing. And at harvest, the spirits of vegetation were (and still are in many cultures) honored in various ways. In Southeast Asia, the rice harvest was practiced in a way that was painless to the essence of the plant. In some rituals, a symbolic rice mother was made from straw and used as a marker in a chosen section of the rice field where offerings were left. In Peru, all useful plants were animated by the Divine. Effigies from quinoa, maize, coca, and potato were made and worshipped throughout the course of a year. In many farming communities of the British Isles, the last sheaf of grain was ceremoniously beheaded. A corn dolly was made and hung above the hearth for protection until the following spring, when the spirit of the grain was returned to the soil.

What we think of as quaint customs are reflections of a complete reliance on the rhythms of nature. Sadly, in this modern age of on-demand living, we have separated the spirit from the grain. Think about it—as modern home gardeners, if our tomatoes contract blight or if cabbage worms destroy the broccoli, we may feel bad, but for the most part it is shrugged off, as we can go to the store and purchase more. Early agrarian societies were at the mercy of their gods, as the threat of starvation was one bad harvest away.

Witches' Thanksgiving

In gratitude for the harvest, festivals and feasts emerged, with the whole community invited to participate. For the ancient Romans, Ceres, Goddess of the Corn, was venerated. For the Greeks, it was Demeter, and for the Amorites, Dagon, their god of fertility and agriculture. Tributes were offered to the gods in the form of fruits, grains, or meat. Originating in Britain, ingathering celebrations were hosted by landowners and embodied the jubilation felt after the hard labor was done. This celebration still exists in parts of the British Isles and goes by many names, including Harvest Home. Other harvest festivals you may recognize include Sukkot, which in Jewish tradition celebrates the gathering of the harvest and commemorates the miraculous protection provided for the children of Israel when they left Egypt.[4] The Chinese Mid-Autumn Festival or Moon Festival is a movable festival that celebrates the harvest and encourages the harvest-giving light to return the coming year. Similar festivals are also celebrated by other Asian countries, including Vietnam, Singapore, the Philippines, and Malaysia. In Korea, Chuseok celebrates the harvest and the ancestors. And in Ghana, Homowo is tied to the Ga people's migration to Ghana and celebrates bountiful harvests.[5] Every culture celebrated the harvest, for this was a time of relief and gratitude that no one would go hungry during the long, dark winter to come.

Mabon is also called Witches' Thanksgiving, and our family has always celebrated it in true Thanksgiving style, complete with pumpkin pie. It makes more sense to us to celebrate the harvest in September instead of our traditional American date of the fourth Thursday of November, long

4. Arthur Waskow and Larry Goldbaum, "The Festival of Sukkot," University of Massachusetts Amherst, accessed May 8, 2023, https://www.umass.edu/orsl/festival-sukkot.
5. African Studies Program, "Thanksgiving and the Homowo Festival," University of Wisconsin–Madison, November 21, 2016, https://africa.wisc.edu/2016/11/21/thanksgiving-and-the-homowo-festival/.

after the harvest is done. As this is a time of balance and harmony, I keep magick low key for the equinox with introspection and meditation. Under the golden light that filters through big-leaf maples near the river, my coven and I typically spend a quiet afternoon making tea or incense blends. This is also the time we bless apples and carve them into effigies that will be used to guard our Samhain fire. For us, Mabon is about enjoying each other's company, eating good food, and drinking local hard cider.

Using apples in divination is a great way to incorporate this late summer and autumn favorite. As a symbol of abundance, a plentiful apple crop was thought to be an indication of a prosperous harvest to come. Connected to the Goddess, an apple cut crossways reveals our sacred pentagram in the layout of the seeds. Count the total number and divine using numerology.

One Seed: Initiation, action, independence

Two Seeds: Empathy, harmony, balance

Three Seeds: Creativity, communication, innovation

Four Seeds: Growth, grounding, responsibility

Five Seeds: Freedom, adventure, spontaneity

This is a great time to celebrate the harvest after a year of labor in your Witch's garden. Whether you grew a single zucchini plant or a pantry full of herbs for magickal or medicinal purposes, celebrate your efforts. Decorate altars with homegrown or locally grown fruits and vegetables, garlands of leaves, stalks of wheat, and gathered cones or nuts. Take time for yourself by indulging in favorite tea blends, journaling, seeking advice from your guides via an oracle or tarot deck, scrying, or consulting any form of divination.

Food for this sabbat can encompass a full-on Thanksgiving-style spread or a simple tea with dessert. It can also be fun to incorporate foods that are associated with harvest deities.

Demeter

Demeter, Greek goddess of agriculture, milling, motherhood, and fertility, had numerous shrines throughout the ancient world, including temples and sanctuaries dedicated to her mystery cult. The foremost of these was the celebrated Mysteries of Eleusis overseen by the Athenians. Demeter was usually worshipped in conjunction with her daughter Kore/Persephone, goddess of spring and the underworld. Plants associated with Demeter are mint, wheat, barley, and poppies. Her sacred animals include swine and serpents.

Set your harvest table with a cornucopia brimming with the fruits and vegetables of your harvest. Intertwine faux snakes throughout the décor. Serve pork, desserts laced with poppy seeds, pomegranate, and plenty of homemade bread.

Poppy Seed Crescents

- ¼ cup poppy seeds, plus 1 teaspoon for sprinkling
- ½ cup hazelnuts
- ¼ cup chopped dates
- ¼ cup milk, plus another ¼ cup
- 2 tablespoons sugar
- Zest and juice of 1 lemon
- 2 tubes of crescent rolls (or your favorite crescent roll recipe)
- 1½ cups confectioners' sugar
- ¼ teaspoon almond extract

Preheat the oven to 400 degrees Fahrenheit. Use a food processor to mince the poppy seeds, hazelnuts, and dates until crumbly. In a saucepan, heat ¼ cup milk with the sugar over medium heat. Add the poppy seed mixture and cook until thickened, stirring constantly. Stir in lemon juice and zest. Let cool.

On baking parchment, separate your dough into triangles. Place 1 teaspoon of the filling on each triangle 1 inch from base, spreading the dough out slightly. Roll up to the point and curve the ends slightly to create a crescent shape. Bake for 12 to 15 minutes until golden brown.

For the glaze, combine confectioners' sugar, ¼ cup milk, and almond extract until smooth. Drizzle the glaze over the crescents when cooled and sprinkle with the remaining poppy seeds.

Attis

Attis was an agricultural deity and consort of the Mother Goddess who in his self-mutilation, death, and resurrection represents the continuing cycle of the grain. He was worshipped in Phrygia, Asia Minor, and later throughout the Roman Empire. Plants associated with him are the pine tree, almond tree, and violets. Animals associated with Attis include the hare, goat, and boar. Set your harvest table with pine boughs and cones among potted purple pansies, along with crescent moon and sun ray symbols.

Want to simplify your harvest celebration? Try your favorite almond cookies with a soothing pine tea.

Pine Tea

- 2 cups water
- ⅓ cup chopped pine needles
- 2 cinnamon sticks
- Honey to taste (optional)

Pour 2 cups boiling water over needles and cinnamon sticks. Allow the tea to steep for about 10 minutes. Strain and enjoy with honey. Serves 2.

Pomona

Roman goddess and protector of orchards, gardens, and fruit trees, Pomona took delight in cultivating her garden and carried her pruning knife along with her. She was wooed by and later married to Vertumnus, god of the changing seasons and growth, to whom she was always loyal. Her sacred grove, called the *pomonal*, was located outside the city of Rome. She is associated with apples and all other fruiting trees.

Set your harvest table with a large bowl of apples, nuts, grapes, or other fruits from your garden. Surround it with leaves and rose hips and a few of your garden tools that served you well over the growing season. Of course, anything made with apples will be welcome at this feast.

Savory Apple Tart

- 12-inch round premade piecrust or homemade piecrust
- 1 tablespoon butter
- 1 tablespoon olive oil
- 1 small onion sliced into rings
- ½ cup sour cream
- 1 teaspoon dijon mustard
- ½ cup shredded gruyère cheese
- ½ cup shredded swiss cheese
- 1 teaspoon fresh chopped thyme
- 1 Granny Smith apple, cored and thinly sliced
- Salt and pepper to taste

Roll out your premade dough on a lightly floured surface to fit two 6-inch tart pans. Refrigerate for 30 minutes. Preheat the oven to 375 degrees Fahrenheit. Line the dough with parchment paper and pie weights (or dried beans) and bake for 20 minutes. Remove the weights and parchment and bake another 10 minutes until golden brown. Remove the crusts from the oven and set aside to cool. Reduce the oven temperature to 350 degrees.

In a skillet over medium heat, melt the butter and olive oil. Add the onion and cook until it begins to caramelize. Remove from heat.

Mix the sour cream and mustard in a bowl. Spread it evenly over both crusts. Sprinkle half of the cheeses and thyme followed by the apple slices and onions. Sprinkle the remaining cheese and thyme. Bake for about 15 minutes on the top rack until the cheese is bubbly. Allow it to rest for 10 minutes before serving.

Mabon Blessing

We are facing the season of rest and introspection as the days increasingly become darker, and it is truly a time to be thankful. I thought I would share the Mabon blessing of my coven, a thank-you to the earth for the blessings of the year and reminder to embrace the dark half of the year. It will allow us to gather energy for yet another growing season. Feel free to use it as is or modify it to fit your practice.

Hail to thee, blessed element of air. For the knowledge I/we have gained as I/we traverse the spiral path. I am/we are thankful.
Hail to thee, blessed element of fire. For the spark that keeps me/us inspired to continue to make my/our goals a reality. I am/we are thankful.
Hail to thee, blessed element of water. For your calming touch that helps me/us maintain balance in my life/our lives. I/we are thankful.
Hail to thee, blessed element of earth. For your grounding energy that reminds me/us that home is always where the heart is. I am/we are thankful.
Hail to thee, Lord of the Harvest. For as you dip into the Shadowlands, I/we too am/are able to accept the introspective time of darkness ahead of me/us. I am/we are thankful.
Hail to thee, Queen of the Harvest. For the fruits of the earth and your ever-changing light. May I/we hold your lessons dear as I/we continue our journey. I am/we are thankful.
Blessed be the harvest!

Soul Dolly

Apples have long been used in Samhain rituals as the fruit of the dead. Our coven gathers apples at Mabon and peels and carves them into soul dollies to guard our Samhain ritual. Between Mabon and Samhain, they are lovingly dried, and at Samhain our ancestors are invited to occupy the apples and guard our rites.

You will need:

- 1 large apple per person
- Vegetable peeler
- Paring knife
- Lemon juice
- Salt
- 1½-inch dowels or sturdy twigs
- Mason jars

Peel the apples. Use paring knives to carve a face. When finished, coat with a mixture of lemon juice and salt for preservation. Insert a dowel and prop the apple up in a mason jar. Allow it to dry for 3 to 6 weeks.

Chapter 27
Herbs of September

The slanting evening light tells us autumn has come. We raise our glasses in honor of a harvest well done and celebrate by coming together and sharing our bounty. The herbs I have chosen reflect restoration, good fortune, and protection for the coming dark half of the year.

Agrimony (*Agrimonia* spp.)

Planet: Jupiter

Element: Air

Energy: Masculine

Deities: The Dagda, Vishnu

This member of the Rosaceae family was known as a heal-all and has been used since medieval times to speed up wound healing, to staunch bleeding, as a gargle for sore throats, as a mild sedative, and as an antihistamine. Growing up to 40 inches in height, this erect plant has spires of tiny yellow 5-petaled flowers and can be found in many areas, including forest margins, meadows, and along riverbanks. It is native to Europe and North Africa but has become well spread throughout growing zones 6 to 9.

Magickally, it was used in reversal and restorative spells and for protection and healing. Use it in dream pillows to combat nightmares and to ensure a restful sleep.

Shielding Oil

The shielding properties of cinnamon and cedar combine with the uplifting scent of orange and the restorative properties of agrimony to make this a lifesaver for me as a neurodivergent. Keep on hand to use when you're in a situation that may cause overstimulation.

You will need:

- ⅓ ounces carrier oil (grapeseed or fractionated coconut oil are great)
- 5 drops cinnamon oil
- 3 drops cedar oil
- 2 drops orange oil
- 2 drops agrimony oil
- Glass roll-on vial

Mix all the ingredients together and add the blend to the vial. Shake and allow it to sit overnight before use.

Alfalfa (*Medicago sativa*)

Planet: Venus

Element: Earth

Energy: Feminine

Deity: Gaia

Related to peas, this ground cover has a sweet, grassy aroma, and if you've raised farm animals, you understand what a treat it is for them. Grown since ancient times, alfalfa has always been a food that symbolized wealth and was used as a charm against want. Medicinally, alfalfa has a reputation for lowering cholesterol and purifying the body and can be found in both supplement and tea form. It is most commonly enjoyed as sprouts for salads and sandwiches and can be found in almost any grocery store. It is a popular animal fodder, as it is naturally high in protein. It is thought if you place a jar of dried alfalfa in your pantry, your shelves will never be empty. Also use alfalfa for money magick, prosperity, longevity, and good fortune.

New Business Venture Charm Bag

For good fortune and prosperity, place some dried alfalfa along with a couple of coins in a green drawstring bag and tuck it in a drawer at your place of work.

Barley (*Hordeum* spp.)

Planet: Venus

Element: Earth

Energy: Feminine

Deity: John Barleycorn

Barley is a cereal grain that grows on erect stalks and has been cultivated for thousands of years. Compared to other grains, like wheat, oats, or rye, barley can tolerate a variety of climates, which makes it an important food source for those areas where other grains don't grow. It is also malted for beer and Scotch whisky production, as well as used as a food source for farm animals. Rich in vitamins and minerals and high in fiber, barley may help keep your digestion system healthy and reduce the risk of chronic diseases.

The importance of this grain can be seen in folklore. The ballad of John Barleycorn is an example of this, as John is the personification of the grain in his journey of life, death, and rebirth. The Greeks used barley in alphitomancy, a form of divination involving barley cakes or loaves of barley bread used to discern if someone was lying. Members of a group would be fed the barley cakes, and if the suspected person contracted indigestion, they were guilty.

Sprinkle barley around your home for protection or tie dampened stalks into knots. With each knot, imbue it with those things that weigh heavy on your mind. Float the stalks down a running water source (creek or river) as a means of release. Use barley in magick for luck, health, and prosperity.

Mabon Toast

If serving beer or whisky at your Mabon sabbat, raise your bottles and say simultaneously,

> May the barley bring us luck
> May the barley bring us health
> May the barley bring us prosperity
> Hail to the corn!
> Blessed be!

Herb Robert (*Geranium robertianum*)

Planet: Venus

Element: Water

Energy: Feminine

Deities: Robin Goodfellow, Wren, Robin, Fox, Crane

This herb is considered a noxious weed in the Pacific Northwest. Also known as stinky Bob for its strong musky smell, it is native to Europe and parts of Asia and Africa, and it spreads easily and quickly.

This plant in the geranium family has a five-petaled pink flower attached to branching red stems with fine white hairs, and it grows in hedgerows, forests, mountain meadows, and even cracks in the pavement. It is also one of the longest-flowering members of the geranium family, flowering continuously till frost sets in. It has been used in its native countries to cure ails of every variety, from a toothache to cancer. Its leaves can even be rubbed on skin to keep mosquitoes off, and the plant produces a brown dye.

Sometimes called fox geranium, robin flower, wren flower, or robin redbreast, this tiny flower has a connection to mischievous woodland spirits and hobgoblins. It can be used in magick for fertility, luck, faery magick, and protection.

Autumn Garden Protection Offering

- Equal parts of the following:
  - Petals of herb Robert
  - Rose hips
  - Elderberries
  - Haws
- Small wooden bowl
- Bell

Place the ingredients in a small wooden bowl and take it to your faery altar in your garden.

Use a bell to ring in the protection of the fae. Say something like this:

As summer wanes and autumn is in the air (*ring bell*)
I call to you spirits whose shadows draw near (*ring bell*)
To dwell here through the winter's calm (*ring bell*)
And protect my garden from all that mean me/us harm (*ring bell*)

Mullein (*Verbascum thapsus*)

Planet: Saturn

Element: Fire

Energy: Feminine

Deities: Jupiter, Circe

This herb stands guard much like the warrior Crone it represents, with wisdom, strength, and grace. It is an ally who isn't picky about where it plants its roots and grows easily in the poorest of soils. In fact, mullein has probably caught your eye when you were driving along country roads, for this tall biennial beauty can reach up to 8 feet tall, with densely haired leaves and tiny bright yellow flowers, and is at home near roadside ditches. Medicinally, mullein is used for soothing coughs, colds, and asthma and as a poultice for sore muscles, sprains, and joint pain. Magickally, it is an herb of protection from malevolent magick and is said to drive away evil spirits.

Mullein forms long, heavy seed heads and stalks that stiffen, making them the perfect plant to use for torches. It is said that country folk dipped the seed heads in melted lard and used the makeshift torch as a way to lighten dark paths that wound through forests and guarded Witches' rites. Use mullein in magick for protection, courage, health, love, divination, and exorcism.

Modern Hag Tapers

For those of you who would like to try hag tapers as a protective element in your practice but need something a little safer than an actual torch, this is a great way to mix a little old-world witchery into your modern craft. Keep one on hand to kindle your Samhain fire.

You will need:

- 1–2 dried stalks of mullein with seed head attached
- Several teaspoons each of dried rosemary, sage, and calendula (or herbs of your choice)
- 1 sheet of baking parchment
- ½ pound beeswax (You may need to adjust the amount of beeswax depending on size and how many tapers you make.)
- Tongs

Cut mullein stalks into 3-to-6-inch lengths. Mix the dried herbs and spread them out on the baking parchment. Melt the wax in double-boiler over medium-low heat. Use tongs to completely coat the stalks in melted beeswax and roll them in the herbal mixture. Let the tapers dry overnight.

Around the Garden
To-Do List for September

Gather seeds from open-pollinated and heirloom plant varieties to dry and use for the next season. If frost is imminent, pick tomatoes and peppers, harvest pumpkins and squash, divide any perennials that may need it, and dig tender bulbs to store for the winter. Plant spring-blooming bulbs and summer garlic. Weed and mulch garden beds.

In warmer zones, plant containers with annuals for the autumn season. Continue to deadhead annuals and perennials to maintain blooming. And plant cool-weather crops such as kale, cabbage, radishes, and beets.

Grow Your Magickal Knowledge

Pagan Pride Day festivals are typically celebrated during September or early October in cities all over the United States. They're fun, informative, and a great way to enjoy the harvest season with like-minded people.

Celebrate the autumn equinox (Mabon) in a fun and unique way with friends or with your coven by putting together a cider-pressing party. Try apple varieties 'Fuji', 'Gala', 'Jonathan', or 'McIntosh'.

OCTOBER

The garden knows the secret—
apprentice yourself to its ways.

OCTOBER CORRESPONDENCES

Nature Spirits: Kelpie, faun

Colors: Orange, brown, deep green, black

Herbs and Flowers: Calendula, sage, mullein, rosemary, catnip, pumpkin

Scents: Cherry, nutmeg, patchouli

Stones: Opal, tourmaline, citrine, obsidian

Trees: Yew, cypress, elder

Animals: Ram, stag, scorpion

Birds: Crow, raven, dove

Deities: Horned God, Hecate, Kali, Ishtar

Zodiac: Libra, Scorpio

Work spells for divination, ancestral work, shadow work, letting go, and hearth and home.

Chapter 28
The Witching Hour

"What a glorious death," I like to say of an October landscape. Of course, family and friends always raise an eyebrow when I speak of autumn in such terms, though I know they are appreciative of my creativity. But it's true, for in its decay, the earth celebrates with a fiery breath that alights the trees and fills the air with its sweet smolder. We are bewitched by silhouettes in moonlight and dance with wild shrieks by firelight into the arms of the Dark Goddess, who promises transformation for all of those who are willing to follow.

The garden too is preparing for its own transformation. For as the nights become longer and the cool temperatures beckon us indoors, our plants are readying themselves for dormancy. Instead of exerting energy in an attempt to grow, they stop. This protects the plant from water freezing within their sensitive leaves, stems, and trunks and causing harm, and it allows roots to continue developing until spring's return.

With October, the veil once again thins, and we celebrate the darkness that comes with the newborn year. Samhain is the third of our harvest festivals, and the herbs I have so lovingly grown, dried, and blended into incense in honor of my ancestors are ready to release their smoke into the night air. Yes, there is something about October—a magick like no other that beats deep within the soil. It is felt in the wind that creeps in from the north and the rain that gathers around the foothills. For me the season of the Witch is most enjoyed in the forest, where my wild soul feels most at home. The spirits of the forests that surround me are my guides, and together we weave the magick that suits my feral nature.

Magick is also happening beneath the soil that protects the roots of trees in the surrounding forests. There is a network of mycorrhizal threads that connect one tree to another, allowing them to communicate and share nutrients and water. A fungus acts as a distributor, and in return, "the mycorrhizal network retains about 30 percent of the sugar that the connected trees generate through photosynthesis. The sugar fuels the fungi, which in turn collects phosphorus and other mineral nutrients into the mycelium, which are then transferred to and used by the trees," shares the National Forest Foundation.[6] The fruit of the mycorrhizal network fungus are called mushrooms. It's a symbiotic relationship, as one could not survive without the other. This is evident when you find mushroom circles in your yard or see them around a tree in a park.

Seeing fungi growing in lovely shelf-like patterns on downed logs always seems to make the forest feel enchanted. You half-expect a faery being to be perched upon one as you walk by. But these mushrooms have a different job. They are plant pathogens that invade weakened or damaged trees through airborne fungal spores or spores carried by insects to wood exposed by injury. Shelf fungus aid with decomposition in the forest, which provides essential nutrients for new growth.

It is into the forest one should go as the wind churns and leaves turn crimson in October. A lot of mushroom varieties are ready to harvest, and there are fallen nuts, cones, and stones to be found—a treasure trove for the Witch who likes to gather and make their own magickal supplies.

So let us take a walk down a twisted path through trees that seem to beckon us with open arms to delight in the offerings of October. In this land of shadow and hidden treasure, a-hunting we shall go.

A-Hunting We Will Go

There is something gratifying about being able to go into your natural surroundings and forage for food that is in season. Mushrooms and autumn

6. Britt Holewinski, "Underground Networking: The Amazing Connections Beneath Your Feet," National Forest Foundation, accessed June 12, 2023, https://www.nationalforests.org/blog/underground-mycorrhizal-network.

go hand in hand. And with their earthy, meaty flavor, mushrooms are ideal ingredients for stews, soups, and the hearty fare we long for as darkness encroaches. Here, I offer a few precautions for gathering and a short list of some of the most common mushrooms you may find while in the forest. I also encourage anyone interested in foraging mushrooms to contact your local mycological society for more information.

- Never consume anything you cannot positively identify.
- If you are new to mushroom foraging, take an experienced forger with you as a guide.
- Take along a guidebook with clear, identifiable pictures included.
- Mushrooms are delicate—handle gently and use a mesh gathering bag or basket.
- Never take the first one you find, as it may be the only one.
- Never pull mushrooms up by the root; bring a small knife and cut them.
- Only harvest what you'll eat.
- Take pictures of mushrooms you can't identify to look up later.
- Never harvest mushrooms from a poisonous host such as a yew.
- Some mushroom varieties may cause stomach upset. Always cook mushrooms before consuming. Always start with a small portion if you're new to a variety.
- Always thank nature for the bounty it provides in your own way.

Chanterelle (Cantharellus *spp.)*

This easy-to-identify mushroom may pop up anytime between July and October, depending on your region. There are several varieties of this popular mushroom, and its color can range from creamy white to yellow to a bright golden yellow. They have a funnel-shaped cap and ridges on their underside as opposed to having gills. These true woodland beauties grow in groups on the forest floor and are likely to be found around hardwood trees such as oak, birch, or poplar or in the moist, mossy floor near hemlocks, pine, or fir. Medicinally, chanterelles are anti-inflammatory, antimicrobial, and an antioxidant. With a warm, sweet flavor, they are great in risotto and soup recipes. In magick, use this mushroom in spells for love, bonding, psychic development, and dreams.

Chicken of the Woods (Laetiporus sulphureus)

A great mushroom for novice foragers, this shelf-like mushroom grows on hardwood (typically oak) in the eastern half of the United States. *L. gilbertsonii* is another variety that grows in the western United States. Bright orange to yellow in color, they do not have gills. It is thought to have a similar taste and texture to chicken. Try it sautéed or as a meat replacement in a burger. Use chicken of the woods mushrooms in spells for grounding.

Hen of the Woods (Grifola frondosa)

Though the name is similar to chicken of the woods, hen of the woods is not the same mushroom (another example of why it's important to know your scientific names). Also known as maitake mushroom, it grows in feather-shaped clusters at the base of hardwoods (typically oak) and is light brown in color. Medicinally, it is antibacterial and antimicrobial, and its earthy, smoky flavor makes it great roasted or added to pasta dishes. Use hen of the woods in spells for abundance and healing.

Honey Mushrooms (Armillaria spp.)

Honey mushroom is another parasitic fungus that can typically be seen growing against broadleaf plants such as fruit trees. This mushroom grows in clusters with a honey-colored cap that has a sticky texture and hairy scales on top of a thick white stalk. Harvest this mushroom when young, as the stalks become fibrous with age. Cook it thoroughly. Its sweet flavor is great braised or roasted. Use honey mushrooms for wisdom, divination, and protection.

Oyster Mushrooms (Pleurotus ostreatus)

These subtle-flavored gems can be found any time of year, depending on your region and weather conditions. A cluster of shelf-like mushrooms, each 2 to 8 inches wide, is produced annually. The mushrooms are smooth on the upper surface with gills along the lower surface of the mushroom, and colors include creamy white, beige, yellow, and tan. They are typically found growing on hardwoods but will grow on conifers as well. Oyster mushrooms taste wonderful sautéed or used in stir-fry. Use them in spells for mental clarity and cleansing.

Mushrooms Steeped in Folklore

Not all mushroom-hunting explorations have to be about finding edible varieties to nourish one's body. Wandering the forest on a crisp autumn afternoon is also about nourishing one's soul. It's about revelation and wonder and discovering the magick that surrounds us. Take a guidebook and thermos of your favorite hot beverage and see if you can spy any of these mushrooms. A few of them are edible, but some are not and should be appreciated at a distance.

Witch's Butter (Tremella mesenterica)

This is one of the more beautiful mushrooms to find while wandering the forest. Its bright yellow gelatinous clusters remind one that the spirits of the forest are alive and that magick dwells all around us. Witch's butter can be found in temperate deciduous forests on downed logs, stumps, or deadwood. Though edible, the fungus really carries no taste. In folklore, it was known for its use in curses. In eastern Europe it was said to be placed at the entrance of the house of the person a curse was intended for. One could also stick a pin in the gelatinous cap to reverse a curse. Witch's butter can be burned as a means of protecting oneself from malignant spirits. Use it in protective and defensive magick.

Trumpet of the Dead (Craterellus cornucopioides)

Also known as black trumpet or horn of plenty, this is a perfectly edible and delicious mushroom that can be found growing singularly in moist or mossy areas near hardwood trees such as oak or beech. It stands about 4 inches and is black to gray in color. Its folk name comes from its resemblance to a trumpet being played by the dead from below the ground. Its scientific name references its connection with the cornucopia, which symbolizes good fortune, abundance, and a bountiful harvest. Add this mushroom to your Samhain altar as an offering for protection received from your ancestors. Add it to meals for abundance and good fortune in the coming year.

Witch's Hat (Hygrocybe conica)

Also called witch's cap or blackening waxcap, this small group of agaric mushrooms seems at home growing through the leaf litter around the quintessential Witch's cottage. With orange, red, and yellow conical caps that turn black as they age, there's no question how they got their name. They can be found in damp mossy or grassy areas near woodlands and are neither edible nor hallucinogenic. Associated with mysteries of the Otherworld, witch's hat mushrooms can be added to your Samhain altar or used in magick for cleansing, banishing, and protection.

Fairy Ring Mushroom (Marasmius oreades)

You're not going to find these in the deep woods among the leaf litter, but in pastures, grassy meadows, or even your own backyard. This small, brown edible mushroom stands on a tough stalk with a bell-shaped cap and is great in pasta dishes and sauces.

Mushroom rings are truly steeped in folklore—but not all the stories are the sweet tales of dancing childlike fae the Victorians told. A common ancient European belief is that they were created by witchcraft. In Germany they were the *Hexenringe* (Witch ring) and in France, *ronds de sorciers* (sorcerers' rings). But my favorite is from Sussex, England, where they were called hag tracks. So, Witches, if you see a ring of *Marasmius oreades* growing in a circle in your yard, dance in wild circles around it to welcome the Witches' New Year—and when you're done, pick a few of the mushrooms for your next meal. Use them in magick for working with the fae, protection, growth, and courage.

The Fly Agaric Mushroom

A very clear memory for me, as a child of the 1970s, was seeing large groups of young people in a lightly wooded area that stretched alongside the highway foraging for something on the forest floor.

"What are they doing?" I'd ask my parents.

"Picking shrooms" was always the answer.

It took me quite some time before I realized that my parents didn't mean the chanterelles that we would harvest every autumn but psychoactive mushrooms. In fact, the Pacific Northwest is one of the better growing locations for *Psilocybe cyanescens*, or wavy caps, the tiny little shrooms I would watch the young foragers gather.

It was theorized that fungi have been around for hundreds of millions of years, but with the discovery of the extinct *Ourasphaira giraldae* in 2014, it is now believed fungi have been around for billions of years, making them one of the oldest organisms on earth. And the use of psychoactive mushrooms has been a part of religious and ritual practice since human existence. In Central America, the psychedelic mushroom called *teonanácatl* was used in ritual to communicate with the gods, and in snowy Siberia, some legends say shamans sipped on hallucinogenic urine from reindeer who nibbled at the infamous fly agaric to induce shamanic flight—which may have partially inspired legends of Santa Claus and his flying reindeer.

Fly agaric, or *Amanita muscaria*, is that unmistakable bright red mushroom with the white speckled markings we quaintly connect to faery stories and cottagecore. The folk name refers to its past use as an insecticide in some parts of Europe, where bits of the mushroom were sprinkled in milk to kill flies. "Agaric" refers to a type of mushroom having a curved or flattened cap with gills on the underside.

Commonly found across the British Isles, Europe, Northern America, and Asia, fly agaric is known for its psychedelic effects. To minimize some of the less desirable side effects of the fly agaric's strong toxins, ibotenic acid and muscimol, it was processed by drying, smoking, putting in ointment, or steeping in tea. Though deaths are extremely rare involving fly agaric, most people don't realize that other members of the Amanita family include some of the deadliest mushrooms in existence. This includes death angels or destroying angels (*Amanita bisporigera* and *A. virosa*) as well as death cap (*A. phalloides*). It is the amatoxin in this genus of mushrooms that accounts for over 90 percent of deaths associated with poisonous mushrooms.[7]

Fly agaric is commonly known for its uses in ritual practice, but it has also been suggested that Vikings may have used it for its inhibiting effects on the body's fear response and startle reflex during berserker raids.[8]

Appearing late in the year (August to November), typically near birch or spruce trees, these mushrooms are enchanting to stumble upon. Years ago, while visiting my in-laws in Alaska, I wandered the birch forest behind their house and was completely gobsmacked to find dozens of the beautiful fungi lighting up the forest floor. In Germany, the fly agaric mushroom is a symbol of good luck and reverence for nature. I, indeed, felt lucky that day.

Use it in magick for clairvoyance, luck, courage, spirit flight, and fertility.

Charm Bag for Good Luck

The fly agaric is one of Germany's *Glücksbringer*, or lucky charms that are sometimes exchanged during New Year celebrations. You may recognize the symbols that follow, as they are prominent in many German holiday images from the turn of the twentieth century. Add your choice of the following lucky charms to a green drawstring bag along with a piece of pyrite or clear quartz crystal.

Chimney Sweep: Good luck over the year

Four-Leaf Clover: Good fortune, wishes that come true

Horseshoe: Protection, good luck

7. Maxwell Moor-Smith, Raymond Li, and Omar Ahmad, "The World's Most Poisonous Mushroom, *Amanita phalloides*, Is Growing in BC," *British Columbia Medical Journal* 61, no. 1 (January/February 2019): 20–24, https://bcmj.org/articles/worlds-most-poisonous-mushroom-amanita-phalloides-growing-bc.
8. Howard D. Fabing, "On Going Berserk: A Neurochemical Inquiry," *Scientific Monthly* 83, no. 5 (November 1956): 232–37, https://www.jstor.org/stable/21684.

Ladybug: Longevity, healing, good harvest

Mushroom: Good fortune

Penny: Wealth, protection

Pig: Wealth, prosperity

Tie your bag three times and say something like this:

Knot one—this spell's begun
Knot two—my will is true
Knot three—luck come to me

Chapter 29
Veiled in Mystery

I am most grateful for my garden when twilight brushes leaves with amber hues and shadows draw the intensity of color from my blooms. It is as the garden wanes that it is at its most wild. Vines tangle arbors and the calendula that escapes its boundaries wears its shaggy seedhead as a crown. Bees drone drunkenly among the fallen marjoram that carpets pathways, and the breeze tussles with the last of the sunflowers, who lower their heavy heads in acknowledgment of the darkness to come.

It is during this time of year as I gather the last of the harvest and begin trimming back tired perennials that I indulge in the mysteries of the garden. What secrets do plants hold? What magick do they manifest? As humans, we are intricately tied to the realm of plants. They have nourished us and healed us in times of sickness. They have provided us with beauty and have inspired works of art. Plants have weaved a tapestry of mythology and lore that has shaped our understanding of how the world works. They have been talismans to us throughout our lives and guarded our graves long after death.

But some plants wear a darker veil of mystery. They are the ones we are warned about as children not to touch. They are the baneful plants of Witches' gardens and spirit flight. They are the poisoners of ancient history and the means to an end in the tales of gothic romance. As with most plants, when handled properly, these baneful plants have substances that play a vital role in medicine, but they require respect and should not be grown as novelty in your Witch's garden.

The first thing a lot of new magickal gardeners want to do is add classic witchy plants to their garden. Before you go out and do that, let's take a look at some of their deadlier attributes. Remember these baneful allies are no joke, and they do not care whether you live or die. You must take precaution when growing and working with them. Never take them internally and never attempt to make a flying ointment nor purchase one from someone who isn't a well-trusted and educated herbalist specializing in baneful herbs. It's better to use herbs that are in the same family or have the same magickal associations, especially when dealing with the Solanaceae family. *Nicotiana* (tobacco) or even *Petunia* is a wonderful substitution for anything that falls in the nightshade family.

Belladonna (Atropa belladonna)

Like a lot of baneful herbs, the devil's berry, as it's sometimes called, has been both a healer and a poisoner since ancient times. Scopolamine, an alkaloid found in belladonna, is still used to treat nausea and motion sickness and aids in the recovery from anesthesia. Atropine is a key ingredient in the eye drops used by ophthalmologists to dilate eyes.

This bushy perennial whose name means "beautiful lady" is native to parts of Europe and Asia. It grows to approximately 5 feet in height and produces glossy black berries that are slightly sweet. Its roots, berries, and leaves contain atropine, hyoscyamine, and scopolamine that may cause rapid heartbeat, delirium and hallucinations, convulsions, coma, and death. The color and sweetness of the berries makes them an especially dangerous temptation to children or adults who are not familiar with the plant.

Ruled by Saturn and the element of water, *Atropa* derives from the oldest of the Greek Moirai (Goddesses of fate) who dictated the life and death of humankind. She was Atropos, who cut the thread of one's life with her shears. Belladonna is also synonymous with the folklore of salves that carried Witches to the devil's black sabbat. Though considered a classic Witches' herb, this is not something you want in your garden.

Its darker powers include visions, spirit transformation, astral travel, and working with the Dark Goddess. Safe substitutions for your magickal workings include eggplant blossoms, mugwort, and tobacco.

Foxglove (Digitalis purpurea)

It is said if you hear the bells of the foxglove ring, you will soon die. This beautiful plant ruled by Venus and the element of water is known for its tall spikes of tubular bell-shaped flowers. It has the power of both life and death, as it contains digitoxin, a cardiac glycoside used to treat heart disease, but too much will slow the heart completely and hinder blood circulation, causing death. This plant is wonderful in the garden, and if handled with respect, is a great addition to your magickal arsenal. Grow with caution if you have children or pets. Foxglove prefers partial shade in zones 4 to 9.

Its darker powers include defensive, protection, and deflective magick. Safe substitutions include snapdragons and mullein.

Hemlock (Cicuta *spp.)*

A member of the Apiaceae family, this umbelliferous beauty should not be confused with the coniferous and harmless hemlock tree (*Tsuga* spp.). Also called water hemlock, this plant grows 2 to 6 feet tall on divided stems with purple markings and fernlike leaves. It contains the chemical cicutoxin, which acts directly on the central nervous system and can kill quickly, either when taken internally or when rubbed on the skin. It thrives in moist landscapes, shoreline thickets, and the forest's edge. Do not bring this one into your garden.

Ruled by Saturn and the element of water, its darker powers include defensive magick, astral travel, and the removal of sexual urges. Safe substitutions for spellwork include hemlock's safer relatives carrot, parsley, and Queen Anne's lace.

Henbane (Hyoscyamus *spp.)*

Sometimes called devil's eye, henbane lives up to its dubious reputation, as it is a highly toxic member of the nightshade family. There are about twenty species of henbane, and all of them contain powerful narcotic tropane alkaloids, including scopolamine and hyoscyamine. Though long used for medicinal purposes, including as a sedative and painkiller, high doses may induce hallucinations, loss of muscle control, seizures, or cardiac arrest. Native to Eurasia, it has been thought of as a Witch's herb due to the sensation of flying it can produce when rubbed on the skin. Ruled by Saturn and the element of water, it was also an important ritual prophetic herb to many ancient cultures throughout Europe. This biennial should be grown with caution in full sun in zones 4 to 8.

Henbane's dark magick includes divine madness, spirit flight, hexing, and connection to the spirit world. When working magick, try the safer alternatives, tobacco and mace.

Jimsonweed (Datura stramonium)

Jimsonweed is a very witchy plant that blooms deliciously from mid to late summer through frost, and like most members of the nightshade family, it is indeed poisonous. Datura has played a role in ritual for various cultures as a visionary plant for telling the future, receiving counsel from the gods, and for revelation concerning disease and misfortune.

Jimsonweed contains the anticholinergics atropine and scopolamine, and consumption may cause fever, flushing, dry mouth, blurred vision, altered mental state, and in rare cases, coma or even death. Grow with caution in well-drained, humus-rich soil in full sun in zones 6 to 9.

Datura's darker magick includes protection wards, deflection, and communication with the spirit world. Safer substitutions for magick include petunia, tobacco, and bindweed.

Mandrake (Mandragora *spp.)*

Few plants are as richly steeped in magickal folklore as this member of the nightshade family. Ruled by Mercury and the element of fire, its forked roots give it a strange human-like appearance that during the Middle Ages was one of the reasons for its significance as a medicinal and magickal plant, thought to be able to cure anything from infertility to insanity. According to folklore, mandrake being pulled from the ground could produce a scream that if heard by human ears would cause certain death. This folk belief is thought to be a clue to its poisonous nature.

In modern medicine, it has been used to treat conditions including arthritis pain, asthma, and ulcers. But because all parts of mandrake contain tropane alkaloids, large doses may cause hallucinations, blurred vision, abdominal pain, dizziness, vomiting, and diarrhea. In severe cases it can slow the heart rate and sometimes lead to death. Mandrake can be grown in zones 6 to 9 in rich, well-drained soil and prefers full sun to partial shade. Roots can be harvested after approximately three years.

Mandrake's darker powers include exorcism, protection, and communication with the spirit world. Try working with mayapple or gingerroot as a safer substitution in magick.

Wolfsbane (Aconitum napellus)

Also known as aconite or monkshood, this mysterious beauty is native to western and central Europe and grows on 2-to-3-foot stems that have lovely hooded purple flowers and rounded, lobbed leaves. It has a long history of being utilized for acts of homicide and execution, especially in ancient cultures of Greece and Rome. The name "wolfsbane" is connected to its use as a bait poison to kill predators such as wolves or bears. Medicinally, aconite has been used to treat anxiety and restlessness, to disinfect, and to improve circulation. Large doses of aconite can paralyze the nerves, lower blood pressure, and stop the heart. This plant adds a bit of mystery to any garden and grows well in partial shade in zones 3 to 8.

Ruled by Saturn and the element of water, wolfsbane is said to drive away werewolves. Its darker powers include deflection, working with the Dark Goddess, invisibility, and protection from psychic vampires. Tobacco is a safe substation for this plant in your spellwork.

Yew (Taxus baccata)

As the longest-lived tree species in Europe, is it any wonder the yew is synonymous with immortality? The yew, which stands guard over many of Europe's churchyards, has sweeping branches that can root as soon as they hit the ground and replace the original trunk if it falls victim to damage or disease. A dark evergreen with bright red berries, most parts of the tree are poisonous due to a deadly alkaloid called taxine. Symptoms include dizziness, weakness, vomiting, low blood pressure, and slowing of the heart. Yew prefers full sun to partial shade in well-drained soil in zones 4 to 8.

Possibly because of yew's poisonous nature, the tree has been woven into many ghost stories that feature doomed lovers. Ruled by Saturn and the element of water, some folklore dictates that just sitting beneath the tree can cause death. Yew's dark magick includes connection to the spirit world, underworld, death, and rebirth. A safe substitution for your magickal working is sandalwood.

Witches' Flying Ointment

The iconic image of a female Witch straddling her broom has been a part of history since the Inquisition. And though brooms were associated with women and domesticity, it was a man by the name of Guillaume Edelin who, under torture, was the first to confess of broomstick rides to sabbats in honor of the devil.

To power a Witch's transport, it was said a salve was made up of the fat of a child steeped in herbs such as belladonna, poplar buds, hemlock, wolfsbane, and soot. The salve would have been applied to the mucous membranes of the vagina and along the staff of their broom to allow flight to their hedonistic rites.

Of course, medicinal salves have been used for thousands of years, and psychoactive herbs also have a long history of ritual use, but there is no clear evidence of a Witches' flying ointment ever being used in such a way. One thing is for sure: salves using poplar buds have been long used in medicine, with poplar salve (*unguentum populeum*) being one of the oldest formulations. Known for their anti-inflammatory and antimicrobial properties, poplar-based salves also included other herbs, and recipes could be found in many herbals and pharmacopoeias. One such book, *Gart der Gesundheit*, written in 1485, included henbane, poppy leaves, and mandrake, among other herbs mixed with the poplar.[9] One was to rub the concoction on the

9. Claudia Müller-Ebeling, Christian Rätsch, and Wolf-Dieter Storl, *Witchcraft Medicine* (Rochester, VT: Inner Traditions, 1998), 133.

temples and the area around the navel. Salves such as this were well known and used much like we do aspirin today. So, one must ask: Are salves such as *unguentum populeum* the basis for Witches flying ointment?

If you look online today, you will find many sources for modern Witches' flying ointments, complete with a list of added psychoactive or potentially lethal plants. Buyer beware. If you plan on purchasing some, only buy from a professional herbalist with extensive knowledge of baneful herbs.

Soul-Flight Ointment

Poplars, cottonwoods, and aspens all belong to the Salicaceae family. Black cottonwood, or western balsam poplar (*Populus trichocarpa*), grows along the river near my home, and in February, when the buds swell and the scent of their sweet resin fills the air, I collect buds from saplings along the winding riverbank. I loosely fill quart jars with the buds, then fill them with olive oil, and let them steep in my pantry until spring is in full bloom. The oil can be used in soap and salve recipes. My favorite magickal use for cottonwood buds, though, is in making soul-flight ointment. When dabbed on the pulse points and on the third eye, this ointment is a safer alternative to many flying ointments but can still open the practitioner up to soul flight.

You will need:

- 4 parts cottonwood buds
- 1 part dried mugwort
- 1 part dried yarrow
- Oil to cover
- 1 ounce beeswax
- Essential oils of your choice (optional)

Place the buds and herbs in a quart jar and cover with your choice of oil (olive, grapeseed, sweet almond, etc.). Let steep in a warm, dark place for several weeks. Shake daily.

When ready, use a double boiler to melt 1 ounce of beeswax. When melted, add 1 cup of your infused oil and stir until blended. Take off heat and add the optional essential oil of your choice. Pour the mix into 2-ounce tins and allow them to cool fully. This recipe fills 4 tins.

Follow Me to the Dark Side: Gothic Gardens

Gardens are truly a transitionary space—not quite wild nor completely tamed. They are haunting in the way that they portray the aspect of what they once were: trees and shrubs planted to give us a false sense of order, and flowerbeds that, despite our influence, are more than willing to go back to their wild nature. They are a maze of light and shadow that bewitches our senses, drawing us deeper under their spell. Add a crumbling courtyard, vine-entangled tombstones, mossy pathways, and plants with dark folklore attached, and you have yourself the making of a truly gothic garden.

We can thank the Victorians whose Gothic revival of the late nineteenth century stepped away from former Greek and Roman influences and gave us irregular shapes, pointed arches, and decorative crown moldings. Literature and art of the time presented us with erotic melancholy and a longing for the transcendental among dark ruins and spooky landscapes.

Rural cemeteries, unaffiliated with the church, became places of reflection where one could meander among gravesites in a tranquil garden landscape. People of the time used cemeteries as one would a public park today: day outings were planned, and picnics enjoyed among the graves. Cemeteries also provided sculptors a place to showcase their work. Today, we can appreciate the darker aesthetic a garden has to offer. Gothic gardens remind us of the beauty that one can only find in decaying architecture, dark reflecting pools, and paths that feel a little feral. They help us remember that every plant has a story and the spirits of the wild are ever lingering nearby.

Gothic gardens have made a comeback, incorporating themes found in a dark romance, such as crumbling hardscapes, salvaged wrought iron, and found finials, along with peaked trellising and twisting paths through trees that hang with Spanish moss or are covered in clubmoss and lichen. Your plantings might reflect a traditional witchy garden with a mixture of baneful or medicinal herbs. Or you might prefer something dark and dramatic like an all-black garden with splashes of bright red. Here I offer two garden designs to give your landscape a truly gothic vibe.

Something Wicked This Way Comes Garden

This shady garden design gives a nod to all of us Witches who feel at home in a garden where the neighborhood children are taught not to go. The townsfolk whisper of night flights on broomsticks and dark magick on moonless nights.

Corkscrew Hazel (*Corylus avellana* 'Contorta'): A strongly twisted variety of hazel that grows 10 to 15 feet in height in zones 3 to 9.

Cowslip (*Primula veris*): This old-fashioned favorite of the primrose family grows well in part shade in zones 2 to 8.

Wolfsbane (*Aconitum napellus*): With all its deadly charm, wolfsbane will light up a shaded corner of your garden. Grows 2 to 4 feet in height in zones 2 to 8.

Foxglove (*Digitalis purpurea*): This magickal flower of the fae grows well in partial shade in zones 4 to 9.

Periwinkle (*Vinca minor*): This creeping evergreen with starlike blooms is a beautiful ground cover in a shady area. Grows in zones 4 to 9.

Lily of the Valley (*Convallaria majalis*): A low-growing, shade-loving, rhizomatous perennial that exudes magick. Grows in zones 2 in 9.

Mandrake (*Mandragora* spp.): A bit of bewitchment for your partly shaded garden. It has purplish tobacco-like leaves and clustered flowers that turn to yellow fruits (Satan's apple) in summer. Grows in zones 6 to 9.

Toad Lily (*Tricyrtis hirta*): With spotted blooms on 2-to-3-foot stems, this shade-loving lily is simply enchanting for a late summer and autumn display. Grows in zones 4 to 9.

Vampire's Kiss Container Garden

With plants straight out of a gothic romance, this container garden recalls a rendezvous with a mysterious lover.

Sedum 'Back in Black' (*Hylotelephium* 'Back in Black'): A beautiful late summer to fall bloomer with near-black foliage. Perennial that grows in zones 3 to 9.

'Black Baccara' Rose (*Rosa* 'Black Baccara'): Dramatic blossoms on long stems. Grows 3 to 6 feet tall in zones 5 to 9.

Wood Spurge 'Walberton's Ruby Glow' (*Euphorbia amygdaloides* 'Walberton's Ruby Glow'): An absolutely bewitching evergreen that emerges red and turns a purple-black as the season progresses. Perennial that grows 12 to 18 inches in height in zones 6 to 8.

Cardinal Flower 'Black Truffle' (*Lobelia cardinalis* 'Black Truffle'): Deep, dark foliage and red blooms that last until frost. Perennial that grows in zones 3 to 9 and 3 to 4 feet in height.

Petunia 'Black Magic' (*Petunia ×hybrida* 'Black Magic'): Deep black velvety blooms that will bloom all season long. Tender perennial that is hardy in zones 9 to 11.

Chapter 30
Herbs of October

The door to the dark half of the year swings open as October draws to a close. The herbs I have chosen reflect the transition to the dark half, as they are associated with endings, psychic awareness, wisdom, and inner journeys.

Chrysanthemum (*Chrysanthemum* spp.)

Planet: Sun

Element: Fire

Energy: Masculine

Deities: Izanami, Odin, Hel

First cultivated in China, chrysanthemums (or mums) at one time had a simple daisy-like bloom. But centuries of hybridization have given us the jewel-toned showstoppers that are now synonymous with autumn. Mums can be found for sale in just about every garden center throughout the fall months. But don't be surprised if these decorative plants do not overwinter—they are not bred to be hardy. Instead, plant hardy chrysanthemum varieties in the spring in well-drained soil with full sun in zones 5 to 9. Try varieties like *Chrysanthemum* 'Dernier Soleil' or *Chrysanthemum* 'Herbstkuss'.

Chrysanthemum has traditionally been valued as a longevity tonic for general well-being and has been used to treat sore throats, to aid digestive issues, and to help reduce fever.

In France, La Toussaint, or All Saints' Day, falls on November 1, when chrysanthemums are set upon the graves of loved ones. Commonly used in funerary practices in countries such as France, Italy, and Belgium, chrysanthemum is a flower of immortality. Plant them around your home to protect against evil spirits or wandering ghosts. Use them in magick for funerary practices, protection, immortality, and grief.

Chrysanthemum Herbal Blend

Here's an herbal blend recipe perfect for protection against wandering spirits as the veil thins at Samhain. Use it as an incense, offering, or to dress candles.

You will need:

- 4 parts dried chrysanthemum petals
- 2 parts dried garden sage
- 2 parts dried rosemary
- 1 part benzoin resin

Use a mortar and pestle to grind herbs and resin. Burn the blend over a charcoal tab.

Cosmos (*Cosmos* spp.)

Planet: Jupiter

Element: Air

Energy: Feminine

Deities: Fortuna, Euphrosyne

The wild child of flowers, cosmos give any garden bed a feeling of being a little untamed; that's probably why I love it so. They easily germinate with direct sowing in the spring and will thrive in almost any soil condition. Preferring full-sun but tolerant of partial shade, cosmos have lovely daisy-like, multicolored flowers that sit atop tall slender stems with lacy foliage and will give you beautiful blooms summer through fall.

Medicinally, *Cosmos caudatus*, or king's salad, is known for its anti-inflammatory, antifungal, antibacterial, and antioxidant properties. Edible, its petals are used to brighten a salad or in desserts, and the leaves and shoots can be eaten raw or used in a stir-fry.

Plants of grace, order, and harmony, cosmos remind of us of the infinite power of the Divine. As they are associated with October, a gift of cosmos during that month is a lucky omen.

Use cosmos in magick for feminine energy, harmony, inspiration, luck, order, and grace under fire.

Honey Jar for Harmony

Whether you're looking to add harmony to your home or to your workplace, this sweetening spell might just do the trick.

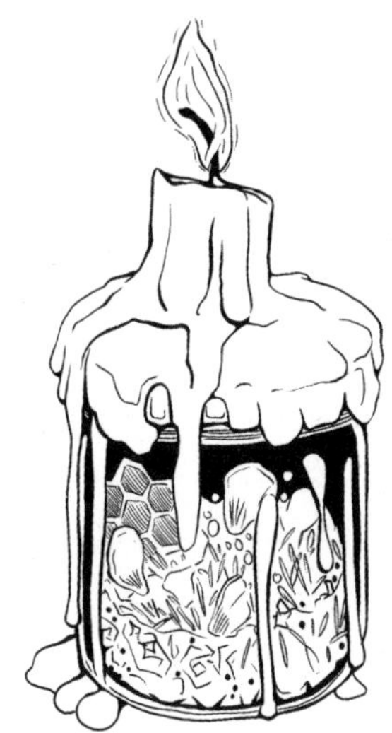

You will need:

- Scrap paper and pen
- Small canning jar with lid
- Cosmos petals
- Lavender petals
- Bay leaf

- Honey
- Small pink tea candle

On a scrap piece of paper, write out or draw symbols that represent where harmony is needed in your life. Fold up the paper and add it to a clean, dry jar along with your herbs. While focusing on your intent, pour honey over the contents until just covered. Fasten the lid. Light your candle and set it on the lid, allowing it to burn down and the wax to seal your spell.

Hazel (*Corylus* spp.)

Planet: Sun

Element: Air

Energy: Masculine

Deities: Diana, Artemis, Hermes, Aengus

Also known as filberts, these trees of hedgerows and moist, loamy spaces are relatively easy to grow in the home garden as they don't require as much space as other nut trees and fruit within three to five years of planting. Depending on the variety, a hazel only grows to around 15 feet tall in growing zones 4 to 9 and can be pruned easily.

Hazel is grown commercially for its wood, which is popular in basket making, for tool handles, and in fence making. The mildly sweet nuts are common in deserts and a main component in the popular chocolaty spread Nutella.

Hazel is sometimes called the poet's tree, as it is connected to inspiration and wisdom. There are several variations of the Celtic story of nine hazel trees growing around a sacred pool. Salmon would eat the fallen nuts, and those who partook of the divine fish absorbed the wisdom. As a favorite wood for walking sticks, it is also connected to travelers. And if you're a traveler lucky enough to find a stick that has been corkscrewed by a honeysuckle vine, the stick is said to make your presence invisible. Use it in magick for psychic awareness, wisdom, inspiration, and traveling.

Hazelnut String for Inspiration

String nine hazelnuts on red twine to invoke the "fire in [your] head." As referenced in the poem "Song of the Wandering Aengus" by W. B. Yeats, the fire in your head is what allows you to go beyond normal thinking and access true inspiration.[10] As you string your hazelnuts, visualize your third eye opening to divine inspiration and say something like this:

Hazel of knowledge, your mysteries astound
Bless these nuts from your glorious crown
One to inspire
Two to inquire
Three for your many charms
Woven together with magickal measure
Creative blockages cause me no harm
Four to be wise
Five to enlighten
Six for your many charms
Woven together with magickal measure
Creative blockages cause me no harm
Seven to visualize
Eight to achieve
Nine for your many charms
Woven together with magickal measure
Creative blockages cause me no harm
Blessed be

Hang your hazelnut string in your creative space, be it office, craft room, or studio.

10. William Butler Yeats, "Song of the Wandering Aengus," *The Wind Among the Reeds* (Cambridge, MA: Cambridge University Press, 1905), line 2.

Mugwort (*Artemisia vulgaris*)

Planet: Venus

Element: Earth

Energy: Feminine

Deities: Diana, Artemis

Mugwort is a favorite herb in my witchy garden. This aromatic perennial is just one of over 500 species in the daisy family, and its wild nature makes it perfect for a meadow garden setting. Mugwort can grow up to 6 feet in height and produces tiny flowers in varying colors. In some areas, this plant is considered an invasive weed as it can spread easily, so make sure to check with your local extension office before planting. This plant prefers full sun but will grow in partial shade and is hardy in zones 3 to 8.

Known as the witch's herb or sometimes cronewort, it was said to be hung on the doors of midwives or healers. Connected to Artemis, mugwort was also known as the "mother of herbs" and was once used to treat women's reproductive disorders. Mugwort has been used more recently as a sedative and as a digestive aid. It has also been used in ointments to relieve dry, itchy skin.

Mugwort is often used magickally to induce lucid dreaming, used for communication with the spirit world, or worn to ward evil. Use it in magick for protection, astral projection, inner journeys, and psychic awareness.

Circle of Light Bath Salts

Don't let the psychic vampires get you down. These bath salts made with protective dried herbs and essential oils are just the thing to soak away those bad vibes and make you feel like you're floating in a circle of light.

You will need:

- 4 cups Epsom salts
- ½ cup baking soda
- 1 cup melted coconut oil

- ½ cup dried mugwort
- ¼ cup dried sage
- 20 drops rosemary oil
- 10 drops lavender oil

Mix all the ingredients together by hand while repeating,

Protect
Purify
Sanctify me

Store the salts in a glass jar and sprinkle 1 cup into your bath.

Pot Marigold (*Calendula officinalis*)

Planet: Sun

Element: Fire

Energy: Masculine

Deities: Áine, Helios, Lugh, Tonatiuh

When I think of autumn, pot marigold comes to mind. Also known as calendula, this popular annual reseeds easily, giving you bright blooms years after year. Single or double blooms are continuous from midsummer through the frost on 1-to-2-foot stalks.

As a common "pot" herb, calendula was used in stews and soups in ancient times and is still used to add a peppery tang to recipes. With high amounts of flavonoids, pot marigold is anti-inflammatory and antibacterial, and it is popular in ointments to treat cuts, bruises, and burns.

It was thought that strewing pot marigold petals would provide protection against thieves. This herb offers us the power of reclamation and the courage to move on from situations that no longer serve us well, and its fiery petals can be used to ignite prophetic dreaming. Use it in protection spells, for psychic powers, and for strength and courage.

Samhain Cauldron Tapers

As October closes and the veil thins between the world of the mundane and that of the Otherworld, we can celebrate this transition with a bonfire kindled with beeswax and sacred herbs. Specific herbs such as mugwort, sage, mullein, rosemary, and calendula all have a history with divination, funerary practices, or communication with the spirit world. Roll them onto beeswax tapers and use them to light a fire of alder wood (a tree associated with the dead), and you have a very magickal bonfire.

You will need:

- 2 lengths of cotton wicking cut about 9 inches long
- 1 honeycomb beeswax sheet (8 by 16 inches) cut in half to make 8 by 8 sheets for 2 tapers
- Combination of any of the following herbs or essential oils:
  - Mugwort
  - Pot marigold
  - Sage
  - Mullein
  - Rosemary

To make the candles, lay the wick along the edge of a sheet of beeswax and start rolling the candle by bending over about ⅛ inch of the wax around the wick. Once secure, roll the candle slowly, making sure to keep it even. When you have come to the end, you can form a smooth edge by gently pressing the edge down onto the side of the candle.

When you are ready to press your herbs into your candles, you can use a lighter to quickly and gently warm the wax in the area you are pressing. Press larger leaves first in a way you find pleasing, followed by smaller petals. If you choose to use essential oil, anoint your candle with it before use.

You can ritually use your tapers to ignite a fire in a cauldron, firepit, or other fireproof container, to call in the spirits—or just to enjoy a fragrant fire on a brisk autumn evening.

Warning: These are not meant to be burned in a candle holder but used only as a fire starter outdoors in a secure firesafe container.

Around the Garden
To-Do List for October

If you live in cooler zones and haven't planted your garlic, shallots, or spring bulbs, this is the time to do so. Frost may already be an issue; this is the time to drain hoses and empty birdbaths to avoid damage. October is the time to trim back perennials and thin out your winter greens. This is also a wonderful time to make notes on which plantings were a success or which were a failure. This will help guide you for next spring's garden. Harvest any remaining summer fruits and vegetables before heavy frost sets in, and remember to leave some seedheads (such as sunflowers, asters, and cosmos) for the birds to eat.

For warmer zones, plant seeds for crops that can grow throughout the winter, such as kale, broccoli, carrots, radishes, and beans. Don't forget easy-to-sow favorites such as parsley, sage, dill, and cilantro. Fill planters with plants like alyssum, dianthus, and impatiens to bloom throughout the winter months.

Grow Your Magickal Knowledge

Used for both positive and negative influences, doll (or poppet) magick is a form of sympathetic magick that has gotten a bad rap thanks to B-rated horror movies. So as the dark half of the year approaches, why not put those beautiful herbs you grew and dried to work as a blessing for yourself (or another willing practitioner, your coven, etc.) by creating a poppet?

Choose the color of the fabric and your herbs based on your intention. Cut out a figure of your choice from fabric you have decorated with your name or meaningful sigils or symbols. Stitch right sides together, leaving a space open to fill. Turn the poppet right-side out and fill it with herbs, crystals, hair, nail clippings, charms, or words of empowerment written on paper scented with essential oils. Stich up the opening. Activate your doll by sticking it with a lovely hat pin or by tapping it with your wand or athame and stating your intention. Place the poppet on your altar or another place of significance to you.

At this transitionary time, October is a great time to harness the power of fire. Pyromancy is a form of divination using the flames from a fire, candle, or another source of flame and interpreting the shapes seen within. Focus on a question as you gaze into the flames. Bright upward flames may indicate a positive answer, and a dull flame may indicate a negative response. Shapes too can be interpreted for meaning.

NOVEMBER

Through the window I watch the garden wither. Sleep now and dream of spring.

NOVEMBER CORRESPONDENCES

Nature Spirits: Bean sídhe, Dullahan

Colors: Purple, white, gray, sage green

Herbs and Flowers: Vanilla, hops, wormwood, hyssop

Scents: Anise, nutmeg, cedar

Stones: Yellow sapphire, topaz, Apache tear

Trees: Pine, chestnut

Animals: Snake, scorpion, bat, eel

Birds: Falcon, owl

Deities: Astarte, Cailleach, Bast, Osiris

Zodiac: Scorpio, Sagittarius

Work spells for healing, hope, shadow work, divination, gratitude, release, and protection.

Chapter 31
Bringing the Garden In

November is as fickle as March—at least that is the opinion of most of us who live in our narrow valley in the Pacific Northwest. "You can't trust the weather, not one bit," I've heard the old-timers say. And it's true, for it can start out clear and cold in the morning, then quickly turn to pelting rain by noon. It isn't surprising to have the mildest of days end with an inch of slushy snow covering the ground or to have dark, tumultuous clouds that settle heavy around rooftops during the day dissipate by nightfall, revealing Orion wielding his sword at Taurus in an attempt save the Seven Sisters. During the dreariest of months, it is those pinpricks of light that remind me that no matter how far away it feels, spring will return and my soul will once again be intoxicated by the scent of green.

November can be hard for many reasons: the realization of the onset of winter, the lack of light that tests even the hardiest among us, and the impending doom of a holiday season that can trigger anxiety or depression in many people. But there is something we can do—we can light up the indoors with a green fire to ease our spirits and provide us with a new magick to explore. How do we do this? By bringing the garden in.

With proper lighting conditions, we can grow many of our herbal favorites indoors. A sunny south-facing window can become an indoor garden oasis. And for those of us who struggle with low light conditions during the winter months, low light houseplants such as philodendrons or jade plants are the perfect solution. In my kitchen, I have two small hydroponic growing systems that provide me with continuous fresh herbs all winter long. If you don't have one, I highly recommend it. They're relatively inexpensive, clean, and easy to use. You can purchase blank pods and fill them with your own seeds or buy seed pod kits.

Keeping houseplants (especially during the winter months) is important for the same reason being in green spaces outdoors is important—because being in touch with nature improves our well-being on so many levels. Houseplants improve the air quality and absorb that negative, stagnate energy that builds in dark spaces. They may boost your mood, which can help you feel more creative and be more productive. They also provide a whole different magickal vibe from an outdoor magickal space.

Our relationship with our indoor green allies is a symbiotic one. We provide them with light, water, and care, and they provide us with clean air and act as magickal partners. Plants such as cacti and ivy are perfect wards to guard against negative influences. Peace lilies or bamboo provide a calm, gentle energy, and succulents like hens and chicks enhance the feeling of hearth and home.

Indoor Magickal Allies

Here are just a few houseplants you may want to consider for your magickal home:

Aloe Vera (Aloe vera)

This popular succulent can grow up to 40 inches tall. Its gray-green fleshy leaves contain a gel that is used to soothe chafed or sunburned skin, and it is widely used in many cosmetic products. Aloe is a clumping plant whose "pups" grow from the base of the mother plant and can be easily transplanted. Plant it in well-draining soil or succulent/cactus potting mix and place in an area that receives bright indirect sunlight. Associated with the moon and the element of water, aloe can be used in spells for luck, money, healing, and protection. Warning: Aloe is toxic to pets.

African Violet (Saintpaulia ionantha)

Available in different colors and with single or double flowers, there is no reason to doubt why African violets are such a popular houseplant. For these plants to thrive, they like their environment warm and humid and prefer bright indirect sunlight. Because they have soft stems that are susceptible to rot, keep the soil lightly moist and avoid overwatering. Associated with Venus and the element of water, it can be used in spells for spiritual growth and working with the fae.

Boston Fern (Nephrolepis exaltata)

The most common fern for indoors, the Boston fern brings a little bit of forest magick into your home. This plant prefers filtered light and lots of humidity, so make sure and keep the soil moist and mist your ally a couple of times per week. Associated with Mercury and the element of air, Boston fern can be used in spells for rain, healing, renewal, protection, luck, and invisibility.

Cactus (Cactaceae *spp.*)

Because cacti come in a wide range of shapes and sizes, you can easily find one that is suited to your indoor (or outdoor) garden display. Cacti are succulents whose fleshy stems are adapted to hold water. For a succulent to be a true cactus, the plant must have areoles where spines, leaves, or flowers grow from. Plant cacti in a mixture of 50 percent organic material and 50 percent inorganic material such as perlite, sand, or gravel, or use a succulent/cactus potting mix. Set the plant in a window that receives at least ten hours of light per day and do not overwater. Associated with Mars and the element of fire, cactus spines are a great addition to Witch's bottles or used as a scribe in candle magick. It was once thought that to place a cactus in a woman's bedroom would keep her chaste. But cacti were also thought to increase the sex drive of men. Use them in spells for protection, sexual stamina, tolerance, and clairvoyance. Warning: some varieties of cactus can be toxic to both people and pets.

Golden Pothos (Epipremnum aureum)

Also known as devil's ivy, this leafy trailing plant is one of the easiest houseplants to care for. It thrives in bright indirect light but is tolerant of low light conditions. Plant it in a well-draining potting mix with an addition of perlite, and water every one to two weeks. Known for its ability to clean the air of pollutants, it is also great for clearing an area of negative energy. Use it in magick for prosperity, protection, and binding rituals. Warning: This plant can be mildly toxic to both people and pets.

Houseleek (Sempervivum tectorum)

A favorite succulent more commonly referred to as hen and chicks, this sweet plant prefers sunlight but can grow in just about any condition. I have them tucked everywhere, from between rocks to inside the belly of an old woodstove, and they continue to thrive. Beautiful rosette-shaped mother plants produce numerous "chicks" that can be easily transplanted. Houseleek will live for approximately four to six years before producing a bloom and dying. The plant is also known as "welcome home husband," and it was said that a wife could place a pot of houseleek at the front door to encourage sexual arousal in her husband upon his return from work. Associated with Jupiter and the element of air, this plant can be used in magick for fertility, luck, hearth and home, love, and protection.

Ivy (Hedera *spp.*)

These hardy and bewitching trailing vines thrive in places other plants will not. They are perfect for brightening up areas with low light, and with their vining nature, they add a touch of wildness to your indoor space. Walking into a room with ivy twisted around windows or among bookshelves is like walking into a warm hug. Their protective nature immediately sets one at ease. Plant ivy in a good all-purpose potting soil. Though ivy likes to be moist, it's easy to overwater it. Water when the top of the soil feels dry. Fertilize about once a month and mist occasionally if you live in a dry region. Add pots of ivy to those spaces where the energy feels slightly off to freshen and beautify. Associated with Saturn and the element of water, ivy can be used in magick for protection, growth, fidelity, love, and healing. Warning: It is toxic to both humans and pets.

Jade Plant (Crassula ovata)

This succulent plant of luck and abundance is reminiscent of a small tree with a thick woody stem and round fleshy leaves. Long living, they can reach up to 3 feet in height and prefer a well-draining soil mixed with inorganic material such as perlite, or you can use a succulent/cactus potting mix. Jade plants need to have at least six to eight hours of bright indirect sunlight per day to thrive. Place them in a room where you work or are creative to feel its positive energy radiate around you. They have starry blossoms that appear around the winter solstice that can be used in prosperity spells. Associated with Venus and the element of water, jade plant can be used in magick for wisdom, abundance, luck, and prosperity. Warning: It is toxic to both humans and pets.

Lucky Bamboo (Dracaena sanderiana)

Both lovely and resilient, this plant is the perfect good luck charm for your home. The funny thing is that lucky bamboo isn't a bamboo at all, but a member of the Asparagaceae family (the same family as asparagus). Traditionally, it is given as a gift to promote luck, growth, health, and good fortune. What I think is great about this plant is that it can be grown either in soil or water, and though it prefers bright indirect sunlight, it can handle some low light conditions. In feng shui, lucky bamboo can be placed in the *xun* position to promote wealth and abundance.[11] The magick of lucky bamboo can also be manifested by the number of stalks brought into your home and grouped into an arrangement:

1: Good fortune

2: Love

3: Happiness, wealth, and longevity

4: Stability, power

5: Wealth or fortune

....

11. Tania Yeromiyan, "What Is Feng Shui: A Brief Guide," Chinese Language Institute, last modified August 9, 2021, https://studycli.org/chinese-culture/what-is-feng-shui/.

6: Prosperity
7: Good health
8: Growth or wealth
9: Good fortune
10: Completeness or perfection
11: Blessings

Warning: Lucky bamboo is toxic to pets.

Moth Orchid (Phalaenopsis *spp.)*

With gorgeous blooms that grow along tall stalks that last up to four months, this variety of orchid is magickal indeed. Moth orchids like indirect sunlight but can tolerate low light conditions. In nature, they grow out from the bark of trees, so plant them in a medium of bark or moss and only water when your planting material is dry. Associated with Venus and the element of water, orchids have long been used in love spells. Use moth orchids in spells for love, lust, passion, and enchantment.

Peace Lily (Spathiphyllum wallisii)

The name alone gives a hint to the calm energy that radiates from this easy-growing houseplant. Not a true lily, peace lily is a member of the Araceae family, whose blooms are tiny flowers crowded on a fleshy stalk and often surrounded by a large, colored bract called a spathe. Plant peace lily in a rich, well-draining potting mix and be careful when watering. Peace lilies prefer being underwatered, so allow the soil to dry out before watering. Use it in magick for familial love, comforting vibes, and peace.

Spider Plant (Chlorophytum comosum)

A popular houseplant, the spider plant has thin, arched foliage with a spider-like appearance complete with "pups" that hang from the mother plant as if dangling from a web. Plant it in a well-draining potting mix and place in an area of indirect sunlight. Because it does not like to be too wet nor too dry, water just as top of the soil is dry to the touch. Spider plants become potbound easily and will need to be repotted approximately every two years. Hang spider plants in the bedroom as a symbol of fertility, or hang one near your front entrance to filter away negative energy. This plant is associated with Mercury and the element of air and can be used in spells for protection, spiritual boundaries, fertility, and abundance. Warning: Spider plant is toxic to both people and pets.

Magick under Glass

I was gifted a very old and beautiful hand-blown glass cloche from the estate of my magickal mentor, Stella. Its glass was warbled and thick, and I knew as I carried it carefully into my home that I would cherish it forever. Stella is one of the people who shaped me into the Witch I am today. She was a healer, an herbalist, a powerful hedgewitch, and a friend. And though she passed thirty-five years ago, I still miss her every day.

The old bell jar was with me for years. It sat on my altar as a symbol of wisdom and held the treasures I would find that I knew, with every fiber of my being, were messages from Stella intended for me during times of doubt or insecurity. One bright, chill spring morning, as I dug out comfrey that had spread beyond its boundaries and worried over a decision that would have a profound impact on me and my family, I noticed blue feathers scattered underneath a pink spirea bush. Pushing aside the brush, I saw the delicate skull of a Steller's jay who had lost his life at that very spot. I gently picked up the skull and smiled as memories of Stella on a similar spring morning filled my head.

"Ah," Stella had said, as she blew off the debris from a small skull she had discovered. "See what I found."

"A bird's skull. How beautiful." I ran a finger over the delicate find.

"It's a Steller's jay. Poor dear." She clucked her tongue. "Steller's jays are clever birds who know a good opportunity when one opens up to them."

"Apparently that one didn't." I chuckled.

"Ah, but the sweet soul took a chance, Monica." She bent over and buried the skull where it was found. "Is life really worth living if we don't take chances every once in a while?" She stood and wiped her hands on her apron. "That's why I like Steller's jays—they're fearless and resourceful." She smiled. "We should all be more like a Steller's jay."

As I looked at the skull, I knew it was a message from Stella. *Be resourceful and fearless, Monica,* I thought. I took the skull into the house, gently cleaned it, and tucked it under the cloche. I did this every time I found a meaningful treasure, and as the years passed, it became a beautiful shrine to the wisdom of my friend.

But alas, sometimes accidents happen, and though they are not all life-altering and do not necessarily leave big scars, they can still hurt. I was cleaning up around my altar. You know how it is—incense ash and collected dust, spilled salt and droplets of oil tend to happen when one has a working altar. And as I wiped away several months of accumulated grime, somehow my arm hit the cloche just right, and the next thing I remember was the sound of shattering glass. My kids heard the commotion and ran inside to find me crying as I gathered the broken shards.

They sweetly helped gather the pieces. Josh found the super glue and attempted to glue the cloche back together as my younger two helped me clean bits of glass from the treasures that it once held. Of course, the super glue wasn't enough to fix my beloved cloche, and I ended up tucking away the remnants in a box in the attic. Over the years, my family has purchased several cloches for me as way to make up for the loss. And though nothing can replace the one that was Stella's, each one is truly a testament to the love that surrounds me.

The Glass Bell Jar

A glass cloche (or bell jar) is a wonderful addition to your indoor Witch's garden, as it holds warmth and provides a constant level of humidity for plants that thrive in tropical conditions. And because the closed environment acts as a mini ecosystem, it is low maintenance.

Bell-shaped glass jars with open bottoms were invented around 400 years ago in Italy as a way to prevent frost damage and promote early growth for outdoor spring plantings. They quickly became popular with gardeners in France, Britain, and the Netherlands and eventually made their way to the United States. Originally, only the wealthy could afford these utilitarian works of art because glass was far too expensive for the average person. It wasn't until the cost of manufacturing glass became cheaper that bell jars were found in the typical cottage garden. Even today, glass garden cloches meant for outdoor gardening can be very expensive for most gardeners. PVC versions that include a vent for temperature regulation are a cheaper alternative that will last you for years with proper care.

But if you're looking to bring a vintage garden aesthetic indoors, you can purchase relatively inexpensive thin-glassed cloches at any craft or home store. Besides keeping your indoor plants under glass, they are wonderful for grouping seasonal décor or your favorite witchy collections. Faery gardens too can be designed to be a miniature world under glass. I have a large glass bowl with an ornate glass lid (also known as a closed terrarium) that sits on my dining room table (a.k.a. seasonal altar) that houses a tiny graveyard with moss and ferns, and I have to admit, sometimes I gaze through the glass and imagine myself in that little gothic landscape. A miniature faery garden is a nice way to bring the spirits of nature indoors or give your indoor garden an enchanting vibe.

Plants that thrive in closed terrariums or under a cloche are those that require warmth and high humidity. Soft-stemmed tropical plants, ferns, and carnivorous plants all do well under glass. Depending on the size of your cloche, individually potted plants can be set under the dome, or you can plant them in the shallow dish that is sometimes provided with cloches or purchase one that fits under your cloche.

Here are few plants to consider:

African Violet (*Saintpaulia ionantha*): Spiritual growth, faery energy

Baby Tears (*Soleirolia soleirolii*): Peace, tranquility, hearth and home

Begonia (*Begonia* spp.): Balance, harmony, gratitude

Fern (*Tracheophyta* spp.): Healing, renewal, protection

Flame Violet (*Episcia cupreata*): Spiritual growth, faery energy

Ivy (*Hedera* spp.): Protection, growth, fidelity, love, and healing

Moss (*Bryophyta* spp.): Faery energy, luck, prosperity

Nerve Plant (*Fittonia albivenis*): Generosity, self-awareness, calm

Orchid (Orchidaceae spp.): Love, passion, enchantment

Philodendron (*Philodendron* spp.): Rejuvenation, forgiveness, adaptation

Polka-Dot Plant *(Hypoestes phyllostachya)*: Happiness, faery energy, peace

Venus Flytrap (*Dionaea muscipula*): Strength, courage, protection

Planting a closed terrarium or cloche base is simple but does require several important layers to keep your plants healthy and happy. Place a handful of clean pebbles in a clean cloche base for drainage purposes. Follow this with a piece of terrarium mesh that fits your base to separate your drainage layer from your soil layer. Add a single layer of activated charcoal to help absorb pathogens. Then add a layer of a terrarium substrate mix (a planting medium available online or in any gardener's supply store).

Remove the plants from their pots, gently removing any excess soil, and plant them into the substrate mix. Add decorative pieces, stones, driftwood, and the like. Place the cloche lid over the plants, and situate the cloche in an area that provides bright indirect light. Water using a misting bottle approximately once a month.

Faery Garden Cloche

This tiny faery garden is designed to welcome the spirits of nature into your home.

You will need:

- Cloche or closed terrarium of your choice
- Clean pebbles
- Terrarium mesh

- Activated charcoal
- Terrarium substrate mix
- Planting material (try moss, ferns, ivy, and/or flame or African violets)
- Paper and pen

Follow the instructions on the previous page for planting. If you're wanting to give your faery garden an enchanted feel, add a pebble path or miniature pieces that fit your aesthetic. Consider tiny resin mushrooms, toads, or snails. Or how about miniature garden tools and twig furniture?

If you're interested in adding this to your altar, instead of the kitschy accessories, add crystals, acorns or hazelnuts etched with sacred symbols, bones, or other natural witchy finds.

On a piece of paper, draw the seven-pointed faery star or a protective sigil or symbol of your choice and place your planted cloche on top of it.

Place your hands over the cloche and say something like this:

As darkness falls and cold sets in
I ask for protection for those who dwell within
Home and hearth and kith and kin
Spirits of nature, watch over us until spring begins

Chapter 32
Stir the Pot

It is in the month of November that one finds me in the kitchen. As the rain falls in glossy sheets across the landscape, I remake old family favorite recipes and allow my mind to linger on the stories of my ancestors. Pulling raspberries from my freezer for my grandmother's tart recipe, I think of my grandparents and great-aunts and great-uncles who worked the family raspberry farm—the echo of laughter as they picked, the straw hats and berry-stained aprons they wore, gossiping about neighbors in hushed tones. As I add dried herbs to a stew recipe Stella had given me, I think of her in her rubber boots and wool sweater with dirt under her fingernails and twigs in her hair, always teaching, inspiring, and seeing her defeats as learning opportunities. The pumpkins and winter squash that I take from their storage bins to turn into soup or other hearty fare bring to mind the hands of each family member that lovingly saved and passed down the seeds, and I am thankful for their generosity and care.

This is my idea of a proper Thanksgiving, connecting food to family and friends who have influenced and shaped me as person. It is honoring them in quiet contemplation. It is memorializing them through recollection and the recipes they passed down at my own slow pace.

We all have traditions that have influenced the way we celebrate the Wheel of the Year—that favorite recipe that is always made, those silly activities that are repeated within your family or friend group, those get-togethers that become ritual. In our home a favorite tradition is B-movie night, when everyone drops the DVD of their favorite horrible B-movie into a bag. Someone is elected to draw one, and we all are forced to watch it together. We eat plenty of snacks and heckling is encouraged, but leaving the room because your movie wasn't chosen is definitely not allowed. I always pick the 1973 original musical *The Wicker Man*. And I love to watch the twisted faces of my family when it's chosen. And it's chosen a lot. This is an example of how tradition is born; it links us together and creates a closeness between friends and family members. Tradition gives us a sense of belonging. Of course, food is a big part of our traditions. Sharing special meals draws us together and is a way of connecting us to our past and building memories for the future.

Both magick and medicine, food is linked to many of our folk beliefs. I think of the young women who eagerly used their apple peels to divine who their true love may be, the patterns in tea leaves scattered on the bottom of porcelain cups thought to forecast one's future, and salt thrown over a shoulder to preserve one's luck. The gathering and production of food were done as ritual with customs, blessings, and prayers to give thanks to the spirit of the plant (or animal) that was harvested. Over wood-burning hearths where cauldrons gently rolled, many more cultural and spiritual traditions began. Recipes, medicine, folk remedies, and simple rites were passed from hearth keeper to hearth keeper.

The Magick of Food

November is the perfect month for rediscovering the magick of food. Seek out family recipes and let the taste, scent, and texture reconnect you to your own past traditions. Or consider amping up outdated recipes with fresh ingredients to create new traditions with family or friends.

Here are a few common ingredients whose magick was intertwined with daily life:

Chili (Capsicum *spp.*)

Chili peppers add that touch of heat that give recipes an extra kick. Chili peppers are packed with vitamins and antioxidants, so adding them to your diet has many health benefits, including supporting bone health, reducing inflammation, and helping support the immune system. With more than thirty species in the pepper family and even more varieties, the level of spice is measured using the Scoville heat scale. Mild peppers such as sweet banana range from 1 to 500 Scoville heat units, while a scorcher like 'Carolina Reaper' can reach 2.2 million.

As chilis are featured in many cuisines around the world, is it any wonder they are steeped in folklore? In India, seven green chili peppers and a lemon are hung outside of a home or shop to appease the goddess of poverty and misery, Alakshmi, and bring good luck instead. In many cultures, chili peppers are known as a cleanser for bad luck, bewitchment, and the evil eye. If a friend asks for a pepper to use in a favorite recipe, never hand it to them directly, but instead place it on their table so as to not bring discord to the friendship.

With the chili's connection to Mars and the element of fire, it's prefect for adding to a romantic meal to stir up some passion. To provide a little extra power to your spellwork, add chili powder or chili oil. Use chili in spells for hex-breaking, protection, lust, fidelity, and fertility.

Line of Fire Protection Spell

To protect your Witch's kitchen, line chili peppers along your kitchen windowsill. Use your power hand to activate your own personal power by tracing the symbol of Mars in front of the window. As you do so, say something like this:

> Power above
> Power within
> Negativity out
> Love and joy in

Garlic (Allium sativum)

First cultivated in both Egypt and India over 5,000 years ago, garlic is among the oldest food crops. Well known even in ancient times for its healing and restorative power, garlic was used in both medicinal and spiritual practices.

Native to central Asia, garlic is a bulbous flowering plant and is closely related to onions, leeks, and chives. Its intense flavor and added health benefits, including boosting the immune system and antibiotic properties, make it a popular ingredient in many cuisines.

Garlic has a long history of protective uses in the household. It was said that midwives hung garlic in the birthing rooms to safeguard newborn babies from malevolent spirits. Sometimes garlic bulbs were added to the last sheaf of grain and hung in the home for protection. To prevent illness, cloves of garlic were tucked under pillows or hung in bedrooms.

Associated with Mars and the element of fire, garlic can be used as a ward for psychic vampires, to guard against negativity, or in spells for passion. Hang garlic braids in your kitchen to protect your home from negative energy. Sacred to the goddess Hecate, garlic-infused foods can be added to meals associated with her worship. Leave garlic at the crossroads or at an altar dedicated in her honor.

Braided Garlic

Braided garlic is a lovely (and useful) way to add a touch of old-world enchantment to your home. I braid all my garlic and just snip the bulbs from the braid when I need to add a few cloves to add to a recipe. But I always make a small garlic braid that hangs in my kitchen all year long for protection. I sometimes tuck other protective herbs into the braid, such as sage and rosemary, for an added magickal oomph.

You will need:

- 10 to 12 intact bulbs of softneck garlic
- Twine

Gently rub the garlic bulbs to remove excess dirt and trim up any shaggy roots. Pick out your three largest bulbs and lay them down with one in the center with its leaves pointing toward you. The other two should lay to the right and to the left with their leaves crisscrossed to form an X over the center bulb.

You may want to secure them with a piece of twine tied around the base of the three bulbs.

Lay a fourth bulb in line with the center bulb. Lay two more bulbs to the left and to the right with their leaves lined up with the previous bulbs' crisscross layout.

Begin braiding by taking both sets of leaves from the right and move them under the center leaves. Repeat this with the leaves to the left. Continue two more times.

Add three more bulbs and braid in the same manner as above. Continue this process until you have braided in all your garlic. When finished, continue braiding the remaining leaves and tie off with twine.

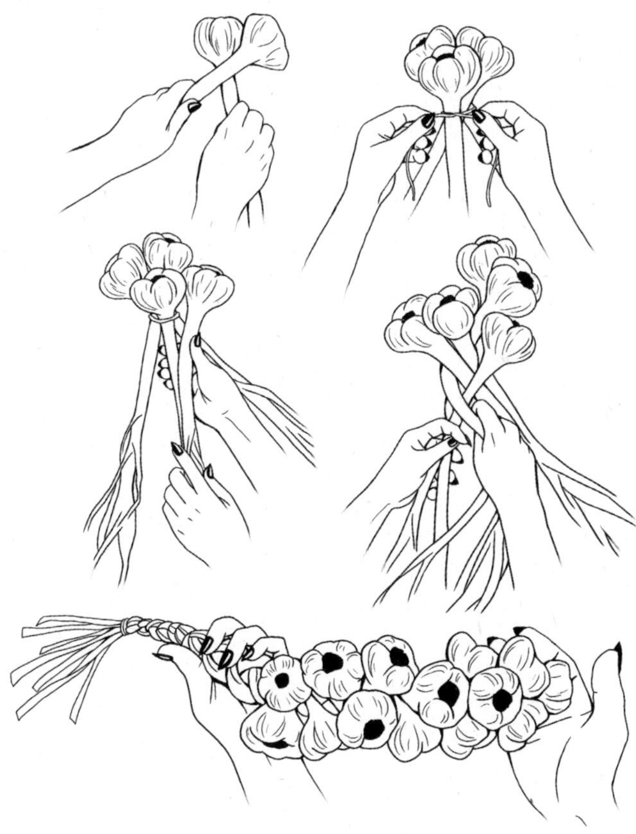

Olive Oil

Originating across many cultures throughout the Mediterranean and Middle East, olive oil has been used in food, medicine, and rites since ancient times. Extra-virgin olive oil is made from pure cold-pressed olives, which gives it a greenish tint and herbaceous taste. Regular olive oil, which is paler in color and has a more neutral flavor, is a blend that includes both cold-pressed and processed oils. Olive oil is rich in healthy monounsaturated fats and contains antioxidants, which makes it a wonderful multipurpose cooking oil.

Italian superstition dictates that spilling olive oil is considered bad luck. Olives or meals laced with olive oil were thought to increase sexual potency, and olive branches hung in the home or near the chimney kept evil from entering. Connected with the sun and the element of fire, olive oil can be used as a carrier oil for anointing blends for protection, peace, lust, and healing.

Abramelin Oil

This ceremonial anointing oil is used by several magickal traditions. The recipe was found in the grimoire *The Book of Abramelin*, originally written in the fourteenth century by Abraham von Worms and later translated by S. L. MacGregor Mathers.[12] This recipe is a variation of the 1897 Mathers version.

You will need:

- 2 parts cinnamon stick
- 2 parts myrrh resin
- 1 part galangal powder (Thai ginger)
- 8 parts olive oil

12. S. L. MacGregor Mathers, trans., *The Book of the Sacred Magic of Abramelin the Mage*, 2nd ed. (London: John M. Watkins, 1900), 76–77.

Use a mortar and pestle to grind the first 3 ingredients. Add it to olive oil and store the blend in an amber bottle. Use it to invoke deity, to anoint candles or tools for spellwork, and to enhance spiritual knowledge.

Sage (Salvia officinalis)

Sage is a Mediterranean herb with downy gray-green leaves that grows up to 2 feet tall. With softly colored tubular flowers that grow on spikes, this member of the mint family is a favorite for pollinators. Used to strengthen memory, ease digestion, and ease the effects of the cold or flu, sage is packed with nutrients and well known for its antibacterial, antifungal, antiviral, and antioxidant properties. This highly aromatic herb is commonly used to infuse flavor into dishes with high fat content, including hearty meat dishes, soups and stews, and bread.

Sage was used by ancient Romans to clean teeth and gums, and both Egyptians and Romans used sage to preserve meat and to promote fertility. In household folklore, sage leaves under the doormat were said to protect against ghosts. It was said that if the sage in the garden withered, it was a sign that sickness would befall the home. It was also used as a cure for warts, which may be due to its antibacterial properties. An old English saying dictated that eating sage during the month of May would grant immortality. This purifying herb associated with Jupiter and the element of air can be used in magick for wisdom, longevity, communication, and protection.

Sage and Lavender All-Purpose Cleaning Spray

Vinegar is a natural cleanser that is safer and better for the environment than commercial cleaners. Infuse it with sage and lavender for antibacterial and antifungal properties and to cleanse built-up negative energy and add loving vibes.

You will need:

- 2–4 fresh sage leaves
- 1 teaspoon lavender buds

- ½ cup distilled white vinegar
- 16-ounce glass spray bottle
- 2 cups water
- Sage essential oil (optional)
- Lavender essential oil (optional)

Infuse sage leaves and lavender buds in ½ cup vinegar for approximately 10 to 14 days.

When ready, strain out the herbs and add the infused vinegar and the water to a spray bottle. Optionally, add an additional 10 drops each of sage and lavender essential oils.

Giving Thanks with a Dumb Supper

I've never been a fan of the traditional American Thanksgiving. Not only because of the highly diluted history attached to the holiday, but because the end of November seems like a poor choice for a harvest festival. By that time, thoughts of Yule are already simmering, and if I'm being completely honest, half of my house is already decorated for the midwinter festivities.

As I already mentioned, November, for me, is about quiet contemplation. It is listening to the sound of rain on the roof and sipping herbal tea. It's the crackling of the fire in the woodstove and slow food cooked with intention, love, and gratitude for those who came before me. So it is during this month of darkness and reflection I find the perfect setting for a solitary dumb supper.

Dumb suppers have a long history in Southern, Ozark, and Appalachian traditions, but the roots stretch all the way back to the English love of divination games. Dumb (mute) suppers were held by young women with backward meals and settings in the hope that as the clock struck midnight, the spirits of their husbands-to-be might join them. Over time, dumb suppers evolved to soulful, silent memorializations of the dearly departed typically celebrated near Samhain.

This is something I do on my own, so my husband is expected to treat himself to dinner and a late movie. I never theme my dinner but plan the meals based on special memories or handed-down recipes. I set my table with the "good" dishes and wear something that makes me feel pretty. Per tradition, I set my table backward, meaning the silverware and glasses are set on the opposite side decorum dictates. I light a candle and leave an item at the place setting of each of my dearly departed guests that represents them in some way. I also place a handwritten thank-you note at each of their place settings. Before serving my meal in reverse (dessert first), I bow to each of my settings as a quiet welcome. At midnight, I eat and savor each bite, each memory, each person who made a mark on my life. For me this is a private and sacred ritual—no divining the future nor attempting any type of spirit communication. This is me giving thanks to those who came before me; I'm a better human because they existed.

To make a dumb supper part of your own tradition, remember these guidelines:

Dumb refers to "mute," so there is no talking allowed. The menu is up to you. Try meaningful or favorite recipes. If inviting guests, be sure they clearly understand the concept, and welcome them in silence.

Lay out table settings in reverse. Set a place at the head of the table for the dearly departed. Avoid electrical lights while dining. Use candles or lanterns to set the mood. Make sure to light a candle at the head of the table in recognition of the honored spirits.

At midnight, serve the meal in reverse order: dessert, main course, then appetizer. If using this time for divination, do so in silence. Was an apparition sensed in the empty seat? What messages did they share? Write them down.

If you are sending messages to your dearly departed, have each guest write them on slips of paper and one-by-one go to the seat at the head of the table. They may either be burned in a small lit cauldron or just placed at the setting to be burned later.

When ready, acknowledge or thank the head of the table in your own way. Guests are to depart in silence. Extinguish the candle at the head of the table and clear the table. Meals set up for dearly departed can be saved as leftovers for another meal or ritually disposed of as you see fit.

Chapter 33
Herbs of November

Darkness has settled and we may find ourselves tucked up in a cozy nook with a hot cup of tea. For that reason, hearth and home are the focus of November's herb selection. These herbs reflect warmth, healing, abundance, and protection.

Clove (*Syzygium aromaticum*)

Planet: Jupiter

Element: Fire

Energy: Masculine

Deities: Apollo, Oya

This fragrant evergreen tree from Indonesia grows up to 40 feet tall with clusters of tiny blooms that gather at the tips. It is the unopened flower buds that we use is the kitchen today. Cloves are full of vitamins and minerals, including manganese, essential for building strong bones and brain health. Clove trees grow in zones 11 to 12, require full sun, and prefer well-draining, fertile, loamy soil.

A purifying herb, clove can be burned as incense before a ritual or used to drive away negative energy in your home. According to folklore, carrying clove upon yourself will draw love to you. Use it in magick for protection, purification, love, healing, and focus.

Protective Pomander

Bright, citrusy oranges studded with protective clove and cinnamon are the perfect good-luck charm and make wonderful Yuletide gifts. Add a gold ribbon for hanging or place them in bowls to enjoy their uplifting scent.

You will need:

- Toothpick
- Whole oranges
- Whole cloves
- Ground cinnamon
- Ribbon (optional)

Use a toothpick to pierce holes in any pattern around whole oranges. Place whole cloves into the piercings. Dust with cinnamon and add the optional ribbon for hanging. Pomanders take several weeks to dry.

Elderberry (*Sambucus* spp.)

Planet: Venus

Element: Water

Energy: Feminine

Deities: Hel, Holda, Venus, Hilde

The elder tree is a small tree that grows along country paths and along hedgerows. The European elderberry (*Sambucus nigra*) grows taller (up to 20 feet) than its American cousin (*Sambucus canadensis*), but both bear clumps of sweet-smelling white flowers in the spring and deep blue berries that hang in massive clumps during the late summer and early autumn months. There is also a red variety (*Sambucus racemosa*) that produces berries that are slightly toxic, and of course, there are many other cultivars available at your local nursery or garden center that have been hybridized as ornamental shrubs or for maximum fruit production.

This bent but formidable tree, which imbues the magick of the Crone, leads us through the dark half of the year in more ways than one. The berries of the elder tree, which are harvested in early fall, are rich in vitamin C and chemical compounds called anthocyanidins, which makes syrups and tea made from elderberry a powerful medicine for combating wintertime colds and flus.

Elder guards the gateway to the Otherworld, and meditating under her branches brings you closer to the land of fae. Never take from the elder without asking the spirit of the tree kindly for a piece of her wood. Plant an elderberry in your garden to protect your property and to enjoy its delicious and healthful fruit. Use it in spells for healing, prosperity, exorcism, and protection.

Elderberry Tea

This earthy tea blend warms the soul on cool November evenings.

You will need:

- 4 parts dried elderberries
- 2 parts dried cinnamon
- 1 part dried nettle

Blend the ingredients together. Place the blend in a tea ball in your favorite mug. Pour boiling water into the mug, cover, and let steep for 5 minutes. Remove the tea ball and enjoy. Add honey or cream to taste (optional).

Hops (*Humulus lupulus*)

Planet: Mars

Element: Air

Energy: Masculine

Deity: Ninkasi

Common hops are a climbing perennial bine (vining stem), sometimes called the brewer's companion, whose flowers are a key ingredient in modern beer making. Growing hops for your own home brewing or for the sedative qualities of the cone-shaped flowers has become quite popular due to their easy care. Growing up to 25 feet and weighing twenty pounds or more, they require a strong trellis, but because they are vining stems, they will die back to the ground every winter. Plant in full sun in rich, well-draining soil. The plants will produce copious hop flowers by the second year. Grow them in zones 5 to 9.

Use hops in tea to relieve anxiety and digestion and to aid sleep. Hop-infused water can be used as a hair rinse. It's also great in salves for anti-inflammatory and antioxidant qualities and to relieve dry, itchy skin. Commonly used in dream magick, hop blooms can be added to your dream pillows or in magickal tea blends. Use them in spells for sleep, dreamwork, and healing.

Energy-Clearing Bath Soak

To clear away negative residual energy, try this bath soak recipe.

You will need:

- 4 cups Epsom salts
- ½ cup baking soda
- 1 cup melted coconut oil
- ¼ cup dried hops
- ¼ cup dried lemon balm
- ¼ cup dried sage
- 30 drops lavender oil

Mix all the ingredients together. Store the salts in a glass jar and sprinkle 1 cup into your bath.

Pumpkin (*Cucurbita* spp.)

Planet: Moon

Element: Water

Energy: Feminine

Deities: Lunar deities

The pumpkin is a vining plant in the gourd family native to North America and believed to be one of the earliest domesticated crops. A versatile and important food, the pumpkin is high in vitamins A and C, potassium, fiber, and beta-carotene and is wonderful in both sweet and savory dishes. Pumpkins grow well in zones 3 to 9 and prefer full sun and well-composted soil. Because they need lots of room to spread, plant pumpkins near the edge of the garden and direct the vines away from other plants. Some varieties, like 'Hooligan' or 'Sugar Pie', can be easily trellised if you have limited space.

Full of seeds, pumpkins are the perfect representation of abundance, growth, and new possibilities, and when carved, they become protective wards for the home. Carving pumpkins is a tradition that originated with the Celts, who carved turnips as defensive lanterns. Try carving a pumpkin with protective symbols to light up the darkness as the veil thins or hollow out a large pumpkin as a cauldron for autumnal spells and rituals. Use pumpkin in magick for abundance, fertility, growth, new beginnings, wishes, and protection.

Pumpkin Seed Wish Spell

Draw symbols of growth, abundance, and wisdom on three pumpkin seeds. Take your three seeds to any flowing water source near you (creek, river), and contemplate how these words pertain to you. As you toss each seed in the water, say something like this:

> Seed for the Maiden—allow growth to begin
> Seed for the Mother—manifestation comes from within
> Seed for the Crone—may I be as wise as she
> Seeds of new birth—blessed be

Rowan (*Sorbus* spp.)

Planet: Sun

Element: Fire

Energy: Masculine

Deities: The Dagda, Thor, Brighid, Pan, Vulcan

Rowan (or mountain ash) grows in the forest openings of the upper elevations near my home, and foraging for their berries (pomes) in the autumn is a favorite activity. Bitter raw, they are best enjoyed cooked and are great in jams and jellies, when pickled, or in alcoholic beverages. Medicinally, they provide many nutrients, including high amounts of vitamin C, and may boost the immune system, aid in respiratory function, and aid in digestion.

Rowan is a small tree that grows well in full sun to partial shade. It has compound pinnate leaves and clusters of creamy flowers in the spring, which turn to orange-red pomes by autumn. The berries, left on the trees, will attract birds (especially thrush, robin, and waxwing) well into winter.

A symbol of death and rebirth, rowan was used on funeral pyres and planted in cemeteries to protect the dead from evil spirits. Planting near entrances or on either side of the garden gate is said to protect the inhabitants of the home from misfortune. Twigs tied with red thread to make a solar cross work as a protective talisman that we can use to remind us of our own inner strength during the darkest days. As it's a faery tree, its wood was used to make walking sticks to protect travelers and to make cradles for babies. Use rowan in magick for protection, clarity, healing, psychic powers, and success.

Sacred Wood Bundle

Gathering twigs and bundling them together for your sacred fire is something that can be done all year long. Establish your magickal intention and pick your wood accordingly. Here is one for protection using rowan.

Gather three twigs from each of the following trees: rowan, oak, maple, and alder. Tie each end with red twine.

As you wrap the ends, repeat something like this:

Sacred wood, I bind thee tight
To bring protection and insight
Bind thee tight and bind thee well
To bring enchantment to this spell

Around the Garden

To-Do List for November

In a lot of regions, there is still time for some of you to collect seeds for next year's planting. As the weather chills in colder zones, fill up those bird feeders for our feathered friends to help get them through the winter months. Remember, you can pot up herbs such as parsley, sage, and rosemary that might not survive outdoors and bring them inside for continuous use. You might also want to try potting up some garlic cloves for fresh garlic chives to enjoy in recipes all winter long. This is also a wonderful time to start wintertime-blooming favorites such as amaryllis and paper whites for lovely flowers by the winter holidays. Your gardening tools are going to last longer with a little maintenance; it's time to clean, sharpen, and oil up garden tools for storage..

In warmer zones, continue to practice succession planting to maximize your harvest and trim flowering trees once the blooms have faded.

Grow Your Magickal Knowledge

Add favorite indoor plants to your garden BOS. What magick do they hold for you?

Try stirring up some kitchen witchery. If you are planning on making Yule gifts for your witchy friends or family, you may want to consider these:

- Fire starters made from beeswax poured into a lined muffin tin. Add dried herbs, spices, or wood to suit your intended magickal purposes.
- Hand-burned wooden spoons. Sketch (or stencil) simple witchy designs and go over them with a woodburning tool.

- A small collection of creatively packaged seeds that you collected from your garden.
- Homemade magickal incense or tea blends, salves, or tinctures.
- Sacred wood bundles or smoke-cleansing bundles.
- Protective pomanders.
- Dream pillows.
- Homemade spell candles or cauldron tapers.

DECEMBER

Blessed is the Witch whose green fire lights up the darkest nights.

DECEMBER CORRESPONDENCES

Nature Spirits: The Fates, the Norns

Colors: Red, black, green

Herbs and Flowers: Mistletoe, ivy, poinsettia, narcissus

Scents: Geranium, frankincense, myrrh

Stones: Onyx, turquoise, topaz, serpentine

Trees: Holly, fir, pine

Animals: Horse, elk, bear, mouse

Birds: Owl, robin, wren, rook

Deities: Hathor, Frau Holle, Odin, Saturn, Osiris, Hecate

Zodiac: Sagittarius, Capricorn

Work spells for renewal, regeneration, divination, peace, prosperity, love, and strength.

Chapter 34
Winter Delights

The earth keeps her promises. But admittedly, doubt always creeps up on me in the month of December. For it feels like the darkness will never lift, and I sometimes wonder if the land can recover from the killing hand of winter.

"Patience, dear one." The words of my mentor, Stella, reverberate in my head. "Transformation takes time. In the meantime, we must look for other sources of light."

To busy myself as the darkness encroaches and the wind and freezing temperatures enforce feelings of loneliness and isolation, I find joy sparked from little things: the glow of candlelight in my window, moonglow breaking through the cracks in the clouds. I kindle the light within myself as well, as crafts that have been set aside throughout the year spark new interest. You may find me curled up in a chair, happily crocheting yet another hat, or engaged in pyrography by burning bees and flowers into wooden spoons or boxes. This is also the time of year I create herbal blends, brews, and infusions with the plant material I have dried throughout the growing season to help chase the darkness away. The scent of the herbs always takes me back to summer, when my world was bright and alive with the humming of nature at its pinnacle. It can be difficult, but we have to remember that light is born from darkness in December when many of us feel winter's isolation the deepest. Yule comes to us as a promise that the light is indeed inching back, minute by minute, and one day spring will return.

But in the meantime, if you are a Witch like me who can't keep out of the garden even during the chilliest of days, let's take a look at some season-extending gardening techniques so you can enjoy healthful garden delights well into the dark days of winter.

Under Cover

There are so many styles of cold frames designed to enhance your winter gardening by insulating the growing environment and thus lengthening your gardening season. But my favorite has to be the simple straw bale cold frame because it's a temporary structure that requires absolutely no building skills and can be put together in minutes. Not only can it be used to grow fresh greens throughout the winter, but it can be put to use in the garden all season long.

Spring: Straw bale cold frames can be used to sow early spring vegetables such as peas, greens, and radishes. They are also handy for hardening off seedlings that were started indoors or in a greenhouse.

Summer: Recycle the bale to use as a straw bale garden (yes, you can grow plants in them). Use the straw from wasted straw bales as mulch or to add it to your compost.

Autumn: You can place straw bales around your existing autumn vegetables to protect them from early frost.

Winter: If you don't have room to cold-stratify spring-blooming bulbs in your refrigerator, use a straw bale cold frame to do the work. Place pots of planted bulbs into the frame and allow them to chill during the winter months outdoors. Straw bales set around tender herbs such as rosemary, lavender, and artichokes provide insulation to help get them through the cold months. And of course, straw bale cold frames can be used to extend your gardening season.

Hay versus Straw

People tend to use the terms *hay* and *straw* interchangeably when they are actually two different things. Hay is the cutting of a whole grassy plant such as timothy or alfalfa. It will contain the leaves, stems, and seedheads of the grass and is intended for animal feed. Straw, on the other hand, is the stem cuttings from cereal crops such as wheat or barley. They contain few to no seedheads and are intended for animal bedding, farming use, or garden use.

The problem with using hay in the garden comes down to the seedheads. If you use hay as mulch, you will most likely have grass sprouting wherever it is used. So always ask for straw, as most farm and garden centers carry both, and you do not want to accidently plant grass in your garden bed.

How to Make a Straw Bale Cold Frame

Essentially a mini greenhouse, straw bale cold frames are basically a box made from straw bales with an old window or poly sheeting stapled to a wooden frame as a lid. If you are making a cold frame for winter gardening, it is best to start this project in early autumn.

You will need:

- Straw bales
- Old windows or a piece of 6-mil polyethylene sheeting on a frame made of 1-by-2-inch lumber

How many straw bales you will need really depends on how big you want your cold frame. Arrange your straw bales on bare soil in a sunny location in a rectangular pattern. Add 4 to 6 inches of good compost. Add your starts.

To top it, you can use one or more old windows or 6-mil poly sheeting stapled to a frame made from 1-by-2-inch lumber.

These are a few things to consider when using a cold frame:

Ventilation: Especially in the late autumn months, the temperature can rise, causing your plants to overheat. Use a brick to prop one end of the window frame up or remove it completely for a couple of hours.

Watering: During the autumn months, you will need to water regularly. Over the winter, you can reduce your watering to once every few weeks.

Snow: Snow is a great insulator, but it is important to remove it from your glass or poly sheeting lid to prevent blocking the sunlight.

Low Hoop Tunnel

Another easy option for winter gardening is to make a low hoop tunnel using row cover (garden felt). Low tunnels can push spring four to six weeks forward by increasing air and soil temperatures, and they protect autumn and winter crops from wind, hail, and moderate freezes. You can purchase a complete kit at any DIY store or online, or follow the instructions below:

You will need:

- 33-by-40-inch metal hoop supports
- Row cover (wide enough to have 12 inches overhang on either side and on each end)
- Plastic garden clips

Place the ends of the hoops' supports directly into the soil on either side of your plantings approximately 3 feet apart. Lay the row cover over the hoops and secure it with clips. You can use rocks, bricks, or sandbags along each side and the ends to secure the garden felt to the ground.

Consider these things when using a low hoop tunnel:

- **Ventilation:** When the temperatures are above 55 degrees, open one side so your plants will not overheat.
- **Watering:** Row covers (or garden felt) allow rain through, but plan on watering every few weeks in a dry environment throughout the winter.
- **Snow:** This setup is prone to collapse under extremely snowy conditions, but a low hoop tunnel can be reinforced with a layer of 6-mil polyethylene sheeting on top of the row covering for added strength and protection.

Perfect Plants for a Winter Garden

To be a successful winter gardener, you have to grow the right plants. Those plants will look different from region to region, but for most of us living in colder hardiness zones, the plants I have listed will best tolerate the harsh weather and frigid temperatures that are associated with the winter season. Remember, winter gardens need to be started well before winter sets in (typically late July to early August). Always read your plant start's or seed packet's guidelines thoroughly for a successful winter garden.

Cabbage (Brassica oleracea *vars.*)

When picking hardy cabbage varieties for late-season gardens, look for "storage" or "overwintering" cultivars. Often growing the largest heads, they are great for making sauerkraut and can withstand temperatures to 20 degrees Fahrenheit. Try 'Late Flat Dutch' or 'Brunswick'. If you live in a region where temperatures dip below 20 degrees, consider a cold frame or low hoop tunnel for protection. Cabbage is associated with the moon and the element of water and used in magick for protection and money.

Carrots (Daucus carota)

Winter carrots are so sweet and delicious and wonderful as a snack or used in your favorite winter recipes. All carrot varieties do fine during the winter months, but you may like to try 'Bolero' or 'Napoli' for best winter hardiness. Cover the bed with a layer of straw to insulate. Carrots are associated with Mars and the element of fire. Use them in magick for love, passion, fertility, and grounding.

Collard Greens (Brassica oleracea *vars.*)

This cool-season annual sweetens after being touched by frost and is hardy to 15 degrees. It grows best in colder regions in a cold frame or low hoop tunnel but can survive without protection in zones 8 to 10. Try 'Vates' or 'Morris Heading'. Collards are associated with the moon and the element of water. Use them in magick for protection and money.

Kale (Brassica oleracea *vars.*)

Rich in vitamins and beta-carotene, kale grows sweeter after a frost, which makes it a wonderful addition to your winter garden. It is also a vegetable that is hardy enough to grow without cover in most regions, as it is hardy to -10 degrees. Try 'Lacinato' (dinosaur kale), 'Dwarf Siberian', or 'Red Russian'. Kale is associated with Mars and the element of fire and can be used in spells for protection and money.

Lettuce (Lactuca sativa)

Lettuce is cold hardy to 20 degrees, so it is best grown in a cold frame, greenhouse, or low hoop tunnel. Added to wintertime meals, it gives one a sense that spring is always near. Try 'Winter Wonderland' romaine, 'Winter Marvel', or 'Green Forest'. This watery plant is associated with the moon and can be used in magick for peace, love, and money.

Swiss Chard (Beta vulgaris *ssp.* vulgaris)

If your winters never get below 15 degrees, it's possible to overwinter swiss chard in your garden. Like many greens, it becomes sweeter after a light frost. In regions of severe cold, grow it in a cold frame or low hoop tunnel for continuous harvesting. Associated with Saturn and the element of earth, swiss chard can be used in magick for love, beauty, and money.

Turnips (Brassica rapa *ssp.* rapa)

Turnips are a cool-season crop that can be left in the ground and pulled just before the ground freezes. Use a cold frame or low tunnel for an extended season. Try 'Purple Top White Globe' or 'Just Right'. Turnips were once hollowed out with candles placed inside to chase away evil spirits that roamed when the veil between the worlds thinned. Associated with the moon and the element of earth, turnips can be used in magick for protection and endings.

Leeks (Allium porrum)

The leek is an allium, related to garlic, shallot, chive, and onion. Its sweet, mildly onion flavor is a wonderful addition to risottos, soups, egg dishes, and pasta. It is winter hardy and can withstand temperatures as low as 12 degrees. For regions that experience severe cold, mulch with straw or use a low tunnel or cold frame for protection. Try 'Blue Solaise' or 'American Flag'. Leeks are associated with Mars and the element of fire and can be used in magick for love, protection, and strength.

Leeks for Love

As the wind blows the snow about, wrap yourself up, go into your garden, and pull up a few leeks (or pick up a few from the grocery store). Upon your return, light a candle in your kitchen and invoke your favorite deity of the hearth and home. As you prepare your vegetables for a creamy leek soup (see recipe on page 360), focus on loving vibes and a special evening for two. Leeks are associated with love, and to share them with another is fortuitous indeed. Parsley and carrots are added to invoke passion, as well as bay and onion for protection. As you slowly stir the soup as it bubbles and the scent rises, filling the kitchen with its earthy goodness, chant something like this:

Stir thee with power
Wrap thee with love
Protect thee from negativity
Wrap thee with love

Bright blessings in darkness
Wrap thee with love
Surround thee with passion
Wrap thee with love

Serve the soup in red bowls in a romantic setting in front of a cozy fire and see where the night takes you.

Creamy Leek and Potato Soup

- 3 pounds leeks (about 8 leeks), chopped (use only white and pale green parts)
- 1 large carrot, chopped
- 2 celery ribs, chopped
- ½ cup butter
- 2 cups cubed potatoes, ½-inch pieces
- 1 cup white wine
- 3 cups chicken broth
- 1 bay leaf
- 2 cups half-and-half
- 1 cup fresh flat-leaf parsley leaves, chopped
- Salt and pepper to taste

Sauté the leeks, carrot, and celery in 4 tablespoons butter in a heavy pot over medium heat until softened. Add the cubed potatoes along with wine, broth, and bay leaf. Bring to a boil, then reduce heat and simmer, until vegetables are tender, about 15 minutes. Remove from heat and cool slightly before adding the half-and-half and parsley. Simmer 5 more minutes and discard bay leaf before serving. Serves 4.

Chapter 35
Deck the Halls

It is during the darkest days of the year that one is reminded to stay indoors, light a candle in the window, and hang a wreath on your door for your own protection. For during this time when the sun stands still, one has to be leery of unruly spirits that tromp through the forests looking for a home to torment. It was known, while the long nights around Yule lingered, that we must remember to pour the libations upon the Yule log to appease the household gods and set out shiny objects to distract dark elves who slip uninvited through windows and chimneys. But most importantly, we dare not answer the call of the huntsmen who ride the sky in search of souls to join them on the wild hunt.

For ancient peoples in a seasonal climate, nature's rhythm stopped as darkness engulfed the land near autumn's end. It was a frightening time when ghosts wandered, and evil was present in the howling wind and drifting snow. Aromatic smoke was used to cleanse the home of malevolent spirits, rituals were employed to entice the sun's rebirth, and offerings were left to placate wandering souls. Greens were hung not only for protection but to remind one of nature's fecundity. For with the solstice, the sun god would be reborn, and with him, the promise of spring's return.

Today, candles are lit and carols played as we adorn our homes with greens, proudly stand our holiday tree in a place of honor, and wonder if we might be lucky enough to steal a kiss from that special someone caught standing beneath the mistletoe. For some, these rites have religious connotations; for others, they are just festive traditions, passed down along with favorite holiday recipes and ornaments that have graced family trees from one generation to the next. But do we really know why a tree is brought into the home or why we hang holly and ivy? And where did the tradition of kissing under the mistletoe begin? Let's look at some of wintertide's most iconic plants and their longstanding symbolic associations to the holiday season.

Guardians of the Forest

Conifers (Pinophyta) are evergreen, needle-bearing trees that are a familiar part of our Yuletide celebrations and have played a role in many northern European wintertide festivities since ancient times. Mythologically speaking, trees, in general, served as links between this world and the supernatural, where gods and messengers could access worlds by traveling along its trunks and branches. Forests were dense, dark spaces where danger lurked, and for those who settled along their borders, it was a place of mystery and rich with symbolism as it held the secrets of the spiritual world. The oldest sanctuaries were groves of trees, where under shady branches deities were sanctified and worshipped with ecstatic dancing, feasting, and communication with the spirits of the land.

Plants that remained green all year had a special significance, especially during the darkest days of the year, for ancient peoples. It was believed the sun needed assistance to be revived, so evergreen boughs were hung above doorways and around homes. Celebrations around the winter solstice that included the hanging of evergreens can be traced back to the Egyptians, who decorated their homes with green palm rushes to symbolize life's triumph over death.[13] The Roman Saturnalia found familiar holiday trappings as well, including the adorning of evergreens, gift giving, and feasting.

In northern Europe, a Yule log was brought in and burned over the twelve days of Yule, sometimes in combination with herbs and resins, and of course, kindled with a fair share of libation to honor the household gods. The ash and bits of charcoal and wood left from the fire were truly magickal. Charred pieces of wood might be tucked in the crooks of fruit trees to ensure fertility, and the ash from the fire would be added ritually to

13. Dorothy Morrison, *Yule: A Celebration of Light & Warmth* (St. Paul, MN: Llewellyn Publications, 2000), 4.

the fields while still dormant to safeguard a fruitful harvest in the coming season. Of course, we know now that adding ash to a garden bed increases the soil's pH level, as potassium, calcium, and magnesium found within the ash are essential for plant health.

The Christian church claimed Pagan sites, raising cathedrals where holy trees once stood. The idea was that consecrating Pagan holy days to Christ would more easily convert Pagans to Christianity. Winter solstice rites soon celebrated the birth of Jesus and the evergreens that represented hope, fertility, and protection were adorned with apples and used in "miracle plays" to detail the birth and fall of humanity.

The first Christmas trees can be credited to Germany, where in the sixteenth century trees were brought into the marketplaces and small tabletop trees brought into the homes. Christmas trees were popularized in 1848 when Queen Victoria had an engraving done that featured the queen and her family around a Christmas tree, a tradition brought to England by her husband, Prince Albert, from his home in Germany.

A popular conifer found decorated in homes during the holiday season is the fir tree (*Abies* spp.), which is found in many regions around the world, grows upward of 200 feet tall, and is native to Europe, Asia, Northern Africa, and North and Central America. Among the most popular choices for holiday trees, balsam is on top for fragrance. Douglas fir is chosen for its conical shape. Fraser firs have stiff branches and are long lasting. Connected with Jupiter and the element of fire, fir boughs can be hung above entryways to ward negativity and harm from entering the home. Fir can be burned in incense, or a small branch can used as an aspergillum for blessings. Use it in magick for protection, resilience, and rebirth.

Spruce trees (*Picea* spp.) are distinguished from firs by their down-hanging cones and whorled needle placement. Spruce can be found in North America, Europe, and parts of Asia. Colorado blue spruce is a popular variety of holiday tree for its conical shape and stiff branches and because it rarely sheds its needles. Place one in the household to represent the guardian spirit of the forest. Use it in incense or in smoke-cleansing bundles to add calm to a room. Use spruce in magick for protection, renewal, and strength.

Pine trees (*Pinus* spp.) are the largest of the conifer family, with 115 species, and are native to the Northern Hemisphere, but they are now grown in most temperate and subtropical regions. Scotch pine is a popular holiday tree, like the Colorado blue spruce, for its stiff branches and because it rarely sheds its needles. Pine resin can replace frankincense, and its wood is a good replacement for palo santo. Connected to Mars and the element of air, pine can be used in magick for protection, fertility, renewal, and healing.

Protective Yule Wreath

A simple wreath of conifer greens is a lovely way to add old-fashioned Yuletide charm to a home. It is a perfect symbol of renewal, protection, and the never-ending cycle of life.

When clipping greens from conifer or evergreen plants, do so with the utmost respect to the tree or shrub.

You will need:

- Circular floral form (choose a size that best suits your home)
- Cuttings from several conifer and/or evergreen trees or shrubs (e.g., fir, cedar, spruce pine, holly, bay, eucalyptus)
- Ribbon in the color of your choice

Soak the floral foam in water for approximately 15 to 20 minutes. Trim the tree cuttings to approximately 6 inches in length. Start inserting greens around the outer edge of the floral form. Repeat along the inner edge. Use small bunches of three stems each of various evergreens and conifers to fill in the front of the wreath. Have fun and be creative—there is no wrong way to do this. When you are happy with your wreath, add a ribbon of your choice. You might also wire in cones or add holiday picks found in the floral department of any craft store.

As you hang your wreath, say,

Let this wreath be a reminder of the never-ending cycle of the seasons
With darkness there is always light; in death there is rebirth
Blessed be all friends who enter here

Hope in the Darkness

What vibrancy holly (*Ilex* spp.) has to offer in a monochromatic winter landscape! It's no wonder early Europeans thought holly special, with glossy leaves that reflect the pale winter sunlight and bright red berries that stand out against a snow-covered land. Green was the color of hope in the dead of winter when one wondered if spring would come again, and red the color of the life force that runs through us all.

To the Romans, holly was a plant of good fortune and immortality, and they used it for decoration and gift giving during their midwinter Saturnalia celebration. For the Celts, holly was a protective plant and typically grown near the home, as its spikey leaves were thought to snag evil spirits. It was also brought into the homes during the darkest days of winter, not only to shelter faery folk, who during this time would bring no harm to the inhabitants, but to provide cheer with their reflective leaves and bright red berries. And as tradition dictated, one never felled a holly tree. If you were to take a sprig into your home, you would ask the tree for permission first and, if possible, leave a piece of silver at its roots.

The Holly King is probably the most legendary image associated with the tree. He is a representation of the spirit of nature and an echo of the wild gods of a more ancient time. Robust and covered with branches and leaves, with a holly bush for a club, he is the assurance that the cycle of the seasons is ongoing. The Holly King is mirrored by the Oak King—two sides of the same coin whose roles are equally important. The Holly King resides over the dark half of the year, the season of introspection and dormancy. The Oak King rules the light half of the year, the season of growth and fecundity. The dual for supremacy is ongoing, and as winter solstice approaches, the Holly King relinquishes his reign to the Oak King.

With the spread of Christianity, holly was brought into the church and became symbolic of the crown of thorns Jesus wore at his crucifixion, with the red berries representing his blood. Associated with Mars and the element of fire, holly can be used in magick for courage, strength, luck, protection, and dreamwork.

Winter Solstice Ritual for Renewal

On the winter solstice, we bid fare-thee-well to the Holly King and raise a glass to the Oak King and the season of light. This simple ritual can be performed solitary or as a group.

You will need:

- Cauldron or firesafe container
- Sprig of holly for each participant
- Lighter or match
- Glass of favorite libation for each participant

Call the quarters in your own way. Have everyone gather around the cauldron with a sprig of holly. Have an elected member light the cauldron. Hold up your sprigs and say,

> Hail to thee, Holy King, I/we thank you for this time of dormancy
> For in darkness, we gain resiliency
> In darkness, we learn gratitude
> In darkness, we find our inner source of light

Toss your sprigs of holly into the flame and say,

> Fare-thee-well
> We honor the lessons of the season and will take them with us as the Wheel of the Year turns

Raise your full glasses and say,

Hail to thee, Oak King, I/we welcome the newborn sun and the season of illumination
For in light, we find hope
In light, growth is facilitated
In light, we discover our full potential

Pour a little of your libation onto the earth, take a drink, and say,

Hail the Oak King! Bearer of light!

Close circle in your own way.

Protection at the Door

What a strange plant mistletoe (*Viscum album*) is indeed. It's a parasitic plant that is propagated by birds. The birds eat the berries, and with luck, the seeds held in the bird's droppings will germinate in the crown of a tree. When they do, you have a plant that seems its most vibrant during the darkest time of the year, with leathery leaves that develop from all sides and mother-of-pearl berries that appear around November. To the Celts, because mistletoe grew without being connected to the earth, it was truly magickal—especially during the time of the winter solstice. On the sixth day of the moon, it is said the druids cut the mistletoe from oak trees with a golden sickle into a white cloth, never allowing the plant to touch the ground. Gratitude for the sacred plant was given through a sacrifice of oxen.[14] The plant was used for healing, protection, and fertility rites.

Mistletoe was also thought to guard against thunder and lightning and was thrown upon the roofs of houses in many areas, including Germany, where it was sometimes called "thunder broom." Also known in the ancient world for its protective powers, it was hung in entries to keep witches and dark spirits from harming the inhabitants. This folklore might explain why

14. James Frazer, *The Golden Bough: A Study of Magic and Religion* (New York: Macmillan Company, 1971), 764.

mistletoe is hung as part of our holiday tradition, but it doesn't explain where the tradition of kissing under the mistletoe originated.

Some believe the tradition began because of a tale found in Norse mythology in which mistletoe was the only weapon able to kill Frigg's beloved son, Baldur. The trickster god, Loki, deceived the blind god, Hodr, into launching a spear made from the plant and killing Baldur instantly. Though alternate, later versions of the myth give the story a happier ending, which includes blessing mistletoe as a plant of peace and love or having Frigg's tears fall onto the arrow, which turn to white berries and heal her son, the original story has him remain in the underworld even after attempts to bring him back fail due, once again, to Loki's trickery.

Most likely, kissing under the mistletoe started because of the plant's connection to fertility. The Celts believed that mistletoe could restore fertility. In areas of Germany, the plant was tied to fruit trees around the winter solstice to ensure the trees would be fertile and provide a good harvest the following season. In Austria, it was placed in the bedroom of parents wanting to conceive a child. In England, young girls would place mistletoe leaves under their pillow to dream of their future husband. And in Switzerland, mistletoe was added to bridal bouquets as a charm for a fertile union.

With the Middle Ages came the "kissing bough," which was originally greens wound together into a spherical shape with a clay figure of the infant Jesus tucked within. It was hung as part of their midwinter celebrations, and those who passed beneath would be granted a blessing from the holy child. A beloved tradition with the Tudors, kissing boughs, became large intertwining hoops covered with evergreens such as holly, ivy, bay, and mistletoe. They were hung over entries to welcome guests, which often included a kiss. The Victorians revived the tradition and added other meaningful herbs, such as lavender, rosemary, thyme, and apples. It was all about romance, as Victorian ladies stood beneath the fanciful display of greens waiting for their potential suitors to sweep them off their feet. With time, mistletoe came to stand alone. Sometimes berries were plucked with each kiss, and the fun stopped when the berries were gone, but for the most part, it has become one of those fun traditions that we take part in but never really think about why we do it. Now you know.

Make a Protective Witch Ball

During the seventeenth and eighteenth centuries, glass orbs with threads of glass within their centers were used as wards against dark spirits, illness, bad fortune, or curses. They were hung in widows, hung in trees, or propped up in pottery, and it was believed that an entity that meant harm would be attracted to the object and become caught up within the glass threads inside. Other uses may have included averting the evil eye or preventing Witches from entering the property.

Over time, glass blowers added colors and patterns, and soon their uses became more decorative than preventative. Modern incarnations include gazing balls that can be added to gardens to add spots of color and to reflect the light.

We can easily create our own magickal Witch ball by adding tinsel, dried herbs, berries, bark, crystals, or charms to clear glass ornaments. Here's a reflective one you can hang in your window or add to your Yule tree.

You will need:

- Clear glass ornament
- Red metallic acrylic paint
- Egg carton
- Bay leaf
- Cinnamon stick
- Mistletoe (plus a small sprig for embellishment)
- Black tourmaline or smoky quartz crystals or protective charms of your choice
- Tinsel (to act as the threads of glass)

Remove the metal top from the ornament and pour approximately 1 teaspoon of red metallic paint into the glass ball. Move it around to completely cover the inside. When the inside is completely covered, place the bulb upside down in an egg cartoon to drain out any remaining paint. Let it dry for 24 hours.

Add herbs, crystals, and any charms you might like, top with tinsel, and replace the metal top. Wrap a decorative ribbon around the metal top and hot-glue the additional sprig of mistletoe to the ribbon.

Chapter 36
Herbs of December

From darkness, light is born. The herbs chosen for December are a reflection of this time of celebration and ritual. They were chosen with love, renewal, and abundance in mind.

Carnation (*Dianthus caryophyllus*)

Planet: Sun

Element: Fire

Energy: Masculine

Deity: Jupiter

Native to Europe and Asia, carnations are perennial flowers that are widely grown for use as cut flowers, as they are not only bright and cheerful but also long lasting. With fringed blossoms and a light, spicy fragrance, carnations grow up to 30 inches tall and thrive in zones 7 to 9. Colors include red, pink, coral, and white, though white varieties take dye easily and are sold in a variety of brightly dyed colors to match just about any occasion.

Medicinally, they have been used to treat coughs and colds, reduce inflammation, and relieve anxiety. Carnations are surprisingly sweet and can be steeped in wine, candied, used to make a simple syrup, or used in desserts or salads. If you plan on trying carnations in your cuisine, remember to look for *edible* carnations in your local specialty grocery store or use home-grown ones.

A symbol of betrothal, carnations were part of wedding garlands and sometimes worn by women as a sign that they were taken. Carnations were also thought to be protective and were worn in buttonholes by men to prevent their demise on a scaffold. According to legend, wherever the Mother Mary's tears dropped upon seeing her son, Jesus, carrying his cross, they turned to carnations. Because of this story, the flower became connected to motherly love. In 1907, the carnation became associated with Mother's Day in the United States.

Use carnations in magick for protection, healing, love, and strength.

Color Magick with Carnations

This little trick is a great way to work with color magick and a really fun project if you have young Witchlings.

You will need:

- Clear mason jar, vase or drinking glass
- Food coloring of your choice
- White carnations (either from the garden or your local floral shop)
- Scissors

Fill your jar, vase, or glass ¾ full of water. Add at least 30 drops of food coloring. Use scissors to snip the stem of the flower diagonally. Place it into the colored water and leave it overnight. The carnation will slowly take in the color through the stem and absorb it into the petals, and it will be ready to be used in your favorite spells, charms, or rituals relying on color magick.

Camellia (*Camellia* spp.)

Planet: Moon

Element: Water

Energy: Feminine

Deities: Artemis, Luna

With beautiful peony-like blooms and evergreen foliage, varieties of camellias offer those in zones 7 to 10 flowering elegance from late fall into early spring. They prefer dappled light and well-drained soil, and with their regal beauty, they add elegance to any garden.

Camellia flowers have long been used for cosmetics in East Asia, as they're native to the region. Oil extracted from the blooms of *Camellia japonica* contains omega-6 fatty acids, which may plump the skin and promote elasticity.

The delightfully feminine bloom may be planted to attract abundance in one's life. Camellia can be used in rituals for self-love, eternal love, abundance, full moon magick, and prosperity.

Prosperity-Drawing Powder

Powders are finely ground herbs that are used in spell crafting. You can use your mortar and pestle for this recipe, but it is easiest to use an electric grinder. Use this prosperity-drawing powder to roll candles in, to trace a focal point for visualization, or to use during ritual.

You will need:

- 2 parts dried camellia flowers
- 1 part dried orange peel
- 1 part dried basil

Grind your ingredients until they form a fine powder. Store in an amber jar for up to a year.

Patchouli (*Pogostemon cablin*)

Planet: Saturn

Element: Earth

Energy: Feminine

Deities: Hedone, Pan, Freya

A tender perennial that flourishes in zones 10 to 11, patchouli is a member of the mint family and native to tropical regions of Asia. In colder hardiness zones, patchouli is a wonderful addition to a witchy container garden, as it not only provides a perfectly enchanting scent but is also easily accessible for your spell-crafting needs. Patchouli is not a long-lived plant, typically dying after only a few years, but with its shrub-like qualities, it's nice for adding contrast in a cottage-style garden.

Popular in aromatherapy, perfumes, and cosmetics, patchouli essential oil has antiseptic and anti-inflammatory properties and can be used as a natural insect repellant. Patchouli leaves can be used to brew a tea that is said to calm the nerves. Leaves can also be used in cooking; dried leaves are used as a seasoning and to flavor alcoholic beverages. Patchouli oil is used to flavor baked goods, candy, and chewing gum.

Use patchouli to get your creative juices flowing and help you birth your next project. Crumble dried leaves as a replacement for graveyard dirt in spells. Burn it in incense to release its earthy scent in spells to attract a new lover. Use it in magick for money, love, lust, and fertility.

Patchouli Money Draw Spell

Remember, money spells don't guarantee you an anonymous check appearing in your mailbox. But they may open a door as a means to access money—a side-gig or a new job, perhaps.

You will need:

- Dried patchouli leaves
- Bay leaf
- Small cauldron
- Charcoal tab

With a mortar and pestle, finely grind patchouli leaves. As you do this, focus on bringing money into your life. On your bay leaf draw a symbol, sigil, or rune of your choice for money or wealth. Light the charcoal tab and place it in small cauldron. As you place the bay leaf into the cauldron, repeat something like this:

Money flows and wealth grows

Sprinkle the patchouli into the cauldron. As the smoke rises, focus on your intention.

Juniper (*Juniperus* spp.)

Planet: Sun

Element: Fire

Energy: Masculine

Deities: Astarte, the Morrigan

A member of the cypress family, juniper is native to North America, Europe, Asia, and Africa. Junipers prefer zones 4 to 8, and when planted in the right spot, they are easy to care for. That's because these wide-spreading conifers can grow in many different climates, from alpine tundra to temperate rainforests.

Some varieties produce edible berries (female cone seeds) that can be used in desserts, in savory dishes, and to flavor drinks. Though nutrient-rich, containing high amounts of antioxidants, vitamins, and minerals, juniper is not advised in any form while pregnant, as it is also a uterine stimulate, which may increase the chance of miscarriage. Of course, juniper berries are best known for their role in the distillation of gin—it is the berry's signature "pine" note that gives the alcohol its distinctive flavor.

Juniper was hung on the door for protection from evil spirits and was said to guard against theft and sickness. Juniper wood is highly aromatic and great burned as incense for purification before ritual and to stimulate clairvoyance. Use it in magick for psychic awareness, protection, health, love, and exorcism.

Wintertide Infused Vodka

Toast the newborn sun with a brew of botanical goodness. This drink has all the spicy flavors of winter along with added citrusy notes to remind us that spring will surely come again.

You will need:

- 3 tablespoons juniper berries
- Peel of 1 orange
- Fresh sage leaf
- Sprig of fir or spruce
- 1 cinnamon stick
- 1 star anise pod
- 1 cardamom pod
- ¼ teaspoon coriander seeds
- 12 ounces vodka

In a sterilized jar, add the dry ingredients and cover with the vodka. Seal and shake the jar. Let the blend infuse for approximately 3 days. Strain with a cheesecloth and enjoy at your Yule celebration.

Poinsettia (*Euphorbia pulcherrima*)

Planet: Sun

Element: Fire

Energy: Masculine

Deities: Kali, Huitzilopochtli

As the quintessential holiday plant, poinsettia blooms are one of the most recognized emblems of Christmas. But those large, cheery red flowers are not flowers at all: they are its bracts' response to shorter winter days. Its flowers are the tiny yellow berry-like structures at the center of each leaf bract.

Native to Mexico, poinsettia was called *cuetlaxochitl* by the Aztec people. Today, it is known as *flor de nochebuena* (Flower of the Holy Night/Christmas Eve). Though introduced to the United States by Ambassador Joel Roberts Poinsett in 1825, it is Paul Ecke Jr. who is considered the father of the poinsettia industry due to his discovery of a technique that caused seedlings to branch and grow bushier.

In magick, poinsettia's bright fiery bracts remind us of sun's rejuvenation and rebirth. Use the plant in spells to kindle hope on dreary winter days. Use it in magick for renewal, joy, hope, and balance.

Yule Incense Blend

This is a wonderful blend to use for your Yule ritual.

You will need:

- 6 parts dried orange peel
- 4 parts fir needles
- 2 parts dried red poinsettia bracts
- 1 part mistletoe leaves
- 2 cinnamon sticks
- ½ part pine resin

Use a mortar and pestle to grind the ingredients together and then burn the incense over a charcoal tab in a fireproof container.

Around the Garden

To-Do List for December

If a freeze is in the forecast, move potted plants under eaves or close to the house. You can also cover them with a frost cloth or other heat-retentive blanket. Stop fertilizing, as winter is a time of dormancy, and any new growth will be harmed by below-freezing temperatures. If using a wood stove or fireplace to heat your home, use some of the ash to improve pH levels that are below 6.0 in your garden bed. Remember to check stored bulbs to make sure there is no rot. Protect tender plants with row covers.

Grow Your Magickal Knowledge

Bring evergreen and conifer cuttings into the home for protection and to symbolize resiliency and renewal. String dried orange slices and cranberries to symbolize the return of the sun. Celebrate the darkest days of the year by bringing in the light: light candles in the windows or hang twinkle lights in those dark corners. Honor our animal and feathered friends by decorating outdoor trees with nuts, apples, and suet treats. Use the solstice to reflect and set your intentions for the upcoming year.

Because the holidays can be hectic, allow yourself time for self-care. Work on ritual that allows you to recapture and honor your personal power. Meditation, ritual baths, and chakra cleansing may all be included.

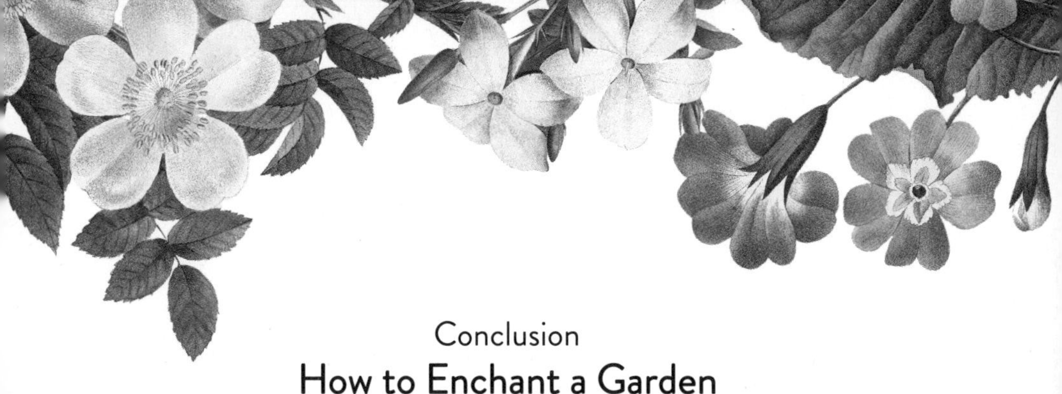

Conclusion
How to Enchant a Garden

An enchanted garden doesn't have to be that of a fairy-tale setting—no mythical creatures or talking animals required. Neither does it require sprawling fields of flowers or a thatched cottage tucked within the trees to make it magickal. What makes a garden enchanted, then? Well, dear Witch, the answer is you. Whether your garden is indoors or out, is just a few containers on a balcony, or takes up the entirety of your backyard, if it fills your soul with bliss, then it is indeed enchanted.

I hope you've enjoyed our journey together and that it inspires you to continue along the garden path. Remember to envelope yourself in the rhythms of nature, for each cycle has knowledge to share. Embrace your own illuminating light during the dormancy of winter and cultivate your intentions as spring's regenerative force releases its own green fire. Know that summer invites us to grow beyond established boundaries and explore those things we never thought possible for ourselves. And as autumn ushers in the time of the harvest, celebrate those accomplishments (big and small) that helped you grow into the person you are.

Remember, your power is a seed that lies dormant within, and our journey together through the pages of this book is intended to coax you to plant them deep and well. So plant those seeds, dear Witch, and allow *your* magick to bloom.

Blessed be as you continue along the enchanted garden path.

Appendix

Herbal Magickal Properties

African Violet: Spiritual growth and working with the fae

Agrimony: Reversal spells, protection, healing, and restorative spells

Alfalfa: Money magick, prosperity, longevity, and good fortune

Aloe Vera: Luck, money, healing, and protection

Angel's Trumpet: Seduction, working with the Dark Goddess, divination, communication with the dead, and protection

Angelica: Protection, visions, and healing

Apple: Love, healing, abundance, fertility, health, immortality, and garden magick

Ash: Protection, wisdom, divination, healing, wealth, love, and transitions

Baby Tears: Peace, tranquility, and hearth and home

Barley: Luck, health, and prosperity

Basil: Prosperity, passion, cleansing, protection, peace, courage, strength, purification, and love

Bay Laurel: Divination, creativity, wisdom, protection, strength, and prosperity

Bean: Love, protection, sexual potency, and funerary rituals

Bee Balm: Prosperity, peace, clarity, and banishing negative energy

Beech: Communication, wisdom, revelation, wishes, luck, and creative power

Begonia: Balance, harmony, and gratitude

Belladonna: Visions, spirit transformation, astral travel, and working with the Dark Goddess

Birch: Protection, new beginnings, purification, clarity, and exorcism

Blackberry: Wealth, transition, regeneration, protection, and fertility

Blackthorn: Protection, setting boundaries, purification, and hexing

Bleeding Heart: Love, unrequited love, self-love, and healing

Blueberry: Protection against psychic attack, peace, rebirth, and motherhood

Borage: Courage, happiness, and psychic powers

Broom: Cleansing, purification, protection, and divination

Cabbage: Protection and money

Cactus: Protection, sexual stamina, tolerance, and clairvoyance

Calendula: Protection spells, psychic powers, strength, and courage

Camellia: Self-love, eternal love, abundance, full moon magick, and prosperity

Campion: Liminality and working with the fae and the dead

Carnation: Protection, healing, love, and strength

Carrot: Love, passion, fertility, and grounding

Cedar: Protection, prosperity, purification, clarity, and wisdom

Chamomile: Divination, love, money, sleep, and purification

Cherry: Divination, unification, love, and intuitive insight

Chicken of the Woods: Grounding

Chickweed: Love, attraction, rebirth, and fidelity

Chili: Hex-breaking, protection, lust, fidelity, and fertility

Chrysanthemum: Funerary practices, protection, immortality, and grief

Clove: Protection, purification, love, healing, and focus

Collard Greens: Protection and money

Cosmos: Feminine energy, harmony, inspiration, luck, order, and grace under fire

Cottonwood: Attracting money, hope, healing, encouragement, transformation, and soul flight

Crocus (Autumn): Love, lust, psychic abilities, strength, and wisdom

Crocus (Spring): Love, merriment, friendship, new beginnings, and visions

Daffodil: Luck, fertility, love, and abundance

Dahlia: Resiliency, acceptance, protection, self-love, grace, reconciliation, elegance, and dignity

Daisy: Love, lust, joy, divination, abundance, and creativity

Dandelion: Adaptability, transformation, wishes, strength, and release

Elderberry: Healing, prosperity, exorcism, and protection

Evening Primrose: Beautification or self-love rituals

Evening Rain Lilies: Protection, familial love, and working with ancestors

Fairy Ring Mushroom: Working with the fae, protection, growth, and courage

Fern: Healing, renewal, protection, invisibility, and faery magick

Fig: Fertility, divination, and love

Fir: Protection, resilience, and rebirth

Flame Violet: Spiritual growth and faery energy

Fly Agaric Mushroom: Clairvoyance, luck, courage, spirit flight, and fertility

Four o'Clocks: Dreams, sleep, love, and adding sweetness to your spells

Frankincense: Protection, spirituality, and exorcism

Fritillaria: Love, healing, and wisdom

Garlic: Warding against psychic vampires, guarding against negativity, and spells for passion

Ginkgo: Mental clarity and accessing ancient wisdom

Golden Pothos: Prosperity, protection, and binding rituals

Gooseberry: Assurance, healing, and loving protection

Grapevine: Fertility, merriment, money, and abundance

Hawthorn: Communication with the fae, Beltane rites, fertility, happiness, and protection

Hazel: Psychic awareness, wisdom, inspiration, and traveling

Hellebore: Protection and exorcism

Hemlock: Defensive magick, astral travel, and the removal of sexual urges

Hen of the Woods: Abundance and healing

Henbane: Divine madness, spirit flight, hexing, and connection to the spirit world

Herb Robert: Fertility, luck, faery magick, and protection

Holly: Courage, strength, luck, protection, and dreamwork

Honey Mushrooms: Wisdom, divination, and protection

Honeysuckle: Psychic awareness, wisdom, inspiration, and traveling

Hops: Sleep, dreamwork, and healing

Houseleek: Fertility, luck, hearth and home, love, and protection

Huckleberry: Luck, protection, and dream magick

Hyacinth: Protection, love, and happiness

Ivy: Protection, growth, fidelity, love, and healing

Jade Plant: Wisdom, abundance, luck, and prosperity

Jimsonweed: Protection ward, deflection, and communication with the spirit world

Juniper: Psychic awareness, protection, health, love, and exorcism

Kale: Protection and money

Lamb's Ear: Healing and protection.

Lamb's-Quarter: Healing, invisibility, protection, and abundance

Larkspur: Reclaiming spells and rituals, ward negative spirits

Lavender: Tranquility, peace, dreamwork, divination, love, happiness, and protection

Leek: Love, protection, and strength

Lemon: Love, fidelity, longevity, luck, home blessings, and lunar magick

Lemon Balm: Healing, happiness, spirituality, and peace

Lettuce: Peace, love, and money

Lily of the Valley: Faery magick, intuition, and creating

Lucky Bamboo: Wealth and abundance

Mandrake: Exorcism, protection, and communication with the spirit world

Maple: Power, protection, strength, and vitality

Marjoram: Love, happiness, money, protection, and health

Mayapple: Fertility, love, healing, protection, and prosperity

Meadowsweet: Funerary rites, handfastings, liminal magick, love, divination, and happiness

Moon Flower: Dreams, psychic abilities, and women's mysteries

Moss: Faery energy, luck, and prosperity

Moth Orchid: Love, lust, passion, and enchantment

Mugwort: Astral projection, inner journeys, and psychic awareness

Mullein: Protection, courage, health, love, divination, and exorcism

Nerve Plant: Generosity, self-awareness, and calm

Nettle: Binding, protection, exorcism, lust, and healing

Night Phlox: Harmony, productivity, communication, and love

Oak: Strength, healing, luck, working with solar deities, midsummer rites, health, and money

Onion: Protection, healing, lust, prosperity, and prophetic dreams

Orchid: Love, passion, and enchantment

Oyster Mushrooms: Mental clarity and cleansing

Patchouli: Fertility, money, lust, and love

Peace Lily: Familial love, comforting vibes, and peace

Peach: Love magick

Pear: Love and lust

Pearly Everlasting: Improve health and longevity

Peony: Elegance, prosperity, and healing

Peppermint: Unblocking your third eye, peacefulness, and prophetic dreams

Periwinkle: Protection, mental clarity, love, lust, fidelity, happiness, and funerary rites

Philodendron: Rejuvenation, forgiveness, and adaptation

Pine: Protection, fertility, renewal, and healing

Plum: Protection and love

Poinsettia: Renewal, joy, hope, and balance

Polka-Dot Plant: Happiness, faery energy, and peace

Pomegranate: Divination, luck, fertility, persistence, wishes, and prosperity

Poppies: Remembrance, release, death, luck, wealth, love, dream magick, sleep, and invisibility

Pot Marigold: Protection, psychic powers, strength, and courage

Primrose: Connect with the faery world, new beginnings, protection, beauty, and love

Pumpkin: Abundance, fertility, growth, new beginnings, wishes, and protection

Radish: Protection, strength, and courage

Raspberry: Protection and love

'Red Flare' Water Lily: Clarity, direction, and the creative process

Reed: Liminal magick, protection, and fertility

Rhubarb: Love, sex, fidelity, and protection

Rose: Love spells, divination, purification, peace, friendship, and happiness

Rosemary: Remembrance, purification, protection, love, dispelling nightmares, fertility, and sea witchery

Rowan: Protection, faery magick, clarity, and psychic powers

Rue: Love, clarity, and healing

Sage: Wisdom, balance, fertility, and longevity

Snapdragon: Protection, hex breaking, bravery, and passion

Snowdrop: Hope, grief, friendship, triumph, strength, and new beginnings

Spider Plant: Protection, spiritual boundaries, fertility, and abundance

Spruce: Protection, renewal, and strength

St. John's Wort: Protection, healing, Midsummer rites, luck, divination, happiness, and strength

Strawberry: Love, fertility, success, luck, and healing

Sunflower: Joy, fertility, loyalty, wishes, wisdom, and health

Sweet Alyssum: Calm, protection, peace, and faery magick

Sweet Pea: Friendship, protecting children, chastity, and courage

Sweet Woodruff: Protection, purification, prosperity, Midsummer or Beltane rites, and victory

Swiss Chard: Love, beauty, and money

Thyme: Purification, reversal spells, healing, love, dreamwork, courage, sleep, and psychic powers

Tobacco: Dreams, connecting with animal guides, psychic abilities, cleansing, and protection

Trumpet of the Dead: Abundance and good fortune in the coming year

Tulip: Love, protection, prosperity, and divination

Turnip: Protection and endings

Valerian: Love, sleep, dreams, purification, and protection

Venus Flytrap: Strength, courage, protection

Violet: Prophetic dreams, faery magick, friendship, love, luck, healing, lust, and wishes

Willow: Love, healing, and female rites of passage

Witch Hazel: Healing after loss, protection, and finding lost objects

Witch's Butter: Protective and defensive magick

Witch's Hat: Cleansing, banishing, and protection

Wolfsbane: Working with the Dark Goddess, invisibility, and protection from psychic vampires

Wood Betony: Protection, purification, and passion

Yarrow: Communication, psychic ability, and vivid dreams

Yellow Woodsorrel: Healing, health, love, and communication with the faery realm

Yerba Buena: Clarity, focus, love charms, and sleep

Yew: The spirit world, the underworld, death, and rebirth

Bibliography

Bradley, Fern Marshall, Barbara W. Ellis, and Ellen Phillips, eds. *Rodale's Ultimate Encyclopedia of Organic Gardening: The Indispensable Green Resource for Every Gardener*. Emmaus, PA: Rodale Books, 2009.

Cunningham, Scott. *Cunningham's Encyclopedia of Magical Herbs*. St. Paul, MN: Llewellyn Publications, 1985.

Fabing, Howard D. "On Going Berserk: A Neurochemical Inquiry." *Scientific Monthly* 83, no. 5 (November 1956): 232–37. https://www.jstor.org/stable/21684.

Foxx, Christine L., Jared D. Heinze, Antonio González, Fernando Vargas, Michael V. Baratta, Ahmed I. Elsayed, Jessica R. Stewart, et al. "Effects of Immunization with the Soil-Derived Bacterium *Mycobacterium vaccae* on Stress Coping Behaviors and Cognitive Performance in a 'Two Hit' Stressor Model." *Frontiers in Physiology* 11 (January 2021): 524833. doi:10.3389/fphys.2020.524833.

Frazer, James. *The Golden Bough: A Study of Magic and Religion*. New York: Macmillan Company, 1971.

Graves, Robert. *The White Goddess*. Reprint, New York: Noonday Press, 1992.

Houdret, Jessica. *Practical Herb Garden*. New Castle, PA: Hermes House, 2003.

Inkwright, Fez. *Botanical Curses and Poisons: The Shadow Lives of Plants*. London: Liminal 11, 2021.

Jakubczyk, Karolina, Katarzyna Janda, Sylwia Szkyrpan, Izabela Gutowska, and Jolanta Wolska. "Stinging Nettle (*Urtica dioica* L.)—Botanical Characteristics, Biochemical Composition and Health Benefits." *Pomeranian Journal of Life Sciences* 61, no. 2 (2015): 191–98. https://doi.org/10.21164/pomjlifesci.78.

Král, Martin. *Of Dahlia Myths and Aztec Mythology: The Dahlia in History*. Seattle, WA: American Dahlia Society, 2014. https://dahlia.org/wp-content/uploads/2018/01/Dahlia-Myths-Part-1.pdf.

Lowenstein, Tom, and Piers Vitebsky. *Native American Myths and Beliefs*. New York: Rosen Publishing, 2012.

MacGregor Mathers, S. L., trans. *The Book of the Sacred Magic of Abramelin the Mage*. 2nd ed. London: John M. Watkins, 1900.

Moor-Smith, Maxwell, Raymond Li, and Omar Ahmad. "The World's Most Poisonous Mushroom, *Amanita phalloides*, Is Growing in BC." *British Columbia Medical Journal* 61, no. 1 (January/February 2019): 20–24. https://bcmj.org/articles/worlds-most-poisonous-mushroom-amanita-phalloides-growing-bc.

Morrison, Dorothy. *Yule: A Celebration of Light & Warmth*. St. Paul, MN: Llewellyn Publications, 2000.

Moura, Ann. *Grimoire for the Green Witch: A Complete Book of Shadows*. St. Paul, MN: Llewellyn Publications, 2003.

Müller-Ebeling, Claudia, Christian Rätsch, and Wolf-Dieter Storl. *Witchcraft Medicine*. Translated by Annabel Lee. Rochester, VT: Inner Traditions, 1998.

Nichols, Ross. *The Book of Druidry*. Reprint, New York: HarperCollins, 1992.

Patterson, Jacqueline Memory. *Tree Wisdom: The Definitive Guide*. London: Thorsons, 1996.

Penicka, Sarah. "*Caveat Anoynter! A Study of Flying Ointments and Their Plants.*" In *The Dark Side: Proceedings of the Seventh Australian and International Religion, Literature and the Arts Conference 2002*, edited by Christopher Hartney and Andrew McGarrity, 181–95. Sydney: RLA Press, 2004. https://core.ac.uk/download/pdf/229401822.pdf.

Rätsch, Christian, and Claudia Müller-Ebeling. *Pagan Christmas: The Plants, Spirits, and Rituals at the Origins of Yuletide.* Translated by Katja Lueders and Rafael Lorenzo. Rochester, VT: Inner Traditions, 2006.

Yeats, William Butler. *The Wind Among the Reeds*. Cambridge, MA: Cambridge University Press, 1905.

Index

A

B

D

E

F

G

H

I

M

N

O

P

R

S

T

V

W

Y